D1809395

B 1 123755 4

Research in adult education in the British Isles

Abstracts and summaries, principally of master and doctoral theses presented since 1945

by Alan H. Charnley

National Institute of Adult Education
(England and Wales)
35 Queen Anne Street
London W1M 0BL

© National Institute of Adult Education
(England and Wales)

This book is sold subject to the condition that
it shall not, by way of trade or otherwise, be
lent, resold, hired out or otherwise circulated
without the publisher's prior consent in any
form of binding or cover other than that in
which it is published and without a similar
condition including this condition being
imposed on the subsequent publisher

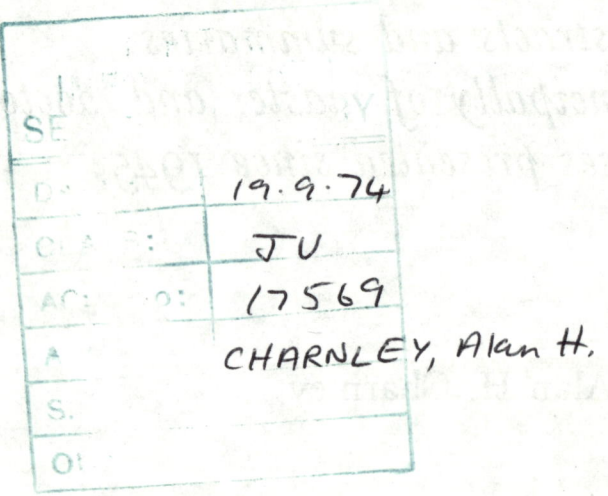

SE

D·   19.9.74

CLA   JU

AC: o: 17569

A   CHARNLEY, Alan H.

S.

O!

First published 1974
ISBN 0 900559 14 4

design/computer·composition/print in England
by Eyre & Spottiswoode Ltd at Grosvenor Press

Contents

Acknowledgements

I am indebted to the authors of the original texts for granting me permission to view and review their work, and to authors, universities and publishers for giving copyright clearance. The very process of summary and abstraction entailed in condensing theses, some of which exceed 800 pages, inevitably introduced an element of dogmatism which was not evident in any research paper that I read. I wish to emphasise that any such fault, transgression committed in selecting the text for abstraction or any idiosyncracy of interpretation is solely my responsibility.

Acknowledgement is made of the splendid help received from the academic and administrative staffs of the universities, from officers of associations concerned with adult education and from librarians; their locations will be readily inferred from the contents.

It is with deep appreciation that I record the sustained encouragement and support of Professor H. Arthur Jones, Professor Thomas Kelly, John Robinson and Arthur Stock. I have had the advantage of their constructive criticism at every stage of the work from its inception and they have indeed been most generous in giving me the benefit of their expert knowledge of the whole field of adult education.

Special mention must be made of the part played by the Cambridge Institute of Education; I wish to convey my gratitude to the Director, W.O. Bell, and to the members of the Senior Common Room for their hospitality, and to mention especially the Librarian, Marjorie Bocking, and her Senior Assistant, Patricia Smith. It is largely because of the excellence and efficiency of the library and the library service that this project has been completed within the allotted time.

Carole Sutherland, who shepherded the manuscript to publication, deserves grateful acknowledgement, as does my wife, who has given so much of her time to the preparation of the manuscript and to the administration of copyright clearance.

A. H. CHARNLEY

Introduction and reader's guide

The subject matter of adult education is complex, being concerned with many areas of interest and types of activity. Consequently, it is unusual to read a thesis or a research paper which is limited, either in content or relevance, to a single, specialist issue within a rigidly defined discipline.

The theses and publications summarised in this volume are those which are available on inter-library loan. We thought it important that the reader should be able to follow up the summary by reading the original work, and consequently availability became one of the major criteria of selection. As new theses are deposited in the libraries we hope to issue supplements to this volume.

A system of descriptors for computer use has been devised by the Educational Resources Information Center (ERIC), the Adult Education section of which is located in the Center for Careers Education, Northern Illinois University, Dekall, Illinois, USA, and a similar thesaurus is being constructed by the Council of Europe, the European Documentation and Information System for Education (EUDISED). Since the latter has not yet been published, and as the former is specifically for computers and thus is too sophisticated for this text, I have relied upon Professor Thomas Kelly's *A select bibliography of adult education in Great Britain,* 2nd edition 1961, and on a preview of the contents list in the 3rd edition, to be published by the National Institute of Adult Education in 1974, to provide a basis for the arrangement of theses in this volume. The links between Professor Kelly's Bibliography and this volume are explained in Appendix I. For many reasons, including availability on inter-library loan, some theses thave been noted in Professor Kelly's book which are not summarised in this volume. A reader who wishes to have a comprehensive bibliography should therefore refer to Professor Kelly's work. I have also been influenced by Dr Edward Hutchinson's classification in *Research in adult education,* NIAE 1970.

The theses have been grouped into eight main sections, given in the Contents, and subdivided in the text into topic areas by the use of subheadings.

Sequence of summaries and abstracts

The principal topic of each thesis or paper determines its place in the volume.

Example — if a thesis is *firstly* concerned with the origins of an institution, and *secondly* with a description of the social background of its contemporary student enrolment, it will be listed in Contents under 'Historical and descriptive surveys'.

Each summary/abstract

Title — the title of the original text, specifying the subject matter, author or editor, degree, university and date, and publisher where appropriate.

Aim — indicates the original author's principal objectives and sometimes clarifies the title; for example, 'adolescent' in the title will be defined by age range in this section.

Method — describes the outline of the methodology or the original research programme, the extent of the statistical work, the numbers in the sample and any further information of that character. Comparison of the summaries in this section will suggest to the professional research worker the various degrees of technicality, but at the same time the more general reader will not feel overwhelmed by statistical minutiae which, out of the context of the full original text, could be meaningless.

Discussion — provides the principal general argument of the *original* author and informs the reader of the subject matter covered in the main body of the original work. 'Discussion' is, therefore, my account of the author's reasoning; I have tried to avoid interposing my own views, assumptions and attitudes, and the objective has been to exercise empathy without presumption.

Findings — offers the principal conclusions, expressed succinctly and without qualification: these concise versions cannot be more than indicative; the original text is the authority. It is emphasised that research workers detail their conclusions with many caveats, and state precisely and fully in the original texts the specific conditions and the degrees of certainty which are applicable.

Coding — the coding letters at the end of the theses are explained in Appendix I, and are provided for the reader who requires a more detailed classification.

General comments

This volume refers to at least five-hundred man-years of highly intensive and original work so that, in the space of 350 pages, it has only been possible to give a general impression of the total research effort at this academic level, and merely to indicate the 'flavour' of each thesis or paper.

Because several institutions are described in detail, sometimes critically, it must be stressed that, by strict definition, this is not a description of the contemporary scene; both the theses and the circumstances are matters of history. Nevertheless, the deeper concerns of the methodology of, the practice of, and the attitudes to, adult education which are revealed in this text defy time. Consequently, although the techniques of teaching ascribed to Institution X may be now out-of-date, the special spirit of that Institution's service continues; indeed, perhaps that ethos is just that much more alive because of the invigorating effect of a properly conducted research enquiry.

Thus I have tried not only to establish the nature of the research that has been conducted by many types of institutions, but also to demonstrate, through the account, both the variety of provision and the breadth of vision of the adult education movement in the British Isles.

Section 1

Historical and descriptive surveys

THE DEVELOPMENT OF ORGANISED LEISURE-TIME ACTIVI-
TIES FOR YOUNG PERSONS IN ENGLAND, WITH PARTICU-
LAR REFERENCE TO LONDON by S. E. Barnes, M.A.(Ed) thesis,
University of London 1947.

Aim

To describe the development of organised leisure activities for young
people between the ages of about 14 years (the school-leaving age in
1947) and 21 years, from 1800-1947.

Discussion

It is perhaps worth noting that, when this thesis was written in 1947,
a 17-year-old youth had lived through two major world social
convulsions, the economic depression of the early 30s and the World
War conditions of the early 40s. The author's own experience of
youth work covered precisely this period so that, having seen with
his own eyes the interrelation of social conditions and individual
education, he affirms in the introduction that 'Education must be
regarded as a continuous process . . . Recreational leisure and education are not opposed to one another; the more they are syn-
thesised, the more we shall get the right kind of both'.

With this general approach to his subject, the author describes the
principal educational movements of the 19th century until the Act
of 1902 in Chapter 2, and developments during the years 1901-1918

8

in Chapter 3. On the whole, adolescents benefited from educational developments during this period by accident rather than design. Often an improvement in primary and secondary (or elementary) education improved their conditions; similarly, adolescents often took advantage of improvements in adult education, such as the University Extension movement and the WEA. However, there were certain services specifically for young people. For example, midway through the 19th century, the Army and Navy started the Cadet movements. The Girls' Friendly Society (formed in 1875), the Boys' Brigade (founded 1883) the Church Lads' Brigade (founded 1891), provided diverse activities for young people. The principal objective of these organisations was 'the advancement of Christ's Kingdom . . . through fellowship in worship, study, work and play'. In 1900 the Girls' Guildry was formed in Glasgow, with the objective of attracting the adolescent girl '. . . . until she enters the communicant membership of the Church'. The Girls' Life Brigade, formed in 1901, had similar objectives.

There were, of course, politically motivated youth organisations, such as the youth sections of the Co-operative movement, the Junior Imperial League (Conservative) and the Labour Party League of Youth.

In addition, in 1907, the Boy Scout and, in 1908, the Girl Guide movements were started, to develop a sense of citizenship through individual character training. As members were divided into groups according to age (e.g. Girl Guide Rangers were 15-21 years old) programmes were devised which related to the problems of the age group in question.

The major part of the thesis deals with the period 1902-1947, the period in which, increasingly, the state intervened to provide youth facilities or to co-ordinate the efforts of voluntary bodies. In 1916 a Central Juvenile Organisation Committee was set up to stem the tide of juvenile delinquency by positive social and educational work; in 1918 the CJOC was transferred from the Home Office to the Board of Education, where it duly suffered from the general economy drive.

In this period new organisations sprang up; the St John Ambulance Brigade Cadets, the Welsh League of Youth, the Youth Hostels Association and Young Farmers' Clubs. Other voluntary clubs were strengthened by federation, such as the National Conference of Boys' Clubs. At the same time, the state continued to expand its effort, particularly in the area of vocational activities in the Evening Institutes such as, for example in London, the Junior Technical Institutes.

But in 1939 Board of Education Circular 1486 stated 'the social and physical development of boys and girls between the ages of 14 and 20 who have ceased full-time education . . . has for long been neglected in this country'. To remedy this neglect the partnership of the state in the Service of Youth was regarded as fundamental. In 1943 the Advisory Council to the President of the Board of Education issued a report *The Youth Service After the War* which concentrated on strengthening voluntary organisations. A further report, the *Youth Service Report 1945,* looked forward to the Youth Service being part of the education service as a whole, that is, to the implementation of Clause 41 of the Education Act of 1944.

It was also hoped that the community centre element in the Cambridgeshire Village Colleges would encourage more community centres in other local authority areas.

Writing in 1947, the author argued that buildings should be designed so that accommodation should be appropriate, functional and adaptable to all the educational needs of the whole community. He apologised for the obviousness of the comment.

Coding: 1c(vii), 1b(xxii), 1b(xxix)

A STUDY OF THE DEVELOPMENT OF ADULT EDUCATION IN SCOTLAND by J. Griffin, M.A. thesis, University of St. Andrews 1953.

Aim

a To survey the development of adult education in Scotland up to 1950

b To examine some aspects of contemporary provision

c To survey the provision of adult education in certain other countries

d To consider adult learning, the students and their courses e To examine some of the methods of learning

Discussion

The contribution of the Mechanics' Institutes to technical education and to the provision of libraries is a feature of early 19th century adult education in both Scotland and England. Adult schools, on the other hand, never took firm root in Scotland and evening schools, as in England, tended to become institutes of vocational learning.

Scotland had, by 1870, a long tradition of university opportunity for the sons of poor men; in 1867 16% of students attending the universities were sons of artisans and skilled labourers. For this reason the University Extension movement, pioneered by the University of St. Andrews in the 1870s, has peculiarly Scottish characteristics and could not be described as being so successful as that in England and Wales. Access to universities was relatively easy for, until 1892-3, entry was possible without a preliminary examination, and consequently the enthusiasm for University Extension was tempered by the fear that a successful extra-mural movement might in some way restrict the amplitude of internal provision.

A report of a survey conducted in 1939 by University Extra-Mural Committees, Education Authorities, the WEA and three University Settlements noted that, out of 37 County and City areas, only 18 had classes; that out of the 271 classes examined, 173 were held in four large cities, Glasgow, Edinburgh, Aberdeen and Dundee, with over 50% of the students in the Glasgow region.

The post-war development of adult education in Scotland, the contribution of the universities, the WEA, the Comrie, Dumfries and Airdrie experiments in the early post-war years, the re-opening of Newbattle Abbey College, the contribution of the Voluntary Associations, of the BBC and the Carnegie United Kingdom Trust are described in detail. Progress was partly impeded, however, by the absence of direct grants to voluntary bodies and universities in Scotland. The author argues, however, that the comparatively slow development of adult education in Scotland may be ascribed to several factors rather than to any single consideration.

An analysis of student occupations in 1948-1950 compares the composition of classes in Scotland with those in England. Research in the Manchester Extra-Mural Board area, the results of which were published by Professor W. E. Styler, is particularly mentioned. Student occupations in the lowlands were proportionately similar to those in England, but the author suggests that classes in the smaller industrial towns and larger industrial villages of Scotland attracted a larger percentage of manual workers.

Lectures and discussions were the most common methods of instruction, but the thesis describes many uses of the educational technology of the period and includes an evaluation of the effect of, and the use of, wireless from the earliest days of broadcasting.

Coding: 1a, 7a, 3d, 2a, 2b, 5a, 5b, KB557

EDUCATION AND SOCIAL CHANGE IN MANCHESTER, 1780-1851 – WITH SPECIAL REFERENCE TO THE DEVELOPMENT OF SECONDARY, HIGHER AND ADULT EDUCATION by R. B. Hope, M.Ed. thesis, University of Manchester 1955.

Aim
To investigate the effects of the changing social and economic background on the development of secondary, higher and adult education in Manchester between the years 1780 and 1851.

Discussion
Between 1780 and 1851 Manchester was transformed from an agricultural into an industrial community. The concentration of the cotton industry in and around Manchester created a vast network of support industries, commercial activities, transport services and an export trade.

Were all these signs of material advance and social change without their counterpart in the field of intellectual achievement? How did Manchester, as a new, though typical, product of the Industrial Revolution, respond to the awakening educational needs and demands of the area as regards post-primary education?

The author describes the city's response to these problems in a thesis which is divided into five parts: 'Early Ventures, 1780-1803', 'Post-war Developments in Vocational Education', 'The Use of Leisure amongst the Middle-classes in the Post-war Years', 'Progress in Secondary Education 1803-1851' and 'The Rise of the University'.

The origins of many of Manchester's more famous contemporary institutions are given, including the University of Manchester and Manchester Grammar School, and the Mechanics' Institute. The thesis also includes descriptions of many institutions whose period of service to the community was rather more brief; for example, the New Mechanics' Institute. Recorded are the achievements of succeeding generations of families: the Heywoods, Gregs, Fairbairns and Brothertons, all of whom were Whig or Radical in politics and and non-conformist in religion.

The author concludes that, by 1851, the wealth of Manchester's merchants and industries was obviously limited, and it became increasingly apparent that collective action and eventual state assistance was the only solution.

Coding: 1a

AN HISTORICAL SURVEY OF EDUCATION IN A SUBURBAN AREA by P. L. P. Clarke, M.A. thesis, University of London 1956.

Aim
To survey the development of education from about 1800-1950, but particularly from 1850-1950, in the suburban area of Wimbledon, Merton and Morden.

Discussion
The districts of Wimbledon, Merton and Morden were originally three villages which became suburbs of London at different times. Wimbledon was a town in 1902 and was in time to accept responsibility as a Part III authority, whereas Merton and Morden were dormitory areas of more recent growth, and came within the jurisdiction of the Surrey County Council for education purposes. Such institutions as the Wimbledon Technical College, the secondary schools and the branch of the WEA, however, met the needs of the whole locality.

Consequently, the first chapter introduces the 'suburban' area of Wimbledon, Merton and Morden, giving geographical, historical and sociological information. There follows an account of the foundation of local elementary schools, together with details of curricula, and of school conditions, which are related to national developments. Chapters 3 and 4 describe the development of secondary education, the divorce of technical from secondary education, and the growth of the modern technical college, showing the college to be, first, the headquarters of various types of post-elementary education and, later, an establishment of higher education.

The account of part-time and evening technical education in Chapter 4, together with information about the local administration of these services, leads to an examination of the work of two selected voluntary organisations (Chapter 5) in the area — the WEA and the Townswomen's Guild — both of them attempting to meet the needs of a suburban community. Although the author acknowledges that the WEA, in Wimbledon at least, is a valuable organisation as far as progress in further education is concerned, he argues that perhaps there are not enough of the 'working-class' in our dormitory suburbs to support the movement, or perhaps the very word 'worker' is beginning to take on new and less class-conscious connotations. He notes that in 1953 the poorest district, South Wimbledon, provided fewest members, whereas even the wealthiest areas did provide members. WEA membership attending classes in 1952-1953 reached about 9,600.

The work of the Townswomen's Guild — the monthly meetings, classes and groups, and outings — is described as invaluable to individual women tied to family duties in a suburban area. The author estimated that membership in the Wimbledon area approximated to the numbers in a good-sized secondary school.

For comparison, the population of Wimbledon alone in 1950 was about 58,000, and for all three districts together about 133,000.

Chapters 6 and 7 return to the problems of primary and secondary education from 1902-1955. Appendices give, *inter alia,* details of WEA members and classes, and figures for the membership of the Townswomen's Guild.

Coding: lb(x), lb(xxi)

THE DEVELOPMENT OF ADULT EDUCATION IN WARRINGTON DURING THE NINETEENTH CENTURY by W. B. Stephens, M.A. thesis, University of Exeter 1958.

Aim

To study the history of adult education during the 19th century in an industrial town in Lancashire.

Discussion

The growth of adult education in the 19th century in Warrington is essentially a study of the mixed background of a factory town and a cultural centre, of illiterate working men and of a partly-educated middle-class. In 1882 an observer reported an impression of 'dilapidation, dirt and an air of squalid degradation' yet Warrington could claim to have an unusual cultural background; for example, in 1760 Warrington had one of the six libraries in existence in Lancashire and Cheshire.

The thesis describes the way in which the middle classes embarked on a process of self-education from 1800 to 1825, through the musical societies, the scientific societies and the museum and the literary societies and library.

Chapters 3, 4 and 5 consist of a detailed examination of the role of the Mechanics' Institute from 1825 to 1854, and include a discussion of its motives and aims, the methods of instruction, its control by the middle-class, the response of the working-class and a discussion of the reasons for its decline.

The breakdown of the Mechanics' Institute in the 1860s marked the end of that phase of adult education in Warrington in which the middle and upper-classes had sought, from their own resources, to raise the standard of education of their inferiors.

The next period is marked by growing state financial and administrative aid, and an emphasis on scientific and technical instruction. Nevertheless, voluntary societies, such as the Warrington Co-operative Society, continued to contribute.

With this theme in mind, the author discusses the work of the School of Art, the Peoples' College and Continuation School, the Museum Committee's Science classes, the School of Science, the Warrington Society for the Promotion of Technical Instruction, the

Recreative Evening Schools and, finally, the early years of the Technical Institute. Yet, even in 1902, a local writer could comment 'one half of the town does not know how the other half lives. And more's the pity'.

Coding: 1a, 1b(iv), 1b(xiii), 1b(xxvii), KB572

ADULT EDUCATION IN SOUTH-EAST SCOTLAND by J. B. Barclay, Ph.D. thesis, University of Edinburgh 1960.

Aim
A study of the historical development of adult education and of the techniques of learning, with special reference to the Edinburgh region.

Discussion
The thesis does not deal with technical, commercial and recreational adult education found generally in further education establishments but concentrates on liberal adult education, a term defined in the first chapter.

Adult education in South-East Scotland is described in some detail, from its origins to the 18th century when the Select Society, founded in 1754, included in its membership Adam Smith and David Hume. Similarly assessed are the contributions of the voluntary movements of the early 19th century, such as the Schools of Arts and Mechanics' Institutes, which were primarily vocational, and the religious and literary societies which emphasised the more liberal aspects of adult education. By 1870 most voluntary societies experienced financial difficulties and failed to enlist large-scale working-class support. Indeed, many workers' associations tended to be antagonistic towards anything not created by themselves.

After the watershed of the Scottish Education Act of 1872 the University Extension Movement was initiated, but it proved to be less successful than in England, largely because, for example, in 1889, 1-in-800 people attended a university in Scotland compared with 1-in-5000 in England. On the other hand, the Summer School Movement, started by Patrick Geddes in Edinburgh in 1887, steadily

advanced and proved to be an innovation of international importance.

Co-operative associations were influential, particularly from 1886.
The WEA effectively started in Edinburgh in 1912 and its contribution is fully described. Sadly, co-operation between the WEA and
the Trade Union and Labour College movements in the early 20th
century seems to have been minimal.

University extension work increased after 1945, particularly when
Directors of Extra-Mural Studies were appointed by Glasgow University in 1946 and by Edinburgh University in 1949.

By 1959-60, 51% of all classes organised by the Extra-Mural
Department of Edinburgh University used visual aids of various types
— films, slides, micro-slides, tape recorders and so on.

Though the contribution of broadcasting is highly praised, the
difficulties of linking the traditions of lecture and tutorial techniques
to broadcasting date from the 1930s. There is an interesting discussion of the early impact of television in the 1950s on the courses
offered to students and on the techniques of tutors. A comparison is
made between the introduction of the film in the 1930s and
television in the 1950s.

The place of residential adult education, particularly the role of
Newbattle Abbey, is well documented.

Appendices deal with attendance, courses, Armed Services
education, the Edinburgh WEA and prison education, and include
comparative statistical tables.

Coding: 1a, 7b, 3b, 5d, 5f, 5g, 7c(i), 7c(iii), 7c(iv), 7c(v), 7c(xxi), 8a,
2a, KB557

ADULT EDUCATION IN BRISTOL DURING THE 19TH
CENTURY by H. J. Price, M.A.(Ed) thesis, University of Bristol
1965.

Aim

To study adult education in Bristol during the 19th century and to
relate this local experience to the national trends.

Discussion

Part 1 of the thesis describes the national educational background and outlines the local economic and social framework within which Bristol's educational work amongst adults took place. Adult education was part of a wider educational development which grew alongside that of the provision for children. The industrial and social expansion of the 19th century may be associated with a zeal for knowledge, but the aims of adult education were always more complex. It was also regarded as a source of intellectual pleasure and refinement; it was thought to be a means of changing society.

Bristol itself has a special interest for historians of 19th century England, for at the beginning of the 19th century it was the second largest city in Great Britain but by the end of this period, although still an important urban area, Bristol could be described only as one of several great cities.

In Part 2 the author describes the non-specialist Scientific and Literary Societies, the Bristol Library Society, the growth of the public library movement, the contribution of the specialised Scientific Societies, the promotion of the arts through the Artistic and Musical Societies and the founding of the City Museum and University College. Though the working-classes benefited, the author considers these movements essentially as characterising the spread of adult education amongst the middle-classes.

Working-class adult education is the general subject of Part 3, which deals specifically with the Adult Schools, the Religious Education Societies, the Mechanics' Institutes, Co-operative Education and the Bristol Socialist Society.

Part 4 assesses the contribution of state-assisted, or sometimes merely encouraged, further education; for example, the Evening Schools (in Bristol in 1892 85% of the students were working-class), and the University Extension classes. It suggests that, following the 1870 and 1902 Education Acts, adult education became increasingly a partnership between the state and the voluntary bodies.

Coding: 1a, 1b(iii), 1b(xxv), 1b(xxvi), 1b(ii), 1b(v), 1b(vi), KB561

ADULT EDUCATION IN HUDDERSFIELD AND DISTRICT 1851-1884 by J. P. Hemming, M.Ed. thesis, University of Manchester 1966.

Aim

To review the development of adult education from 1851-1884 in one area.

Discussion

The 'Spirit of the Age' is described in Chapter 1; that is the spirit of optimism, self-help, middle-class reformism and working-class aspiration. However, by 1871 of the 74,358 inhabitants of Huddersfield 11,292 men and 6,005 women over the age of 20 were engaged in woollen manufacture. Consequently, the town's prosperity depended on one industry, and social and cultural progress was inseparable from the economic circumstances prevailing in the international woollen manufacturing markets (Chapter 2).

The essential background study is continued in Chapter 3, entitled 'The Social, Cultural and Educational Setting'. Engels described Huddersfield in 1844 as 'The handsomest by far of all the factory towns of Yorkshire and Lancashire by reason of its charming situation and modern architecture'. Whilst the general philosophy of independent self-help was no doubt responsible for some progress, the Borough did not erect a public library until 1897.

Chapters 4, 5 and 6, the largest section of the thesis, are devoted to the study of the Mechanics' Institute movement in the area, and consider respectively 'The Essential Features of the Mechanics' Institute Movement in Huddersfield and District 1851-1884', 'The Huddersfield Mechanics' Institute', and 'The Progress and Achievements of the Minor Mechanics' Institutes of the Huddersfield District 1851-1884'.

The remaining chapters narrate more briefly adult education for females, the contribution of the learned societies, adult education and Working Men's Associations, the contribution of religious organisations, and the details of some of the outstanding contributors to adult education in Huddersfield.

Coding: 1b(iv), 1b(iii), 1b(vii), 1b(xxvi), 1b(ix), 1b(v), KB564

THE FOUNDATION OF THE UNIVERSITY OF SALFORD by
M. C. Gordon, M.Sc. thesis, University of Salford 1967.

Aim

To trace the development of the University of Salford.

Discussion

The author notes the relative decline in British industrial performance between 1851 and 1869. As one explanation, he points to the
difference between technical education at that time in England and
in Württemberg. In 1866, to stand comparison with Württemberg on
a pro-rata basis, England would have required at least 11 technological universities.

He describes the effects on Salford of the Education Act of 1870
and the Technical Instruction Act of 1889, and the opening of the
Royal Technical Institute in 1896, 'a handsome building in Ruabon
brick in a subdued Victorian Renaissance style'. The organisation of
the Institute under its first Principal, Wilson, the predominance of
evening students and Wilson's proposals for educational reform are
described in detail.

The next Principal, H. B. Knowles (1904-1909) faced a lack of
appreciation on the part of employers and trades unions for the
Institute's work. The number of students declined; Knowles was
severely criticised and left to become Headmaster of the secondary
school which separated off from the Institute into another building.
His Vice-Principal, Dr Prentice, took his place and continued as
Principal until 1933. Prentice established good relations with
industry, introduced a diploma scheme and encouraged students to
gain examination successes which were locally and nationally
recognised.

A full description of the war years, 1914-1918, points to the
greatest difficulty, lack of staff. But conditions in general did not
improve in the period 1920-1932, although the old name 'Institute'
was dropped in 1921 in favour of the more gracious 'College', new
courses were introduced and the College shared in a national
development which was to affect all technical institutions, the
creation of a nationally-recognised system of awards in higher
technical and scientific education.

Of the period from 1931-1939, the most startling act of parsimony was the decision of the Education Committee not to replace Prentice in 1932, but to have his post taken over nominally by the Director of Education, J. A. Hartley, assisted by Mr Clark, head of the chemistry department and Vice-Principal. Given such an arrangement, it is not difficult to understand the reasons for little progress during this period.

H. H. Clapham became Acting Principal for the early years of the Second World War but when, in 1941, the College ceased to be controlled exclusively by Salford and became the joint responsibility of Lancashire County Council and Salford City, J. C. Jones was appointed Principal. Jones resigned in 1944 and Dr Richardson, his successor, embarked on a policy of shrewd publicity, including an invitation to the Minister of Education to speak at the College's Jubilee Celebrations and, in the climate of the 1944 Education Act and the 1945 Percy Report, further progress was achieved.

Under the guidance of Dr P. F. R. Venables, Principal from 1947-1956, the College expanded, introduced social studies, gained recognition as providing facilities for the study of advanced technology, developed 'sandwich' courses and planned new buildings. Largely as a result of Dr Venables' work, his successor, Dr Whitworth, was able to steer the College to its new status as a College of advanced Technology in 1961 and subsequently to university status in 1966.

Thus, an institution whose origin may be traced to 19th century adult education movements could plan to take 5000 full-time students by 1974.

Coding: 1c(ii), 1c(xi), 1b(iv), KB779

THE FULL MAN – THE HISTORY OF ADULT EDUCATION IN CARDIFF – 1860-1960 by D. A. Eastwood, M.Ed. thesis, University of Wales 1970.

Aim
To review the growth of adult education in Cardiff 1860-1960, excepting full-time adult education.

Discussion

During the years 1850-1860 Cardiff expanded rapidly. In 1850 the South Wales Railway was opened and there were startling developments in the coal and iron and steel industries. Industrial growth and prosperity went side by side with deprivation in health, housing and education.

A Mechanics' Institute was founded in 1841 but failed shortly afterwards; in 1848 it was reconstituted as the Cardiff Athenaeum and Mechanics' Institute but once more it failed to attract support and was closed in 1856. There was a demand for education, but the demand was for a basic education, perhaps in the three Rs, and it was precisely this demand that the Mechanics' Institute ignored. Consequently, 'self-improvement' was the way through which adults gained this basic education. In Chapter 1 the author describes the Mechanics' Institutes, the Mutual Improvement Societies, the Working Men's Institutes, Penny Readings, the Sunday Schools and the Young Men's Christian Association.

Chapter 2 is mainly about the opportunities that came into being for those who could read, and it is entitled 'The Importance of the Adoption of the Free Libraries Act'. Besides discussing the Library, the author describes the Museum 1869-1927, the Science and Arts Schools 1866-1889 and some of the principal societies.

'University Assistance to Adult Education in Cardiff' (Chapter 3) deals with the Cambridge University Extension Courses 1874-1883 and the extra-mural developments of the University of South Wales. Chapter 4 is concerned with the WEA; the establishment of the WEA branch in Barry in 1907, the work of the WEA by itself, and of the WEA in co-operation with the Cardiff Education Authority Adult Committee and the University College of Cardiff.

Towards the end of the 19th century, and increasingly during the 20th century, the Local Education Authority expanded its services in adult education. Chapter 5, 'The Local Authority takes Control' describes this process. Starting with the Cardiff Recreative Evening Classes Associations 1888-1890, the author considers the Cardiff School Board and the expansion of evening classes, and concludes the thesis with a consideration of the community centres and adult centres. The first community centre was opened at Trelai in 1958; the adult centres consisted of the old evening institutes renamed. The local authority's concern for adult education was confirmed when, in September 1957, an assistant education officer was appointed to co-ordinate the work in adult education under the aegis of the Adult Committee.

Coding: 1a, 1b(xxv), 1b(ix), 1b(x), 1b(xiii), KB562

SOME ASPECTS OF WORKING-CLASS ADULT EDUCATION IN 19th CENTURY CARLISLE by T. B. Graham, M.Phil. thesis, University of Nottingham 1972.

Aim
To examine and analyse the provision of adult education for the working-classes in 19th century industrial Carlisle; to highlight certain developments peculiar to Carlisle on one hand and, on the other hand, to relate local developments to the national evolutionary pattern of adult education.

Discussion
The first chapter deals with the background social and economic conditions of the working-class in Carlisle, with particular reference to the physical and social environment of the hand-loom weaver. The educational background is also examined and the extent of illiteracy in one working-class parish in the city is carefully scrutinised.

The contribution of the middle-classes, the Mechanics' Institute, the company-sponsored organisations such as the Carlisle branch of the Newcastle and Carlisle Railway Mechanics' Institute formed in the city in 1855, the Religious and Social Institutions and University Extension are the subjects of the second section.

The author then chooses as his theme 'working-class self-help' through voluntary association, and discusses the Working Men's Reading Movement as a case in point. This section is quite detailed, including a photocopy of a letter from Charles Dickens in reply to the invitation to attend the opening of Lord Street Reading Room in 1851. The prescience of Robert Elliot is documented and interesting.

Chapter 4 deals with enterprises founded on the expenditure of public money, in three periods: 1850-1870, the state-aided night-school era; 1870-1890, the era when the night-school faded away to be replaced by the 'new concept of the evening school'; and the period 1890-1900, the era of the 'Acland Code' of 1893.

There are several appendices, including a graph of membership of the Carlisle Mechanics' Institute, and histograms of, for example, enrolments in grant-aided evening schools.

Coding: 1b(iv), 1b(ii), 1b(xiii), 1b(xxv), 1a, KB563

THE LAST FORTY YEARS – THE HISTORY OF ADULT EDUCATION IN THE ADMINISTRATIVE COUNTY OF ESSEX, WITH PARTICULAR REFERENCE TO THE PERIOD 1932-1972 by C. J. Thompson, M.A. (Dissertation), University of Kent at Canterbury 1972.

Aim
To show the growth of the county council involvement in adult education from that of following to that of leadership, and to illustrate the efforts of voluntary bodies and the two Universities of London and Cambridge in inspiring and then supplementing the work of the Education Committee.

Discussion
The population of the administrative county of Essex increased from 916,640 in 1901 to 1,196,804 in 1971, reflecting both the national movement of population southwards and the growth of the dormitory belt outside the London conurbation.

In Chapter 1, the author describes how the provision for adult education in Essex followed the national pattern until the early 19th century and how, because of the lack of industrialisation and despite the civilising effect of the railways, much of rural Essex remained in a state of educational stagnation until the 1890s. After the passing of the Technical Instruction Acts of 1889 and 1891, and the Local Taxation (Customs and Excise) Act of 1890 which empowered the county councils to utilise 'whisky money' for the purposes of technical education, the local authority gradually increased its support. However, as a rural area the local authority was relatively poor, so that in the period up to 1932 much depended on voluntary organisations, such as the Essex Federation of Women's Institutes.

Even in the period 1932-1945, the growth of adult education in the area depended to a large extent on the voluntary bodies, the WEA, the University Extension movement, the Rural Community Council and the Women's Institutes. But the voluntary bodies probably could not have been sustained without the increasing financial support of the local authority (Chapter 2).

Chapter 3 is concerned with the Adult Residential College in Essex, Wansfell. Founded in 1947, it increased the number of courses from 42 in 1949/50 to 67 in 1954/55, and the number of students from 933 per year to 1,795. In 1972 it earned about 70% of its expenditure from students' fees. The author notes that the success of the Residential College has depended very much on the enthusiasm of the Principals, i.e. Dr Down, the first Principal, and Mr O. A. Kingsbury, his successor.

Chapters 4, 5 and 6 describe the growth, from 1945, of the Senior Evening Institutes, the Community Centres and the Voluntary Associations. During this period the local authority became directly responsible for a large section of the adult education provision and, at the same time, indirectly increased its financial aid to the voluntary bodies.

The final sections of the thesis include a discussion of staffing, fees policies, and appendices.

The review of progress in this area acknowledges the efforts of the local authority, but notes that, nationally, the adult education sector is the first to be cut back in times of national financial stringency. The author considers that the administrative area would be one of the leading local providers if, firstly, staffing ratios at all levels were improved and, secondly, if more schools could be persuaded to think of themselves as Community Centres.

Coding: 1b(xiii), 1b(xv), 1b(ix), 1b(x), 1c(i), KB554a

Section 2

Particular movements and organisations

Mechanics' Institutes and similar bodies

GEORGE BIRKBECK – PIONEER OF ADULT EDUCATION by
T. Kelly, Ph.D. thesis, University of Liverpool 1956.

Aim
a To study the life and work of George Birkbeck, widely known in
the 19th century as the founder of Mechanics' Institutes, and
particularly remembered as the founder of the London Mechanics'
Institute, now Birkbeck College
b To examine the general development of the Mechanics' Institute
movement

Discussion
Birkbeck was brought up a Quaker and though, in later years, his ties
with the old faith were to be somewhat loosened, there was always
something of the Quaker about him. This influence is seen in his
deep religious convictions, in the simplicity of his mode of life and
not least in the great philanthropic endeavour to which he committed himself.

Chapters 1, 2 and 3 respectively relate the story of Birkbeck's life
from his birth in Settle to his graduation in Edinburgh (1779-1799);
from his appointment to a chair in Anderson's Institution, where he
started a Mechanics' Class, to his resignation from the Institute
(1799-1804); the period when he gradually became a leading figure

in the Scientific Societies of London (1805-1823).

In the early part of the 19th century, the quickening pace of industrialisation, the growth of the movement of spread education generally, the beginnings of fundamental working-class movements in Socialism, Co-operation, Unionism, provide the background from which the Mechanics' Institute movement emerged. Though Birkbeck had undoubtedly inaugurated the Mechanics' Class and assisted in the founding of the Mechanics' Institute in Glasgow, the founding of the Institute in London in 1823 owes much to the work of Robertson, Hodgskin and Place. Nevertheless, at the famous public meeting in November 1823, Birkbeck was able both to preside and to talk about his actual experience in Glasgow; office and experience proved unassailable.

The birth of the London Mechanics' Institute in 1823 did not occur in an atmosphere of complete sweetness and light; the author notes that the controversy reflected real dilemmas. Partly for this reason the story of the London Mechanics' Institute from 1823-1830 is told in some detail in Chapters 5-7. Thus the London Mechanics' Institute was both of considerable importance in Birkbeck's career and of considerable significance to the entire Mechanics' Institute movement.

Birkbeck, however, was not soley concerned with the Mechanics' Institutes; he was equally interested in a variety of good causes — social, political and, above all, educational. Chapter 8, 'The Diffusion of Knowledge' (1824-1837), examines his varied and many contributions in this respect, and Chapter 9, 'Private and Professional' (1824-1837), reminds us that this indefatigable man remained a busy medical practitioner throughout all this period.

From 1838 until his death in 1841, Birkbeck suffered from ill-health, but even in July 1841 he was writing to friends to urge action against the slave system in the Spanish colonies.

Book 2 deals with the general development of the Mechanics' Institute movement, in three sections, 1823-1831, 1832-1841 and the period after Birkbeck's death. At the close of 1823 there were six Mechanics' Institutes in England, Scotland and Wales; by 1831 there were 101. Though the growth of the movement was fairly general throughout this island, the author emphasises that expansion was not even, either geographically or chronologically. One essential factor limited their success; the leaders of the movement sometimes provided what *they* thought the working-classes should receive by way of instruction and facilities rather than what the working-classes themselves wanted or needed.

In the second phase, 1832-1841, a harsh critic thought that the Institutes had degenerated into 'play-centres for serious clerks' but the widening of horizons to encompass, for example, concerts and exhibitions, was quite valid. Whatever else the Institutes achieved, the libraries of the Institutes were an invaluable contribution to a society bereft of a public library system.

After Birkbeck's death, though many Institutes melted away, they left behind them a moraine of useful institutions; technical schools, art schools, day schools, public libraries, museums, etc. Indeed, a few survive as clubs today.

Coding: 1b(iv), KB620

THE ORIGIN AND DEVELOPMENT OF THE YORKSHIRE UNION OF MECHANICS' INSTITUTES by J. Popple, M.A. thesis (2 vols), University of Sheffield 1960.

Aim
To survey the origin and development of the Yorkshire Union of Mechanics' Institutes (Book 1) and to provide notes on the individual societies connected with the West Riding and Yorkshire Unions of Mechanics' Institutes (Book 2).

Discussion
The Mechanics' Institutes in Yorkshire originated in 1824 from the impulses leading to the formation of the London Mechanics' Institution. In the 20s, the suspicions of both higher and lower social orders and the economic recession retarded their growth. The enthusiasm of the Baines family, father and son, could not overcome the lack of good communications between too few societies. However, after the reform of Parliament and the upsurge of the economy in the 1830s, there was a revival of interest in close co-operation, so that in 1837 delegates of 13 institutes met in the Leeds Court House to consider the formation of the West Riding Union of Mechanics' Institutes.

The West Riding Union had two aims. The primary objective, to co-operate to hire, at reduced rates, the most eminent scientific lecturers failed, as did the attempt to engage a permanent lecturer. The second objective, however, succeeded. The Union was able to collect information concerning the management and daily operations of Mechanics' Institutes and, on that basis, issue recommendations for further improvements; for example, the Central Committee issued recommendations for attracting more working-class support. Relations between member Institutes and the Central Committee were encouraging enough for the Central Committee to welcome delegates from the areas of the County to the 1841 York annual meeting and to enlarge the association to become 'The Yorkshire Union of Mechanics' Institutes'.

Between 1841 and 1850 the Yorkshire Union was consolidated and extended. Basic elementary instruction formed the predominant work of the Institute committees, as the provision of wider facilities frequently met with a poor response.

The rise of sub-unions, such as the East Riding Sub-Union, led to increased educational advantages, but proved to be a challenge to the Yorkshire Union. However, by 1850 the Union had appointed its first agent, T. J. Pearsall. It could claim to have the support of most influential members of society and to be able to exert an influence on government and on local educational developments.

The fourth Chapter of Book I deals with the development of external influences upon the work of the Yorkshire Union between 1851 and 1870. The Union grew from 109 societies in 1850 to 143 in 1860-62 but fell back to 114 in 1870. Despite many encouraging developments, such as library provision, a large proportion of the working-classes could not be induced to join. The societies could match neither the classwork of the Working Men's Colleges nor the recreational facilities in Working Men's Institutes or Clubs.

From 1871 to 1924 there was a successive relinquishment of activities. The Education Acts of 1870 and 1902, the Technical Instruction Act of 1889, the permissive legislation of 1850 and 1855 relating to free public libraries, the 1919 Public Libraries Act and other legislation reflecting or innovating changes in the educational system resulted in the attainment of the Union's objectives and consequent redundancy.

Book II consists of summary notes on each society, and includes dates of the Union's Annual Reports in which there was some reference to the individual Institutes.

Coding: 1b(iv), 1b(xxv), KB625

THE DEVELOPMENT OF MECHANICS' INSTITUTES IN WARWICKSHIRE, WORCESTERSHIRE AND STAFFORDSHIRE 1825-1890 — A REGIONAL STUDY by C. M. Turner, M.Ed. thesis, University of Leicester 1966.

Aim

To examine Mechanics' Institutes in the Midland plateau as sociological units to be studied against the social and economic environment at national, regional and local levels.

Discussion

The author uses the term 'Mechanics' Institute' to include all institutes which consciously appealed for the support of working men which were commonly accepted as Mechanics' Institutes.

This study is divided into four chronological sections; within each the fortunes of the individual Institute are touched on generally and briefly, since this is not an attempt to write the history of each institute in the area. More importantly, the special problems of the Movement in each period are described, and examples are drawn from individual institutes.

In the first section, the problems of founding the first Institutes, the character of the instigators, the type of support and of opposition are discussed. The following section examines the political and religious alignments, the nature of class relations and the variations in class control. The difficulties faced by the Institutes in the middle years of the 19th century, particularly in their programmes and membership, are the subjects of the third section. In the last section the work of the Institutes in the final quarter of the century is described, and there is an emphasis on the question of the development of classes related to external examinations.

Findings

The Mechanics' Institute Movement describes a variety of individual types, each reflecting the peculiar demands of the locality. Nevertheless, there were certain national trends in their history. After a period of opposition, the early Institutes attracted the support of all classes; from politically radical beginnings, they began to attract the support of the middle-classes after 1840. However, by gaining middle-class support they began to lose that of the working-class, particularly of the more articulate, politically conscious groups. Thus, by 1860 many Institutes had lost all their working-class members and had failed to rectify the situation largely because their programmes were determined by the middle-class ethos. In the period 1860-1890 the Institutes were often little more than middle-class discussion groups, but some started to provide comprehensive programmes of educational classes for working men and took advantage of the examination structure provided by, for example, the Society of Arts.

Consequently, the Institutes formed the basis for many public libraries and served to promote the vocational ambitions of many working-class members. In many ways a failure, the Mechanics' Institutes nevertheless have one singular achievement to their credit — they brought the printed word to many working-class people.

Coding: 1b(iv), 1b(xxv), KB625

THE OBJECTIVES AND ACHIEVEMENTS OF THE CHESTER MECHANICS' INSTITUTION AND THE MACCLESFIELD SOCIETY FOR ACQUIRING USEFUL KNOWLEDGE by R. C. Wilson, M.Ed. thesis, University of Manchester 1968.

Aim
To investigate the objectives and achievements of two adult education centres which existed in the Cheshire towns of Chester and Macclesfield between 1834 and 1880.

Discussion
The author shows how the people of Chester and Macclesfield were aware of educational activities in both towns and that, in fact, both centres sprang from the insistent drive of the Rev. Edward Stanley, Rector of Alderley. Although the names of the two organisations suggest different aims and origins, it is shown that both were part of

the general enthusiasm for Mechanics' Institutes which were built up after the 1820s and that their objectives were similar: namely, to provide elementary instruction through the media of classes, lectures, libraries and informal discussion. However, Chester's Institution grew from a public library and this aspect of its work was dominant; indeed, the Institution reverted to a public library in 1875 and the building is still used for this purpose. The Macclesfield Society sprang from small groups of silk workers who were meeting for mutual enlightenment before 1835. The Sunday School Movement in that town during the 18th century undoubtedly created a sympathetic attitude to education.

At Chester the classes were never really successful whereas this branch of the Macclesfield Society's work was a conspicuous feature, perhaps because the Macclesfield classes were closely linked to the demands of the town's silk industry whereas Chester had no such industry seeking to improve trade through better educated workers.

The drawing classes in Macclesfield became the School of Design which eventually developed into a College of Further Education. The female classes grew to become a girls' high school in 1879, and eventually the Grammar School for Girls. These examples of continued influence are not reproduced in Chester, where the public library is the sole reminder of previous educational effort.

In both Chester and Macclesfield lectures were usually ignored by the people for whom they were intended, but in both towns the libraries, particularly the newsrooms, were popular.

The Chester Mechanics' Institute derived a steady revenue from its Water Tower Museum which, from the opening of the railway in 1848, attracted visitors but nevertheless, because of constant financial problems, the premises had to be sold to the Town Council in 1875.

In contrast, Macclesfield's difficulties were not financial; indeed, the very success in initiating developments rendered the Society redundant. By 1880 the offspring were so vigorous that the parent society accepted honourable extinction.

The author describes the social, economic and political life and background of both towns and, in appendices, provides details of, for example, library issues from the Macclesfield Society between 1862 and 1877.

Coding: 1b(iv), 1b(iii), 1b(xxv) KB626

THE CREWE MECHANICS' INSTITUTION 1843-1913 by J. H. Williams, M.Ed. thesis, University of Manchester 1969.

Aim

To examine in detail the foundation and subsequent development of the Crewe Mechanics' Institution from 1843-1913 and to relate the Institution's progress to local and national social, economic, political and educational events.

Method

By examination of annual reports, minute books, prospectuses and contemporary press reports.

Discussion

When the first train passed through Crewe in 1837 it was only a hamlet, housing some 27 families. The building of the locomotive works caused an increase in population, to 4,571 in 1851 and to 42,074 in 1901.

The Crewe Mechanics' Institution is unusual in that, from its very inception, it was heavily subsidised by the railway company and dominated by its requirements. Because of the consistency of this support its history was longer than many other Institutions but, on the other hand, the vast majority of Crewe's citizens depended on the economic success of the railway company, and the social and economic fortuities of individual citizens turned upon the industrial activities of the railways.

Having described the social, economic, political and cultural setting in Chapter 1, the author traces the Institution's history in terms of the Presidencies of six men: Francis Trevithick 1845-57, John Ramsbottom 1857-71, F. W. Webb 1871-1903, George Whale 1903-1908, and C. J. Bowen-Cooke 1908-1913.

Findings

The author notes a number of the Crewe Mechanics' Institution's salient features. Firstly, the Crewe establishment was a provider of formal adult education for seven decades. Secondly, whereas, as a rule, other Mechanics' Institutions had a proletarian membership, Crewe was firmly controlled by an undemocratically 'elected'

Council, the vast majority of whom were obedient to the wishes of the railway directors. (Appendices II and III reproduce the rules of the Institution.) Thirdly, the Institution was dependent upon the railway company for financial aid and free accommodation and, perhaps because of this dependence, there was prolonged animosity between the Institution and the County Education Authorities.

The Institution's membership, as distinct from its Council, was largely confined to the artisan class, who received formal adult education, including technical education, and who enjoyed the library, newsroom and social activities. All these activities were typical of the national pattern of Mechanics Institutes.

The thesis includes a short epilogue of the Institution's history from 1913 to 1936, when the Library, containing 23,973 volumes, and the newsroom were transferred to the Borough Council. From 1936 to 1966 the Institution continued as a Social Club.

Coding: 1b(iv), 1b(ix), 1b(xxv), 1b(xiii), KB626

DERBY MECHANICS' INSTITUTE 1825-1880 by A. F. Chadwick, M.Ed. thesis, University of Manchester 1971.

Aim
To examine in detail the establishment and subsequent development of the Derby Mechanics' Institute between 1825 and 1880, and to analyse the type and breadth of education provided in the context of the contemporary educational, cultural and religious background.

Discussion
Having surveyed the origins of the town of Derby and the most important social and cultural events up to 1825 in Chapter 1, the author traces, in Chapter 2, the contribution of the Strutt family to public and civic life. The Strutts formed their friendships, on the whole, from a narrow section of society, from their fellow Unitarians and from fellow mill-owners. 'Never putting money-making first, they were always warm-hearted and open-handed.' Joseph Strutt argued in 1840 that 'it would be ungrateful in me not to employ a portion of the fortune which I possess in promoting the welfare of

those amongst whom I live . . .' Edward Strutt was concerned in the foundation of University College London, and was elected to the Council of London University in 1831. Powerful, philanthropic, typical of Benthamite, non-conformist reformers, the sympathetic interest of the Strutts was an essential in any local social project. In the establishment of the Derby Institute, William Strutt was active in an administrative and financial sense, but the real driving force was Joseph Strutt, aided by Edward Higginson, a Church of England priest.

However, as described in Chapter 3 which deals with the period 1825-30, when the Mechanics' Institute opened in 1825 it owed its creation to a number of causes besides that of the support of the Strutt family. The details of the first years of the Institute are related; of particular interest is the early establishment, in 1825, of an Institute library. In the period 1831-1839, the subject of Chapter 4, the Institute moved to new premises (1833), built a lecture hall (1837) and held an exhibition (1839) which attracted nation-wide attention.

Perhaps the greatest advance in the service provided by the Institute in the decade 1840-1850 (Chapter 5) was the expansion of class instruction, but by 1850 the Institute was forced to accept officially what had occurred in practice for a number of years, that the bulk of the membership was drawn from the upper working and lower middle classes. Furthermore, two institutions came into being which were to some extent, to compete: the Derby Railway Literary Institute, founded in December 1850, and the Working Men's Association, founded in November 1849.

The period described in Chapter 6, 1851-1860, was characterised by a preoccupation with organisation and status rather than with the direct application of the Institute's original aims; the Institute had achieved 'respectability' but had failed to attain its original, fundamental objectives.

In Chapter 7, dealing with the period 1861-1870, the author describes how the Institute solved some long-standing internal problems, how it held off an amalgamation with Free Library, and how it inaugurated a system of technical education in Derby.

In 1880 Lord Belper, (formerly Edward Strutt), the President of the Institute died, and the family's enthusiastic support waned, for by that date the Institute had all but petered out as a provider of informal education. The period 1871-1880 contains a number of interesting incidents, described in Chapter 8, but essentially the decade is one of declining membership and 'inbreeding'; the opening of the first free public library in Derby in 1871 is but one example of new institutions arising to replace the moribund.

A conclusion, an epilogue and 53 appendices bring the historical account up to date and supply further specific information in graphical form. The Institute still exists (March 1971) as a social club and still contains a circulating library of nearly 10,000 books, both fiction and non-fiction. It began initially with a library and, 146 years later, the library continues as an important service.

Coding: 1b(iv), 1b(xxv), 1b(viii), 1b(xxvi), 1b(iii), KB626

Political and religious reform societies

SOCIAL AND RELIGIOUS INFLUENCES IN ADULT EDUCATION IN YORKSHIRE BETWEEN 1830 AND 1870 by J. F. C. Harrison, D.Phil. thesis, University of Leeds 1955. [also published as *Learning and living 1790-1960*, Routledge & Kegan Paul, 1961 and by University of Toronto Press 1961.]

Aim
To examine the dynamics of the adult education movement during the period when it first became socially significant, by reference to an intensive study of a comparatively small area of Yorkshire during the years 1830-1870.

Discussion
In Part 1 the author describes the social environment of the working-classes during the 1830s and 1840s, using Leeds as an example of urban industrialisation, and the North and East Ridings to illustrate rural working life. Against this background, the potential clientele of adult education, the educability of the people, their reading habits and radicalism, are assessed. Attention is paid to those sections of both working and middle-classes who were likely to be susceptible to adult educational influences, to early trade unionism,

Owenite-socialism and Chartism, and the social influences of church and chapel. The non-conformist influence is analysed in some detail, and the work of the Rev. Dr Hook, Tory radical Vicar of Leeds, is similarly treated.

Part 2, called 'The Sowers and their Seed', describes the activities of various groups who sought to use adult education for their several ends, and relates their efforts to the different layers of social and religious aspiration among the working and middle-classes. One chapter is concerned mainly with the Mechanics' Institute movement, another with the efforts of the working-classes to secure adult education by their own efforts in such rudimentary institutions as Mutual Improvement Societies. Thus, the impact of orthodox political economists, Malthusianism, Temperance, and the genesis of the ideas of self-help are considered.

Adult educational methods also appealed to social reformers such as the Transcendentalists, Owenites, Chartists, Co-operators and middle-class radicals. The period 1840-1860 is considered against this background, and particular attention is paid to the difficulties that the middle-working-class alliance experienced in trying to extend the suffrage between 1847 and 1852. To complete the picture of this period, the author analyses the activities of the religious bodies; the attempts of the Anglicans to establish Church Institutes, the efforts of the Anglican clergy in rural parishes during the 1860s and the establishment of adult schools, particularly in York, by the Society of Friends.

In the final assessment, called 'The Fruits of the Harvest', the situation in 1870 is described. Adult education had contributed something towards the social cement which was the prime need of the new urban industrial society. Through adult education the religious bodies had extended their influence to the working classes; the middle-classes had used it to establish their ethic in society at large; some working men had used it as a means of personal and social advancement. But the concept of adult education as a means of social emancipation for working-men was not formulated with sufficient clarity to assume a distinctive institutional form in the period 1830-1870.

A 60-page appendix describes in detail the career of Mr Hole of Leeds, 1820-1895.

Coding: 1a, 1b(iv), 1b(ii), 1b(iii), 1b(xxv), 1b(v), 1b(viii), KB483

THE CHARACTER OF CERTAIN RELIGIOUS ORGANISATIONS AS SHOWN IN THEIR INFLUENCE ON ENGLISH ADULT EDUCATION 1900-1924 by D. J. Cooper, M.Ed. thesis, University of Leeds 1960.

Aim
To describe, review and analyse the contribution of religious organisations to adult education.

Discussion
The introductory chapter notes that there are roughly two views of the purpose of adult education, either to achieve social purpose or to achieve personal dignity through knowledge. The history of adult education throughout the 19th century illustrates that these two aims were intermingled, and rarely separated. In 1909 Bishop Gore made a speech which could almost pass for that of a radical Chartist. In the same year a founder of the Workers' Educational Association, Mansbridge, expressed the hope that the sons and daughters of working people would seek, through their studies 'first to serve, not themselves, nor even the community, but the eternal purposes of the Divine Wisdom'. The author considers that organised Churches need adult education just as much as adult education needs to be concerned with the quest for the mystical and spiritual.

Chapter 2 deals with the relationship of the organised Churches to the people. In the author's view, by 1900 the Church of England, the Salvation Army, Non-Conformists and Catholics were all concerned with popular education. In Chapter 3, 'The Anglican Church and the WEA', the author shows how, through the influence of William Temple, Albert Mansbridge and others, committed Christians both contributed to the expansion of adult education and affected the quality of the service and, conversely, how the methods adopted by the WEA were applied in the Church Tutorial Class movement.

However, whilst many Anglican personalities were liberal, friendly and genuinely deserving of respect, the fact remains that in 1924 there was no real connection between the Anglican Church and the working-classes. Non-Conformists have been more successful in this respect. Chapter 4, 'The Non-Conformist Churches and Adult Education', takes up this theme, describing the work of the Quakers in the Adult Schools, and the Educational Settlements, the Methodists' Wesley Guild movement, and the Unitarian Church's contribution. In Chapter 5 the Catholic Social Guild, inaugurated in 1909, and the Catholic Workers' College (Plater College) launched in 1921, are described in some detail.

There are no conclusions, except perhaps the suspicion that over-secularisation may lead, not to a rational criticism of the organised Churches, but to a refusal to accept that education is concerned with more than the preparation of individuals for competitive advancement.

Coding: 1c(vi), 1b(ii), 1b(x), 1b(xv), 1b(xxvii), KB1083a

INDEPENDENT WORKING CLASS EDUCATION WITH PARTICULAR REFERENCE TO SOUTH LANCASHIRE 1909-1930 by R. Frow, M.Ed. thesis, University of Manchester 1968.

Aim
To study one section of the education undertaken by members of the working-class as revealed in local archive material relating to Manchester, Liverpool, Hyde and Oldham in the period 1909-1930.

Discussion
The adherents of the Independent Working Class Education movement claimed that the difference between their type of education and all other education lay in the aim. All other education, even that which purported to be for workers, was given in the interest of the ruling class. Consequently, the IWCE movement stipulated that classes had to be independent and self-supporting, that tutors had to be workers, that the method of instruction should develop the workers' ability to play a part in the political life of their class and that the content of their studies should lead to an understanding of the need for social and economic change. The author traces back the concept of independence in working class education to the first manifestation of class consciousness in the earliest days of the Industrial Revolution.

The main theme of the thesis begins in 1908 when the authorities of Oxford University attempted to align Ruskin College more closely to the University. In 1909, the students of Ruskin College went on strike and set up an independent Labour College in Oxford, which later moved to London. The strikers eventually dispersed to their own localities to form classes which would impart education in a working-class way. Two of the 1909 Ruskin strikers, Harold Kershaw of Rochdale and Jack Owen of Manchester, perhaps influenced by syndicalist ideas certainly supported by the organisation of the Plebs League and the Plebs Magazine, played a part in developing the IWCE movement in Lancashire. As an example of one of the earliest of such classes, the author describes the Oldham 1910 class in some detail.

Though the IWCE movement was disrupted by the 1914-18 war, it nevertheless survived, largely because of the continued support of the Plebs League. However, the horrors of war and the success of the 1917 Russian Revolution led many men to believe that society ought to be, and could be, changed. Ernest Faulkner was one such and he started an IWCE class in Hyde, eventually playing a part in the amalgamation of classes to form the South East Lancashire Area of Labour Colleges.

Although amalgamation and reorganisation schemes, such as the formation of the National Council of Labour Colleges in 1921, strengthened the IWCE movement, progress was negated by the defeat of the Labour movement in the General Strike of 1926 and the adoption of 'mondism' thereafter.

People like Faulkner, for example, turned to other aspects of the Labour movement. The subject matter, type of class and teaching methods had already changed to reflect the increasing association with, and influence of, the trades unions. As a result of developments affecting the Labour movement as a whole, the number of IWCE students nationally declined from a peak of 31,635 in 1926 to 15,018 in 1936/37.

Coding: 1b(vii), KB755

THE NATIONAL COUNCIL OF LABOUR COLLEGES – AN
EXPERIMENT IN WORKERS' EDUCATION by J. H. Roberts,
M.Sc.(Social Sciences) thesis, University of Edinburgh 1970.

Aim

To study the growth of the Labour Colleges, with particular
reference to independent working-class adult education in Scotland.

Discussion

The National Council of Labour Colleges (NCLC), founded in 1921,
was an amalgamation of groups actively engaged in the education of
adult workers. Organised into twelve divisions, its object was to
provide a socialist-based education in order to equip the working-
class for service in the Labour movement. This task was carried out
at classes, public lectures and union branch meetings. In addition,
correspondence courses, weekend and summer schools were established and a close association was forged with the Trade Union
movement.

The author examines the growth, activities and conflicts in one
division in the NCLC, the Scottish Labour College. Problems of
finance, administration, classwork, of relations between the College
and the National Executive of the NCLC and between trade unions
are discussed throughout the work.

The survey begins, however, with a study of landmarks in the
development of adult education in Britain since 1698, and its link
with the education of children, and continues with an account of the
initial struggles and clashes leading to the foundation of the NCLC
and the Scottish Labour College. Subsequent chapters deal with the
connection between the Labour College and the Trade Union
movement in the light of the growing rivalry between the NCLC and
the WEA.

There follows an investigation of the dissension within the
Scottish Labour College between 1928 and 1933 and its influence on
management and morale. The discussion continues with a description
of the revival of confidence within the College between 1934 and
1939, the growing influence of the Scottish TUC on its administrative machinery and the controversial attitudes towards Newbattle
Abbey, the residential centre.

After describing the effects of the war on the work of the Scottish Labour College, an account of the educational policy of the Trades Union Congress in relation to the Workers' Educational Trade Union Committee and the NCLC is given. The study ends with the demise of the NCLC in 1964, when its activities were taken over by the educational machinery of the TUC, and with a concluding appreciation.

Findings
From its inception the NCLC stressed that educational questions could be solved only in relation to all other problems facing a capitalist-based society. The basic philosophy was 'we have our own historic way to follow, our own salvation to achieve, and by this sign we shall conquer'. But courage was not enough for, in striving for independence, the NCLC rejected orthodoxy; the militant missionary spirit of many of its supporters, by definition, excluded the uneasy compromises that often characterise political or educational success. The lack of financial resources, the early lack of competent administrators, the rivalry of the WEA, the unwillingness of the NCLC to depend on state finance, were all factors in the eventual decline of the NCLC. Nevertheless, the NCLC served some whose needs were not met by other educational agencies; the Trade Unions often provided support at crucial moments, and through the enthusiasm of one particular leader, James Millar, the movement made a substantial contribution to working-class adult education.

On the other hand, there are lessons to be drawn from the NCLC's experience; firstly, apathy towards education, particularly among the semi-skilled and unskilled workers, is by no means easy to overcome, and secondly, administratively incompetent visionaries are rarely much more effective than uninspired worldly administrators.

Coding: 1b(vii), 1b(xii), 1b(x), 3c, 1a, 1b(xiv), KB758a

Co-operative education

A REPORT ON THE CO-OPERATIVE AUXILIARIES, Co-operative College Paper No. 7, 1960 (83 pp) and THE FUTURE OF THE AUXILIARIES — A POSTSCRIPT, Education Department, Co-operative Union Ltd, 1963 (50 pp) by B. Groombridge. Reports commissioned by the Co-operative Union.

Aim

To suggest how the adult auxiliaries in England and Wales, the Women's Co-operative Guild, the National Guild of Co-operators, the Men's Guild and the British Federation of Young Co-operators, can adapt their purposes, organisations and programmes to increase their strength and service to the co-operative movement in modern conditions.

Discussion

In 1938 auxiliaries' membership totalled 103,000; by 1958 membership had halved, to 56,000, and 40% of the Guildswomen and 45% of the Mixed Guild members were over the age of 60. But by 1958 the proportion of older adults in the population as a whole was increasing whilst people under 30 tended not to shop at co-operative stores. Thus, having described the basic situation and discussed the influences for and against auxiliary progress, the author addressed himself to the question 'Are the auxiliaries needed?'

He examined recruitment procedures, including publicity, branch meetings and programmes, accommodation and leadership and the British Federation of Young Co-operators in particular. Essentially, the auxiliaries depend for recruitment and membership on the pool of co-operative shoppers. If this pool is declining or reflects a certain age bias, then the auxiliaries are likely to experience the same trends. [In 1960 the co-operative movement experienced a phase of static equilibrium before the dynamic re-organisation of the 1966-1972 period.]

The author frankly, but sympathetically, urged reform in nearly every aspect of the auxiliaries' activities. Out-of-date attitudes, programmes, publicity, and some quaint traditions are castigated, none more so than the cheeseparing attitude to infinitely small items of expenditure and to officials' salaries. Various recommendations were made, the most important of which was to suggest closer co-operation between those in charge of the daily activity of co-operative retailing and distribution and those who are concerned with the education of a consumer co-operation. He suggested, for example, that the auxiliaries could act as consumers' associations valued by the management, and that the management could, in return, link trade and auxiliary publicity and public relations.

The postscript, written in 1963, records that the Women's Guild had appointed three part-time field workers and seemed to have arrested its decline, that the Men's Guild had done little other than change its name, and that the Mixed Guild had endangered itself by failing to recognise the crisis before it. To encourage further reform the author reassessed the realism of the 1960 Report's recommendations by setting them against the actual possibilities of action in Stevenage and Deptford.

In the event, the author reiterated, at local level, the two themes of his first report; unity, which involves much closer interdependence and co-operation among Guilds, Education Committees and Boards, and service from more professional officers within the auxiliaries and the Education Department. There appeared to be three main causes of ineptness in the auxiliary movement; firstly, that elected committees had neither the professional officers nor the financial support to be effective; secondly, that the managers of the movement generally did not seem aware of the potential of the auxiliaries, both to support their economic activities and their social purposes; and thirdly, that the auxiliaries do not base their work on the degree of commitment which is implicit in becoming a trading member; for example, auxiliaries should not expose themselves solely to the views of the Co-operative Party.

Nevertheless, the author remained convinced that the auxiliaries are an essential feature of British Co-operation, that their rehabilitation concerns the whole movement and not themselves alone, and that the movement requires professional educationists.

Coding: 7c(vii), 1b(vi), KB654

DEMOCRACY IN THE REGIONAL SOCIETIES OF THE CO-OPERATIVE UNION LTD. Report of a Working Party, (Chairman: W. E. Lawn), issued 1969 (27 pp).

Aim

Within the framework of the Regional Plan, to consider and make recommendations on the organisation and educational provisions necessary in a regional society to secure as effective a development as possible of member participation and democratic control.

Method

The use of evidence provided by documents, publications and articles, together with submissions by interested individuals and organisations, and consultation.

Discussion

Democratic control has two aspects; the accountability of professional servants indirectly to the members of the society and, directly, to their representatives, and the need positively to seek participation of the members and their representatives in the exercise of that control.

To exercise an appeal to members who share in the co-operative principles of the movement, it is necessary to:

1 show in the trading activity and leadership of a Co-operative Society that these principles can produce unsurpassed service to the trading needs of the members;

2 express the implications of these principles on topics of public importance and of immediate Co-operative relevance;

3 relate these principles further to wider national and international issues.

In addition to the changing economic, social, political and educational background within which the co-operative movement operates, there have been remarkable changes in the distributive industry which both alter the distinctive economic advantages of membership and alter the nature of the demands made upon members. The increasing size of societies, for example, may lead to a more efficient service, but may also make it more difficult for members to control the professional management for no other reason than the mundane difficulty of travel within the area of a regional society. Nevertheless, the Working Party remained convinced that greater size also offers strong advantages, and its recommendations to increase member participation take into account the trend towards concentration.

Findings
Locally, the Working Party recommended more information; nationally, they recommended more attention to guidance papers. They suggested that advertising should deal not only with commercial advantages but with the social principles and practice of co-operation. So far as auxiliary organisations are concerned, they recommended the possible junction of the Women's Guild and the National Guild of Co-operators, and the provision of professional organisers to help the Guild in co-operation with the Education Department of the Union itself.

In a further section detailed suggestions are offered for improving the structure of control to encourage member participation. The final section re-emphasises the commitment of the movement to education — both of members and staff. The recommendations seek to encourage greater member participation, more executive responsibility for the education committee, and more professional appointments in the movement's educational service. Finally, the Working Party supported the further development of the activities of the Co-operative College.

Coding: 7c(vii), 1b(vi)

University extra-mural teaching and the WEA

A CRITICAL STUDY OF THE ORGANISATION OF UNIVERSITY EXTRA-MURAL WORK IN ENGLAND by S. G. Raybould, Ph.D. thesis, University of London 1951. [published as *The English universities and adult education*, WEA 1951.]

Aim
To study the organisation of extra-mural work in England, considered with particular reference to its effect on the character and quality of the adult education provided by the extra-mural departments of the universities.

Method
A historical review of developments since 1873, but particularly from 1924 onwards, and a critical assessment of contemporary extra-mural work.

Discussion
In Chapter 1 the early years of the extension movement, from 1873-1919, are briefly surveyed. By about 1900, in spite of the many achievements, the extra-mural movement had not succeeded in two respects; it had not reached many 'working-class' students and it had not succeeded in maintaining the proportion of sustained courses, as contrasted to short, popular lecture courses. In 1913/14, 17 Oxford courses extended over 10-18 lectures, as compared with 114 courses of 6-9 meetings.

These features led directly to the founding of the WEA in 1903, and to the launching of the first University Tutorial Class in 1908, for students who reached out for something more than attendance at lectures. The co-operation of the WEA reaching to a working-class student body and of the university providing tutors for rigorous working-class adult studies led to the institution of Joint Committees.

In 1919 the Final Report of the Adult Education Committee of the Ministry of Reconstruction was published. As regards organisation, finance and staffing, the influence of the Report has been great; but the chief factor which determined the types of work that could be done was not the recommendation of any report but the Adult Education Grant Regulations of the Board and the Ministry of Education issued in 1924. Thus, grants and class provision, from 1873-1945, are reviewed in Chapter 2, bearing in mind the crucial effects of the 1924 Regulations. From 1924-1938, the rate of expansion was greater in the courses lasting one session or less than in the case of the tutorial classes, and greatest in the terminal and short-terminal classes which did not involve written work.

The provision under post-1945 regulations is described in Chapter 3, with the greatest expansion taking place in classes where the courses were both short and, as such, did not involve regular study and writing on the part of students. However, both before and after the war, the proportions as between the different types of class varied considerably from one extra-mural board to another.

The reasons for the continuing trends towards the provision by extra-mural agencies of a larger number and proportion of elementary courses are examined in detail in Chapter 4. The author suggests two principal factors. The first was the situation external to the universities and university colleges of an increasing demand for adult education facilities of an elementary kind which the voluntary 'approved associations' were not sufficiently developed to meet. The second was the internal university willingness to meet this type of demand without equally stressing the importance of maintaining a distinctive 'university standard'. The decisive factor was the second reason.

Trends in staffing, organisation and finance are described in Chapter 5; the author notes that very little published research seems to have been produced by adult education or extra-mural departments, and that the principal fact to emerge was that the departments were organised less as departments concerned with the development of a distinctive branch of university study than as agencies for arranging extra-mural courses and providing teachers for them.

Consequently, in Chapter 6, he turns to a discussion of the question of 'university standards' in adult education, and considers particularly the question of subject specially suited to study by adults and the conditions under which it is appropriate for classes in them to be provided by universities. The end is that the students should come, not simply to witness, to understand, and to appreciate the university method and spirit, but habitually to manifest them in their own work. If that is a definition of the purpose of university adult education, is it also one of the purposes of extra-mural work?

Findings
Chapter 7 and 8 are concerned with critical examination of present provisions and suggestions for an alternative policy in extra-mural work, and the changes in staffing, finance and organisation required to implement these proposals. The author recommends that the universities should not continue to provide elementary courses and suggests that these would be better organised and run by the WEA, if the WEA could receive the financial subventions to employ more tutors. He suggests that experienced university staff tutors may act in an advisory capacity to the WEA district, to assist in maintaining teaching and syllabus standards. He emphasises the requirement that universities should promote systematic thought and enquiry about adult education as a distinctive branch of study.

Coding: 7c(i), 1b(ix), 8a, 5a, 1b(x), Kb 690

A CRITICAL ANALYSIS OF THE ORIGIN AND DEVELOPMENT OF THE OXFORD AND CAMBRIDGE UNIVERSITY EXTENSION MOVEMENT BETWEEN 1873 AND 1902, WITH SPECIAL REFERENCE TO THE WEST RIDING OF YORKSHIRE by N. A. Jepson, Ph.D. thesis, University of Leeds 1955. [also published as *The beginning of English university adult education — policy and problems,* Michael Joseph, 1973]

Aim
This is a study of the origin of the Extension Movement at Oxford and Cambridge and of the contribution made by these two universities in the field of adult education from 1873, when Cambridge organised the first extension courses, until the beginning of the 20th century, when the Education Act of 1902 and the founding of the Workers' Educational Association in 1903 appeared to mark the end of the first phase of university adult education. The thesis concentrates on three major aspects: the origin of the movement, the

composition of the student body and the nature and quality of the education which was provided.

Discussion

Section 1 deals with the period from 1850, when William Sewell submitted his paper on 'Suggestions on University Extension' to the time when the Universities of Cambridge and Oxford began to organise extension lecture courses in 1873 and 1885 respectively. Section 2 is concerned with the type of students the founders of the movements aimed to attract and the degree of success that was achieved. Particular attention is paid to the efforts to recruit working-class support.

Section 3 analyses the kind of education which the Extension leaders hoped to provide and the extent to which they succeeded. It examines the problems associated with the development of liberal adult education, the appointment and retention of staff, the provision of conditions in which effective tutorial teaching was possible and the organisation of systematic courses of study. The final section assesses some of the problems which confronted the University Extension Movement at the beginning of the 20th century.

The important part which the Women's Movement in the 1860s played in the origin of the Extension Movement is highlighted, as is the contribution of the Co-operative Society and the Mechanics' Institutes. But the middle classes dominated the movement; 'I cannot deny that it is the large middle-class which forms our backbone' wrote R. D. Roberts in 1891. But 'where success among the artisans had been achieved . . . it had been due, in part at least, to the local management being in the hands of the working men themselves'. Women students formed the majority, comprising, for example, two-thirds of the students attending Oxford University Extension courses in 1888-89.

The adult movement's contribution to secondary and primary education is of interest; in 1893-94, 747 boys and 1800 girls attended Oxford University Extension courses; in 1901-2, 287 out of 304 sessional certificates were awarded to students attending centres recognised by the Education Department in connection with pupil-teacher training.

Coding: 1b(ix), 2a, 3b, 8a, 4, KB705

ADULT EDUCATION IN ENGLAND AND GERMANY — A COMPARATIVE STUDY by R. J. Cook, M.A. thesis, University of London 1955.

Aim

To compare the systems of adult education which have evolved in two countries that represent Western European civilisation.

Discussion

The history of the two countries has been very different, since Germany did not exist as a unified state until 1871, and traces of medieval feudalism left their mark on Germany's educational pattern. State attitudes to education have also been quite different; state elementary schools were founded in Prussia and other German states about 100 years before the founding of the British state system. The effects of the varying state provision of elementary schools on adult education are examined.

The author argues that development of adult education in Britain was not hindered by the same fear of revolutionary ideas as in Germany, but that Britain, on the other hand, experienced the full force of the Industrial Revolution before Germany; consequently, major differences may be accounted for by reasons of both attitudes and economics. The positive contribution of the English universities to the development of adult education is compared to the aloofness of the German universities although some of the effects of the exchanges of ideas since 1945 are examined.

The thesis deals with the effects of economic and social conditions on the content, aims and capabilities of the adult education service in both countries. Similarly, the methods by which policies are implemented are scrutinised.

Three principal points emerge: Britain has been fortunate in avoiding the excesses of authoritarianism (vide 'Impressions of Adult Education in the Ruhr', by W. Burmeister in *Adult Education*, Winter 1952); Britain is privileged in possessing a strong voluntary movement, in particular that concerned with, and run by, women; and finally, adult education in both countries has developed and changed markedly since 1945.

Coding: 1b(ix), 1b(x), 7a, 1a

CHARLES ROWLEY AND THE ANCOATS RECREATION MOVEMENT by J. I. Rushton, M.Ed. thesis, University of Manchester 1959.

Aim

An investigation of the Ancoats Recreation Movement 1876-1938, evaluating the part played by Charles Rowley in its creation, and an assessment of its value as an instrument of adult education.

Discussion

A guide book of 1857 describes Ancoats as the oldest, and the worst, working-class area in Manchester, in which the truest examples of the indigenous Lancashire population were to be found and the true Saxon pronunciation of English was to be heard. There were 69,500 children in Manchester in 1852, of whom 32,400 were at school, 7,000 were at work and 30,100 were variously engaged about the city streets. Such was the society in which Charles Rowley grew up.

Rowley was a radical whose philanthropy was rooted in the romantic, liberal and protestant philosophy and attitudes of the time. But his tendency towards egocentricity, mingled though it was with a genuine humanitarian concern for the poor, obscured the true origins of the Recreation Movement. As the author gathered information, it became clear that other Manchester gentlemen, notably T. C. Horsfall, participated extensively in the activities out of which the Ancoats Recreation Movement developed. In fact, the early work of the Movement proved indistinguishable from that of the Manchester branch of the Sunday Lecture Society, and T. C. Horsfall's picture museum schemes.

The Movement started in 1876 with band concerts, art exhibitions and flower shows. Perhaps the orchestral music, poetry, rambles, etc appeared somewhat alien and middle-class to the working people of Ancoats, but when, in 1896, the Recreation Movement handed over the principal University Extension work to the newly-founded Manchester University Settlement, the latter had a foundation of recreational activity upon which to build.

From 1896 to 1924, when Charles Rowley retired, the Movement became gradually more middle-class; in 1909 Charles Rowley asserted that the Ancoats Movement existed for 'the intelligent, for whom alone we cater'. From 1924 to 1938 the Ancoats Recreation Movement simply declined and finally expired. Though the leadership of Charles Rowley was missed, probably the best explanation for the decline is that the world had changed. Nevertheless, the Ancoats Recreation Movement made a significant contribution to adult education, and Charles Rowley was its prime servant.

The thesis contains many reproductions, including photographs of Ancoats in 1957. Of particular interest is the friendship of Rowley with the leading Pre-Raphaelites, with Michael Sadler of the Oxford University Extension Movement, and the part played by Sadler and Rowley in the Summer School Movement.

Coding: 1b(ix), 1b(xxiv), 1b(xxiii), 1b(ix), 1b(iii)

ROLE DEFINITION AND FULFILMENT IN ENGLISH ADULT EDUCATION – A STUDY OF CERTAIN ASPECTS OF UNIVERSITY AND WORKING CLASS EDUCATION 1900-1950 by B. W. Pashley, M.A. thesis, University of Liverpool 1966. [part of thesis published as *University extension reconsidered,* Vaughan Paper No. 2, University of Leicester 1968]

Aim
To examine certain of the ideas and assumptions, and aims and achievements, of English adult education in the 20th century, as exemplified by three institutions, the universities, the Workers' Educational Association and the National Council of Labour Colleges.

Method
Each adult educational organisation or institution that is examined is given a three-fold treatment; firstly, a theoretical treatment comprising a presentation of the original stated aim and of the theory, if any, behind it; secondly, a descriptive treatment, comprising a factual presentation of the way in which the organisation worked in practice; and thirdly, an analytical treatment to examine how the stated roles were fulfilled. Statistical data is presented; some statistics, however, represent the number of students, others enrolments:

enrolment figures refer, of course, to the number of courses for which each student registers and are, therefore, more impressive.

Discussion
Section 1, on University Extension, traces the development of the movement in the 19th century and deals with two periods, 1900-1924 and 1924-1951, in considerable detail. All adult education under their sole aegis is defined as pertaining to University Extension. However, the alliance with WEA altered the universities' role, or gave them an additional role. Of the period up to 1924, three principal points are made: that the tradition of independent university provision is much older than the WEA alliance, that universities have often been limited in extending their services by a chronic financial problem, and that 'University Extension' is a portmanteau term within which there was no uniformity of practice either between or within the universities concerned.

In the period 1924 to 1950, as a result of grant aid, the new universities began to provide Extension courses, in addition to their Joint Committee work and, particularly in the period after 1945, there was an increase in courses for relatively small groups and this additional extra-mural commitment tended to direct the attention of most universities away from an almost exclusive WEA nexus. University adult education, because it was not limited or prescribed, was in fact free to assume new roles and to respond to changing social circumstances; indeed the dilemma in 1950 arose not so much from the specificity as from the catholicity of role definition.

The second section of the thesis considers adult education for the working-class, considering firstly the WEA. The Association was created to serve, in the main, underprivileged manual workers. The facilities offered by the University Extension Movement were originally used, but to create a more specific service for workers, the WEA began to provide courses itself and to co-operate with the universities through Joint Committees composed of representatives from universities and WEA districts. The resources of the universities were channelled into tutorial and sessional classes supervised by these Committees.

The task of the WEA was to supply manual workers with opportunities for higher education, but the proportion of manual workers declined to a minority even before 1914. Consequently, since 1918 the WEA has faced a dilemma which it partially solved by redefining its aim as being to meet the needs of the working-classes generally who, it was argued, included many non-manual workers. By 1950 the WEA had become a general cultural provider, catering for all sections of society, concentrating upon no specific need and thus fulfilling no specific role.

The WEA, founded on the belief that the interests of the working-class could best be served through an alliance between the working-classes and the world of scholarship dedicated to an objective search for truth, clashed with the National Council of Labour Colleges, which felt that the true interests of the working class could only be served by an independent education formed in Marxist terms. The struggle to find support for their work amongst the trades unions generated a bitter antagonism. To some extent the WEA/NCLC competition could have been resolved by the TUC itself taking more responsibility for the educational provision for its own members.

This thesis deals with the subject of university and working-class education in general terms; there are many local variations of the national theme.

Coding: 1b(x), 2a, 7c(i), 7c(iii), 7c(xiv), 1b(ix), 1b(xi), 1b(xii), KB700

THE DEVELOPMENT OF ADULT EDUCATION IN THE POTTERIES, WITH SPECIAL REFERENCE TO THE FOUNDING OF A UNIVERSITY IN THE AREA by R. A. LOWE, M.A.(Ed) thesis, University of Keele 1966.

Aim
To trace the development of adult education in the Potteries from the early 19th century to the establishment of a Department of Extra-Mural Studies in the University of Keele in 1962.

Discussion
The development of adult education in North Staffordshire had been continuous since the early 19th century, springing first from middle-class attempts to stimulate local industries, mainly through the

Mechanics' Institutions. The failure of these societies to attract the working classes in any number led to a counter-tradition of self-help which, despite inherent disadvantages, became fairly strong.

Cambridge University Extension lecturers were the first to attempt successfully to unite these two streams, and from 1899, when Oxford lecturers took over entirely the work in Staffordshire, the first contacts were made between the local working classes and Oxford University. The Tutorial Classes, begun by R. H. Tawney in 1908, and the North Staffordshire Miners' Higher Education Movement, which developed from them, strengthened this link. In 1921 the voluntary Miners' Movement became a WEA district, and it was possible to send a steady stream of students to Oxford.

Schemes for a local college had been canvassed as early as 1890, but the independent traditions of local municipalities and the difficulties of raising funds from small-scale local industries mitigated against the realisation of such plans. Furthermore, the establishment in 1914 of a technical college, which partly fulfilled these demands and marked the culmination of middle-class patronage, made the possibility of a second college remote.

Nevertheless, those involved in non-vocational adult education continued to press for a university college which would provide an apex of tutorial classwork but, ironically, when their hopes were realised in 1950, the courses offered by the new University College of North Staffordshire owed more to the national debate on the deficiencies of the university system than to the local demands. After a protracted discussion, and because of the persistent faith of many individuals, the responsibility for extra-mural courses was transferred from the Oxford University Delegacy for External Studies to the Extra-Mural Department of the University of Keele (as the college had now become), with Roy Shaw as its first Director.

Four of the twelve chapters of this thesis deal with the period 1945-1962 and particularly reveal the attitudes of the post-1945 leaders of the adult education movement to the nature and purpose of both internal and external university education, and to the responsibilities of universities to their local communities.

Coding: 1b(ix), 1b(iv), 1b(x), 8c

THE MISSIONARY DONS — ENGLISH UNIVERSITY EXTEN-SION IN HISTORICAL PERSPECTIVE by K. Künzel, D.Phil. thesis, University of Bochum 1972. [From a summary provided by the author]

Aim
a To discuss the relevant literature on university adult education with a clarification of terminological uncertainties
b To examine the historical development of the University Extension movement

Discussion
The object of the first chapter is to show how Oxbridge, starting with the Royal Commission in 1850, had continuously expanded and revived both missionary and imperialistic zeal in the field of national education. In order to make this shift in attitude historically transparent, some attention is paid to the change of the internal climate within the ancient universities, for which the term 'University Extension' had at one stage summed up all aspirations of greater usefulness to society at large. On the basis of a more general analysis of the University Reform Movement, William Sewell's and Lord Arthur Hervey's theoretical concepts on University Extension are discussed, linking them with the first 'extra-mural' activities of Oxford, namely the Middle Class Examinations.

In the second chapter, external factors are examined which in the 1870's created a situation in which universities and adult education could merge together. Among these factors, the general state of adult education, the involvement of the educationally-minded working-class movements, and the rising progress of women's emancipation, are specifically dealt with. The actual development of the classical phase of University Extension up to 1902, a discussion of contemporary progress in the general educational system and the re-organisations in educational administration after 1899 are also discussed.

To explain changes within university adult education after the turn of the century, the third chapter deals systematically with some organisational and didactic features of the Extension Movement, and describes the participants and 'new missionaries', not only in working-class education, but in university adult education generally.

Chapter 4 is concerned with the genesis and progress of the WEA and the Tutorial Class Movement up to 1924. It describes the newly-won political aspirations of the working-class movement and links them with the liberal heritage of University Extension to pinpoint the ideological basis of the WEA and its educational spearhead — the tutorial class. The same chapter follows the development of classical University Extension and the tutorial classes after the passing of the 1924 Adult Education Regulations. An unpublished 'confidential' report by the Board of Education on tutorial classes in England from 1922, containing a great deal of useful and interesting material, has been discovered and used. Institutional changes which resulted from the Adult Education Regulations, namely the practice of setting up extra-mural departments, are also depicted.

Chapter 5 is an attempt to sketch the new social and political conditions of post-war England as considered relevant to the further development of extra-mural work, particularly the way in which a new demand, more flexible grant regulations, the weakening of the traditional WEA/university alliance, and the emergence of a new generation of pragmatic extra-mural directors, have shaped both the ideal and practice of today's extra-mural work.

Having provided a typological survey of post-war extra-mural provision, the thesis concludes with a consideration of social and pedagogical issues which, throughout its development, have characterised and modelled University Extension. To mention but a few: university adult education and general educational advance; a discussion of historical interactions between political reform and tutorial class ideology; questions as to the political dimension of workers' education in historical perspective (as provided by the universities); and changing patterns in the concept of 'liberal' adult education.

' Finally the author attempts to discern some fundamental contemporary changes in national education (comprehensive schools, technical education, the Open University), and their relevance to a progressive form of extra-mural activity.

Coding: 1b(ix), 1b(x) 7c(i), KB704

THE EMERGENCE, DEVELOPMENT AND PROSPECTS OF THE
WORKERS' EDUCATIONAL ASSOCIATION, WITH SPECIAL
REFERENCE TO THE SOUTHERN DISTRICT AND THE NEW
MILTON WEA BRANCH by D. J. Booth, M. Phil. thesis, University
of Southampton 1972.

Aim

To review the emergence of the WEA, to describe its evolution in the
Southern District and the New Milton district, to survey and analyse
the attending population and to examine the latent demand for
responsible-body provision.

Method

An account of the growth of the WEA nationally and locally is
followed by a comparative survey of class members and a stratified
sample survey of the population in the catchment area of the New
Milton WEA branch, in 1968-1970.

Discussion

Chapter 1 describes the emergence of the WEA in 1903, the work of
Mansbridge and the changes in policy wrought by McTavish. Mansbridge established a pattern of tutorial classes and forged links with
the University Extension movement and the 'official' educational
system. McTavish, who succeeded Mansbridge in 1915, wished for
stronger links with organised labour and was instrumental in setting
up the Workers' Educational Trade Union Committee in 1919. Under
McTavish's leadership, the WEA issued a series of political documents
which so involved the WEA in radical politics that it was referred to
as 'the educational conscience and mind of the British Labour
Movement'. Thus, by 1929 the WEA's policy was to appeal directly
to the working man engaged in Trade Union activities.

The Southern District of the WEA is described in Chapter 2; in
1929 1,680 students attended classes of all types, in 1967 just over
10,500 students attended grant-earning classes. (In the 1965/66
socio-occupational group analysis, 42% were housewives, 14%
retired, 8% professional and 4% manual workers). The work of the
New Milton Branch is reviewed in detail in Chapter 3. Of particular
interest is the relationship and distribution of provision between the

local WEA and the Further Education Centre. In 1968/69, in terms of student enrolment, WEA and extra-mural enrolments reached 202, whereas the local authority enrolments amounted to 2,138 students. Chapter 4 describes the methodology of the class and population surveys; in the event, there were 111 usable questionnaires for the class survey (82.8% of those issued) and 146 questionnaires (54% of those issued) of the random sample of the non-participant population. These are analysed in Chapter 5.

Findings

Essentially, class members tended toward a predominantly female, middle-class and retired, student body. 54.9% of students were between the ages of 39 and 65, compared to 46.5% in the random population survey. 10% of the class students were below 38 years of age, compared to 21.5% in the random survey. 41.4% of the students had lived at their present addresses between 6 and 10 years, but 26% of the ramdom sample had lived in the area for 21 years or more. The WEA class survey showed that the socio-economic groupings of the respondent's father had, to a large extent, determined the respondent's groupings.

But there is a national increase in employment in the socio-economic groups I, II and III. Consequently, the national trend towards a white-collar population is reflected in New Milton, and patently, as the analysis shows a significant minority of semi-skilled and unskilled residents in New Milton, the likelihood is that there will be a continuing reduction in the proportion of these social classes attending responsible-body classes.

Where did members of classes hear about the classes? 31.5% attended because of personal recommendation, 10.8% had seen a brochure, 6.3% had read a newspaper advertisement, 12.6% because it was a point of previous class provision, 10.8% because of information from the WEA or the university. 15.3% gave no information but the statistics suggest that this group were mainly housewives who probably received personal and social information. It is interesting that 56.7% of females relying on social and personal information about WEA classes had a terminal educational age of up to 15 years.

96.3% of the class respondents attended classes directly from home so in nearly all cases there was a break between work and class attendance. 76.5% attended classes within 3 miles of their homes,

72.9% using a private vehicle or car to travel to classes. 81% of class respondents liked their course, 38.8% for reasons of educational advance, 43.3% because of the tutor ('outstanding tutor and marvellous films'). Class respondents tended to be far more active in other organisations than the sample population of New Milton. Most of the statistical information is compared to the results of the National Institute of Adult Education Survey.

In summary, New Milton is a middle-class, expanding area for executives and retired people; the WEA student representation reflects this local class structure and thus there are two questions. Firstly, does the WEA student body reflect the local class structure in working-class areas? Secondly, does the WEA tap enough of the latent demand in the New Milton area?

As evidence to provide an answer to the second question, the thesis considers the leisure habits, the reading, listening to radio, viewing television, etc. activities of the sample population. A fascinating statistical finding is that, of the New Milton random population sample, about 35% would choose as first preference *serious* radio or TV programmes, about 38% *cultural* programmes and only about 27% preferred *light* or variety programmes (page 312 of the thesis). The author confirms the general view that leisure interests associated with educational outlets are increasingly home-based but that there is a potential demand for leisure activities which ameliorate the loneliness of retirement or the frustrations of work. Thus, he argues that the difference between branches and between regions is greater than previously indicated, and that local class provision can, and does, respond to real demands in an area. But each area does not have the same social purpose. Consequently, the case is put for both a more generous grant from the central government to the WEA and a more liberal attitude to the spending of that grant.

It may well be that the prime task of the WEA in the Southampton area is to provide courses for the retired or for a prosperous urban community; another branch in another area may decide that the target should be to help the working-class through trade union education. A general grant with a specific purpose simply does not allow for local peculiarities.

Appendices, with information about the WEA both nationally and locally, occupy 100 or so pages of the study.

Coding: 7c(iii), 7c(i), 2a, 2b, 3c, 1c(x), 1b(x), 4, 5h, KB732

Adult and further education under the auspices of local authorities

---

THE VOLUNTARY DAY CONTINUATION SCHOOLS IN LONDON by A. H. Surman, M.A. thesis, University of London 1949.

Aim
To describe the development of the Voluntary Day Continuation Schools, which came into existence in the London County Council area in 1922, and which became Day Colleges in December 1948.

Discussion
In order to operate the Day Continuation School sections of the Education Act of 1918, the LCC established 35 compulsory Day Continuation Schools. All 35 closed in July 1932, but 11 eventually survived to become Voluntary Continuation Schools with three essential characteristics. The student body consisted of young persons from school-leaving to 18 years; the curriculum established was general; and attendance was part-time day.

The thesis shows that the Schools were derived from the voluntary pioneer efforts typical of the early stages of an English educational advance. The main interest of the thesis is as an historical study of the limbo that faced the young worker suspended, as it were, between organisations concerned with compulsory secondary education and institutions and movements concerned with adult education. For many young adults in London, the Voluntary Day Continuation School was a welcome lifeline.

Coding: 1b(xiii)

THE PLACE OF THE EVENING INSTITUTE IN FURTHER EDUCATION IN THE EAST MIDLANDS by J. T. Fielding, M.Ed. thesis, University of Nottingham 1950.

Aim
a To survey evening classes generally

b To review conditions in evening institutes in 1950
c To assess the future of the evening institute

Method

The principal examples chosen for detailed study are taken from the East Midlands because the region affords many appropriate illustrations of progressive movements in adult and further education, and is a representative area for evening institute work.

The historical background and development of further education are placed in a sociological background. The organisation, staffing and curricula of evening institutes, the type of student enrolled and the shift towards the recreational approach are considered in the second part of the thesis. The third part evaluates the effect of the provision of county colleges and community centres on a national scale and the implications of such developments in the East Midlands region.

Discussion

With the increased intervention of state and local authorities in further education and adult education, and the evolution of specialised branches for technical and adult education, evening institutes were seen to take a subservient position during the 19th century. To some extent this was due to their long and close association with elementary education.

Findings

Because of limited resources and an almost continuous pressure to provide new day accommodation, education authorities have rarely been able to give much attention to the proper housing of their evening institutes which have, in consequence, remained tolerated but unwelcome guests in many large schools. The majority of staff were drawn from secondary modern schools or were part-time teachers; grammar school staffs rarely applied but in 1949 the Nottingham University Extra-Mural Department agreed to provide and pay a tutor, if the evening institute provided the accommodation.

Between 1936 and 1946 the proportion attending classes concerned with domestic and women's subjects, physical culture, handicrafts and art increased, whereas the proportion attending classes concerned with English, music and elocution diminished.

Examining the concept of the community centre, the author argues that community centres may properly undertake the work of evening institutes, but that community centres are most appropriate in urban conditions and usually impracticable in rural circumstances. He argues for full-time community centre wardens and for self-government and self-responsibility within the centres.

As for the evening institutes, the author suggests a policy of adaptation, experimentation, co-operation and, where rational, graceful retreat.

Coding: 1b(xiii), 1b(ii), 1b(xxvii), 7c(iv), 8a, 4

THE DEVELOPMENT OF HIGHER AND FURTHER EDUCATION IN SUNDERLAND SINCE 1908 by J. Makkison, M.Ed. thesis, University of Durham 1969,

---

Aim
To describe the development of higher and further education in Sunderland since 1908, chiefly the development of the Technical College and, to a lesser extent, the College of Education and the College of Art.

Discussion
1908 marked the end of the first phase of the Technical College's development because in that year, by the provisions of the University of Durham Act, it was granted conditional permission for affiliation. At the same time a separate Day Training College was established instead of a Department of Education of the Technical College. In 1969 the Art and Technical Colleges were combined to form the Sunderland Polytechnic and the College of Education received its own Instrument of Government.

Chapter 1 describes the economic history of Sunderland in general and Chapter 2 details the dominant industry of the town, shipbuilding. Chapter 3 traces the development of further education in Sunderland from 1825, when the first Mechanics' Institute was founded, until 1908, and describes the early history of the School of Science and Art, which was formed in 1860. From these two institutions sprang all the further education provision in Sunderland.

Chapters 4, 5 and 6 are concerned with the development of teacher-training, and shows how the Day Training College became the largest College of Education within the Durham Institute of Education. The growth of the School of Art into a College of Art and Design within the Sunderland Polytechnic is described in Chapter 7.

Further education in general, and technical education in particular, both nationally and in Sunderland, are dealt with in Chapters 8-12. This includes an account of the struggles of the Technical College to gain recognition for its advanced work, its division into the Sunderland Technical College, the Monkwearmouth College of Further Education and the West Park College of Further Education in 1956, and the events after the publication of the Robbins Report.

Brief mention is made in the thesis of the work of evening institutes.

Coding: 1c(ii), 1b(iv), 1b(xiii)

THE DEVELOPMENT OF STATE-AIDED EVENING SCHOOLS FOR ADULTS 1870-1902 by K. A. Percy, M.A. thesis (2 vols), University of Nottingham 1969.

Aim
To study the development of evening schools for adults (a term which includes a whole range of adolescents and adults) who worked full-time for a living, from 1800-1914, but particularly from 1870-1902.

Discussion
The first two chapters describe the 19th century economic, social and political background, the educational attitudes and the origins of the state education system before 1870, the evening schools and evening science classes before 1870. The author traces the significant growth in the 1860s of evening schools and of their provision of basic elementary education for adults, and he shows that the Code of 1871 decisively retarded this growth. Evening schools stagnated

during the 1870s and declined rapidly in numbers between 1878 and 1885, as much because of administrative restrictions as because of a lack of demand. However, evening science classes, under the Department of Science and Art, grew steadily during the period 1870-1890, and the University Extension movement expanded from 1873 to provide an education beyond the confines of the 3Rs. As Sadler wrote of the latter, 'their function has been in the main stimulative'.

A new Code in 1882 encouraged the revival of evening schools and there was some expansion of numbers of students and breadth of curricula in the late 1880s as a result of the pressure of the urban School Boards. The unrelenting pressure on the central government by School Boards, Inspectors, the Cross Commissioners and the Recreative Evening Schools Association resulted in the liberal Codes of 1890 and 1893, which freed evening schools to be providers of continuative and secondary education. In the subsequent expansion of evening schools during the 1890s, School Boards became increasingly the providers of a wide variety of vocational and non-vocational adult education. The financial support given to evening classes under the Code of 1890 by the Technical Instruction Committees was vital for their survival, particularly in country areas.

In 1889-90, about 65,000 scholars enrolled in evening schools; by 1892/93, the number had almost doubled, to about 116,000, 25% of whom were female. However, between 1899 and 1902, evening schools were the victims of the contest between the supporters and the antagonists of the School Boards. The administrative recon-struction which followed the 1902 Act placed evening schools under the control of the technically-orientated local authorities and the South Kensington Department. Those irregular adult classes which survived between 1902 and 1914 in large numbers did so without much official enthusiasm, although the WEA, founded in 1903, tried to exert some pressure on officialdom.

'The thesis also discusses the relationship of artisan evening classes under the civic universities to the activities of the School Boards. The appendices are extensive and informative, and include a diagram illustrating the 'Correlation of Education', issued by the Manchester Education Committee c.1895, showing various routes for contin-uative education.

Coding: 1b(ii), 1b(ix), 1b(x), KB783

THE DEVELOPMENT OF THE ORGANISATION OF RATE—AIDED EVENING SCHOOLS IN LEICESTER 1871-1925 by A. E. Bryan, M.Ed. thesis, University of Leicester 1971.

Aim
To study the development of evening schools for adults and adolescents.

Method
The study is based substantially on the original records of the Leicester School Board and Leicester Education Committee, currently depistied in the Leicester Museum Archives, together with other discovered material hitherto undeposited. Photographs are included in the thesis; for example, the school furniture being used by the photography class in 1930 is shown to be remarkably unsuitable.

Discussion
There are five main sections, each of which is sub-divided chronologically, dealing with: the executive, buildings and equipment, the teachers, the content and method of the programmes, and the older students, their presence and growth in numbers from 1874 onwards.

Local history is now seen to be a necessary supplement, and at times a corrective, to the contributions of national and international history. In the latter part of the 19th century there was a ferment of educational activity, perhaps exemplified by the emergence of such organisations as the Working Men's College; where a School Board employed someone with experience of, or interest in, continuing education, as with Leicester's first Schools Inspector, the foundations were laid for the development of rate-aided evening schools organisation with a positive concern for adults, and which necessitated the designation of an inspector as 'Organising Superintendent' or 'Director of Evening Schools'.

Though a substantial number of the teachers employed in evening schools were certificated teachers, qualified to teach general subjects in elementary schools, from the 1890s onwards a growing number of the teaching staff employed in evening schools were not employed in the day schools. As it was recognised that teaching in the voluntary evening school differed from teaching in the day school situation, from 1912 onwards particular attention was paid to the standards of part-time teachers. Fortunately, in the case of Leicester, there was no differentiation between 'vocational' and 'non-vocational' activities or between 'educational' and 'recreational' subjects, nor were single subject activities excluded in the interests of encouraging the development of a course system.

Total enrolments increased from 270 in 1874/75 to 1,780 in 1909/10, to 5,264 in 1924/25 and the numbers aged 18+ increased from 264 in 1906/07 to 2,017 in 1924/25.

In general Leicester typifies the two principal national problems facing adult education; firstly, how to attract a reasonable proportion of the adult population into adult education and secondly, how to encourage the attendance of those most in need of continuing opportunities, the working-classes whose share of educational resources have been limited.

An unusual feature of this thesis is the detailed description of the role and contribution of Her Majesty's Inspectorate to local developments during this period.

Coding: 1b(xiii), 1b(xii), KB784

Community associations and centres

THE EDUCATIONAL FUNCTIONS OF COMMUNITY CENTRES — WITH SPECIAL REFERENCE TO SOUTH EAST LANCASHIRE by A. Wilcox, M.A. thesis, University of Manchester 1951.

Aim
To study the educational functions of community centres within the area of the Manchester and District Federation of Community Associations.

Method
By conversations ranging from detailed discussions with officials on the work of their centres to a few minutes of apparently casual talk with members of the centres and with members of the public in the localities of the centres. By questionnaire to community association members in Manchester — 217 forms were completed, providing indicative rather than statistical sample results.

Discussion

A community association is a body of men and women who have come together, either as individuals or as representatives of groups, to promote the common good. It is the voluntary and democratic organisation of people with a variety of beliefs and interests which distinguishes community associations from other bodies. The name 'Community Association' implies a general, rather than a limited and specific, service to the neighbourhood, and the successful association features a sense of community based on a continuity of shared experience. Organisationally, local community associations may increase their effectiveness by joining the National Federation of Community Associations set up in 1946.

The author describes a variety of associations individually and in detail: though each serves a specific neighbourhood, they provide for positive action in seeking friends and personal fulfilment in the community, or sometimes simply offer a release from the tensions and overcrowding at home. Usually, though not always, community associations have a community centre at their disposal.

Membership is difficult to calculate accurately. Fees are usually low and often include an individual's family; for example, out of 22 associations within the Manchester Federation, 11 had household membership, and with 5 of these it was the only form of membership.

Sometimes sections arise by 'spontaneous generation' out of associations; sometimes a group with a shared interest joins an association as a new section. Usually there is a restriction on the amount of money a section's treasurer may hold and all assets above this amount must be with the association treasurer.

It is generally accepted that centres should be pleasant, comfortable, welcoming and aesthetically pleasing. In some cases this is so; but the author notes with regret that there is a ready acceptance of second or third rate furnishings. Schools often provide good accommodation for the associations, but school closures for holidays and the general aura of a school as a place for children often deters adults. Indeed, the school is reckoned to be a poor substitute for the adult community's own centre.

There is no common pattern of activities in a community centre. On the whole there is a preponderance of evening over afternoon activities. Though there is no firm line, community association activities are conventionally described under headings: social, recreational and educational — the last often means an improvement in an individual's behaviour pattern towards other members. More commonly, handicraft would be regarded as educational, whist as social and the arts group as being both social and educational. Teachers or tutors, where employed, are chosen more on the grounds of particular skills, for example cake-making, than on the basis of pedagogic qualification.

Surprisingly, leaders of associations are remarkable for their ordinariness; they are products of their neighbourhood, but perhaps steadiness, dependability, practical sense and shrewdness are more valuable in the community movement than personal 'flair'.

The organisation, service and activities of the Manchester Federation of Community Associations — the first in England — is described in detail. Similarly treated is the question of the appropriate relationships between the local authority and the community association.

The results of the questionnaire showed that the need for companionship within the centre is important at all adult ages, that 'club' activities are the most popular and that nearly 45% of all officials and committee members do not belong to any other organisation. The average number of visits to the centre per week was about 3 or 4 for officials and between 2 and 3 for non-officials. Finally, the centre represents all the out-of-home activities for 7% of members between 14 and 17 years and for 51% of members over 60 years.

Coding: 7c(iv), 1b(xxvii), 7c(x), 8a, 4

THE COMMUNITY SCHOOL AND THE SOLUTIONS IT OFFERS TO SOME SOCIAL AND EDUCATIONAL PROBLEMS ON A BRISTOL HOUSING ESTATE by A. E. Walls, M.A. thesis, University of London 1967.

Aim
a To investigate the problems involved in developing Lawrence Weston Comprehensive School, Bristol, into a 'Community School' on on the Lawrence Weston housing estate

b To examine the educational and social problems experienced at the periphery of large conurbations in the context of urban change and movement

c To consider the history and development of the 'Community School' in both the United Kingdom and America

d To formulate some of the criteria for community schools and to make recommendations for future developments

Method

Historical survey and descriptive analysis are the principal methods used, but the thesis includes a random sample, by questionnaire, of 100 residents representing 1½% of those on the voters' roll in 1966, and some statistical analysis of the backgrounds of pupils attending the school.

Discussion

Studies of housing estates have shown that institutions and organisations which provided focal points for activities in the old-established areas have failed to repeat their successes under changed conditions. To obviate some of the social malaise of new housing estates, the idea of the 'Community School' evolved, the prime purpose of which was to serve the whole community. Such a school is the centre of the social, educational and cultural activity in the area and, as such, is both a direct influence on the neighbourhood and responsive to the needs of the local society. Parts 1 to 3 of the thesis consider the implications of urban change for English and American towns, for schools in general and for Lawrence Weston in particular.

Part 4 examines the work of selected community schools in solving social problems and deals with some English experiments in linking school and community. Parts 5 and 6 consider the problems of cultural borrowing and offer recommendations for the future progress. The amelioration of the condition of the young housewife, isolated by family responsibilities, is particularly considered.

Appendices deal briefly with, for example, post-school activities, evening activities for pupils and evening institute activities during a typical week at Lawrence Weston School.

Findings

The estate contains a large proportion of skilled men, and the area is not unpleasant. Nevertheless, problems of isolation and frustration, of social divisions within one class are recorded, as revealed in the answers to the question 'Are you generally satisfied with the opportunities for recreation and entertainment in Lawrence Weston?'

Age group	Yes(%)	No(%)
Adults	27	67
15-21	32½	54½
11-15	26½	58½
Under 11	12½	71½

The type of services to the community normally provided by English schools stops short of any definition of a genuine community school. Whilst evening classes are commonly provided, most English schools have few social occasions. This study confirms how little impact schools have made, or have been considered to make, upon the great social problems of our times. English schools need to be persuaded that they are social, as well as educational, institutions. Some positive steps that they might take are: taking a lead in community associations, particularly by helping young mothers by organising baby-sitting; providing community news sheets; organising festivals; taking an initiative in creating welfare committees; providing boarding house accommodation to avoid children being taken into care; assisting the pre-school playgroup associations; helping young people to find temporary jobs.

Coding: 7c(iv), 1b(xxviii), 1b(xxix), 2b, 2d

THE DEVELOPMENT OF COMMUNITY CENTRES WITH SPECIAL REFERENCE TO YORKSHIRE by D. Payne, M.Ed. thesis, University of Manchester 1968.

Aim
a To examine and assess the present role of the Yorkshire Community Association. A community association represents a coming together of local people, societies and organisations to manage a centre in which to meet to pursue agreed common ends

b To consider if the community centre is a focal point for the social, recreational and educational activities of the neighbourhood and, if this is not the case
c To investigate who forms the membership of the community association and to what extent its facilities are used or its potential realised

Method

In the first survey, 73 out of 99 community associations in Yorkshire replied to a request for information. Wardens, voluntary officers, members and LEA officials were interviewed. In the second survey, the views of individual members, numbering 365 from 16 Yorkshire associations were received, together with those of 102 members from 6 associations outside Yorkshire. Questionnaires were returned by post or completed during the author's visits.

Discussion

Community associations, community centres, tenants and residents associations and other titles are defined and the aims and purposes of community associations and centres are discussed in Chapters 1 & 2. Chapter 3 considers their historical background, both national and local. In 1946 approximately 100 centres had been built; by 1963 940 existed. Community associations are often financially fragile and sometimes face competition from Working Men's Clubs; consequently, their relationship with local authorities (the subject of Chapter 4) is usually an adequate explanation of the distribution of centres throughout the country.

Similarly, the quality of the premises (Chapter 5) is a function of local authority support and interest. Regrettably, the accommodation was usually inadequate and therefore the effectiveness of the community association was considerably reduced.

The activities of the associations are essentially social and expressive; perhaps some associations are too dogmatic in their exclusion of the formal educational, cultural or social service aspect but the resources in professional personnel and in adequate buildings are limiting factors.

Chapters 6, 7 and 8 deal respectively with association activities, survey the membership and review the staffing arrangements. Overall, about 69% live within one mile of the centre; in a Yorkshire sample, about 40% attend once a week, the ratio of males to females was about 1:2, about 66% were aged 41 years and over. Most people joined to meet people, to help people, to enjoy drama, dancing and music. The average age of wardens (Community Service Association Report 1966) was 50.3 years, about one-third of them having responsibilities for youth work.

Findings
Each centre is highly individual; a single leading personality may make all the difference. The primary problem is how to allocate official funds and help without supplanting voluntary local initiative. On the whole, the author suggests, the community centres could reasonably enter into a closer partnership with local authorities and other sections of the adult education movement and that, conversely, local authorities could do more to foster and nurture the Associations.

Coding: 1b(xiv), 2a, 3c, 4, 5l, 8c, 3b, 7c(x), KB820

A COMPARATIVE STUDY OF COMMUNITY ASSOCIATIONS IN EDINBURGH by A. C. Twelvetrees, M.Sc. thesis, University of Edinburgh 1970. [to be published as *Community associations and centres,* Bookstall Services, 1973]

Aim
To discover how far Community Associations in four areas of Edinburgh effectively fulfil the functions expected of such bodies by the National Federation of Community Associations.

Method
Information was obtained from primary sources; constitutions, minutes, reports, and the correspondence of the associations, as well as from interviews with centre wardens, representatives of the Edinburgh and Scottish Councils for Social Service and other informed individuals. The approach is holistic.

Discussion
An introduction to the functions of community associations in general is followed by an account of the policies of Edinburgh and other Scottish local authorities towards them. The next chapter describes the evolution of community associations in selected areas. Subsequent sections compare and contrast these associations, covering the role of the local authority, membership, finance, leadership, internal structure, purposes and functions, communication and professional staff.

Findings
The evidence reveals that a large bureaucratic community association which co-ordinates local organisations is essentially different from a small community group which may also call itself a community association. The bureaucratic type of community association will less easily induce individuals to identify with it and may stifle initiative through being unwieldy. At the same time, it is more likely to undertake a range of activities and cater for a greater variety of interests. On the other hand, a smaller association which does not have a co-ordinating function, or has no responsibility for a large centre, may gain the allegiance of a reasonably homogeneous community, although this may tend to reinforce, rather than overcome, social barriers. Without exceptional local leaders, or professional help, the natural evolution of such an association is likely to be towards an inward-looking 'members-only' club.

A further conclusion is that a community centre can become a focus for the community in only a limited sense, for in any locality there will always be a variety of social or interest groupings, each of which will cover a different geographical area, and all of which can never be served by any one building situated in any one place. Thus, centres should be only part of a range of facilities, the utilisation of which may, perhaps, be co-ordinated by a community association.

The author further concludes that there is a need for small community groups in addition to larger federal, or co-ordinating (community) associations, and that the federal association should not threaten the autonomy of smaller associations.

The eight objectives recommended by the National Federation of Community Associations for a community association are reduced to two by the author; namely, the satisfaction of hitherto unmet community needs and the co-ordination of local organisations.

Consequently, only the federal association can be termed a true community association; individual membership should be restricted to sub-sections of the association, thus separating membership at representative and individual levels into different organisations or into different tiers of the same organisation.

Finally, if community associations are to be effective, they should be given more resources, particularly in the form of professional 'enablers'. For example, 'in 1954 the Community Centres Officer resigned and was not replaced' and 'each of the centres could use more voluntary assistants, particularly *trained* . . .'; notice should also be taken of the terms of a section heading 'The community centre warden: building manager or neighbourhood worker?'.

Coding: 7(x), 1b(xxviii), 1b(xxvii), 8b

Residential education

RESIDENTIAL ADULT EDUCATION IN ENGLAND by L. Speak, M.A. thesis (2 vols), University of Leeds 1949.

Aim
a To survey the development of residential adult education in England from 1899 to 1949
b To examine the contemporary position of individual long-term and short-term residential colleges
c To provide some accurate information about the Danish Folk High Schools
d To assess the future of residential adult education

Method
A historical survey, with appendices, giving statistics of the number of students, residential staff, the length of courses, the subjects offered and details of accommodation, administration, organisation and financial aid.

Discussion
Until 1939 residential adult education in England developed in two

main directions, the residential college offering courses of from six months to two years, and the summer schools. The summer school movement eschewed the principle of the large, crowded type of meeting and favoured the small gathering of students and teachers in which a sense of fellowship could develop and which was sufficiently homogeneous for classwork and intensive study methods.

Between 1899 and 1919 the first long-term residential colleges were established: Ruskin, Woodbrooke, Fircroft and the Labour College. More colleges were founded between 1919 and 1939, widening the scope of residential adult education but retaining the general character and aims of the original colleges.

Other forms of residential adult education developed during the inter-war years, notably the National Adult School Union's six-month winter schools, residential courses for unemployed adults such as those organised at King's Standing in 1933 and, in 1938, the Lamb Guildhouse experiment in Bowden, near Manchester. Even during the war the movement continued to expand and Holly Royde, Manchester opened in November 1944.

The Education Act of 1944 specified the conditions for an extension of adult education as part of the responsibilities of the local education authorities, provided for the raising of the school-leaving age, for continuative part-time instruction and emphasised the importance of education as a whole.

After 1945 the long-term colleges became far more dependent on direct state financial support, and consequently gained a financial stability and potential for growth hitherto lacking. Each college continued to have its own distinctive 'character' and 'tone'; no attempt was made to impose a uniform system.

Before 1939 students attended long-term colleges for individual enrichment, to develop their capacity for social and political service and to improve their occupations. However, after 1945 more students were able to use the long-term colleges as a preparation for undergraduate studies. In the period 1946-1948 inclusive, out of 104 students leaving Ruskin College, 32 went to University; out of 45 leaving Fircroft, 22 went on to further training; out of 127 leaving Hillcroft, 75 continued in further training. Could it be argued that the colleges existed primarily for the enrichment of personal life?

The thesis deals with the upsurge of short-term residential colleges after 1945. Each short-term college was highly individual, but a broad framework of aims emerged; these were to attract new people into adult education, to provide a residential element for those already in the movement and to broaden the outlook and increase the efficiency of those holding responsible positions in industry, commerce and the professions. However, courses often depended on the groups within the local or regional community with whom the college had the closest links.

The final chapters analyse the development of the Danish High Schools, and consider the special features and special value of residential adult education. The author suggests that one of the special unique features of residential education is its suitability 'for educating the feelings' through fellowship.

Coding: 1b(xv), 7c(vi), 7b, 5a, KB825

SOME PROBLEMS OF THE SHORT-TERM ADULT RESIDEN-TIAL COLLEGE IN POST-WAR BRITAIN by A. M. Hughes, M.A. thesis, University of Liverpool 1954.

Aim
a To survey the growth of short-term adult residential colleges since 1929
b To review and examine the purposes and achievements of short-term residential colleges
c To evaluate the needs of students and their experiences
d To evaluate the role of colleges in the adult education service as a whole

Method
A survey of the origins of 24 short-term colleges, including detailed accounts of seven. Questionnaires were presented to 257 students at Burton Manor in 1952 and 1953, and 125 students who attended general courses at Burton Manor during 1950 were asked to recall their impressions by letter. Personal interviews were also conducted with students from industry and with 16 wardens.

Discussion

A short-term adult residential college consists of any adult education centre whose primary function is to initiate, promote and conduct residential courses, usually not exceeding two weeks in duration. The colleges share many common features but it is emphasised that they also exhibit a surprising degree of individualistic variety. Consequently the wardens, when interviewed, tended to give two answers to questions, one which was general to all colleges and another which applied to the special conditions of their college. At that time few wardens had a more than superficial knowledge of the work done in other colleges.

All colleges relied on the lecture, question session, discussion systems, but some were experimenting with group discussions, project work, case studies and role-playing techniques of instruction. Limitations on course technique developments were two-fold, the shortage of staff and the brevity of courses.

About 40,000 students attended courses each year during the period 1948-1952; in June 1953, 8% were between 15 and 19 years, 27½% between 20 and 34, 28% between 35 and 49, 22% between 50 and 64 and 14½% 65 or over. Educational backgrounds varied; in 1950 out of 301 students attending nine courses at Grantley Hall, 174 had secondary school experience, 25 elementary school experience only, 34, 31 and 37 had attended, respectively, universities, technical colleges and training colleges. On the other hand, out of 177 supervisors attending supervisory management courses at Burton Manor in 1950-1951, 66 were elementary school educated only, and only 13 were solely secondary educated.

Many students had no idea of what to expect and often their first favourable reactions were due to a sense of relief that their worst forebodings were not confirmed; for example, 104 out of 257 were agreeably surprised by the informality. 227 considered the opportunities for discussion, the exchange of ideas, the development of self-confidence and mixing with other students as the most important features of their courses. 11 considered the colleges' chief purpose to be a contribution to the general improvement of social relations or to widen the outlook of students. But 74 out of 257 had suggestions for specific changes in the course they were attending and a further 61 were concerned that either the courses were too short or that there should be greater provision for refresher courses.

Findings
The short-term colleges provide an attractive environment for study, and offer positive social benefits which the students appreciate. There is a need to distinguish between the needs of vocational and non-vocational students and between those who are sponsored and those who attend voluntarily.

Greater attention needs to be paid to the problems of the sponsored student, particularly in ensuring that there is an adequate system of follow-up to his short residential course. Such a system implies fuller co-operation between the colleges and other forms of adult education. There is a need for greater clarity of purpose in the case of some colleges and in individual courses at many colleges. More generous staffing arrangements are recommended. Tutors tend to work in isolation and should be encouraged to play a greater part in the adult education movement as a whole. Finally, the colleges' activities should increasingly reflect the voiced wishes of the general public.

Coding: 1b(xv), 3d, 5l, 2a, 2b, 7c(v), 8c, KB836

THE EFFECTS OF LONG-TERM RESIDENTIAL ADULT EDUCATION IN POST-WAR BRITAIN, WITH PARTICULAR REFERENCE TO RUSKIN COLLEGE, OXFORD by J. Blumler, D.Phil. thesis (2 vols), University of Oxford 1962.

Aim
To evaluate the effects of long-term residential adult education upon the activities and attitudes of adult students, particularly upon four aspects of their lives: careers; relations with voluntary association; cultural interests; subjective social status and social relationships.

Method
Over the period 1952-1958 questionnaires were completed by 207 new entrants to Ruskin College, 126 second-year students, 64 leavers, 180 post-war students and 80 pre-war students. In addition, questionnaires were completed by a further 298 post-war students and 173 students of other colleges (Catholic Workers' College, Coleg

Harlech, Co-operative College, Fircroft and Hillcroft). Interviews were arranged with a sample of 164 post-war Ruskin students.

Discussion
Of 207 entrants to Ruskin College between 1952 and 1956, only 7% had not engaged in some form of part-time study before their admission; about 50% had been involved in part-time study for three or more years. Furthermore, 90% of entrants claimed that their main motive for entry was the satisfaction of an intellectual or cultural ambition, though 38% gave vocational reasons as equally important. Indeed, only a college with the distinctive forces that, for example, the Catholic Workers' College can command can persuade large numbers of students to ignore the vocational possibilities of long-term residential adult education. Thus, though long-term residential study often provides the means for change, it may more simply continue developments initiated elsewhere, or equally, and more prosaically, simply satisfy students whose motivation is already confirmed.

Findings
Sample profile of entrants who returned questionnaires 1952-1956:
Terminal Education Age (206 students)

Years	Percentage
14	52
15	18
16+	30

Sex: 89% male; 11% female

Age

Years	Percentage
21-25	36
26-30	31
31-35	25
36+	7

Social status (207 students)

	Percentage
high status	21
routine clerical	32
skilled manual	30
semi- and unskilled	15
unemployed	1

Careers — Most students ultimately moved into higher occupational groups, although a large minority initially returned to their previous work. Residential college courses aid and suggest employment improvements but are not necessarily the cause of transfers into new occupations. 54% of Ruskin entrants estimated that they were 'definitely likely to find other work'; 70% felt no duty to return to their old job; 86% wanted jobs 'where I could express my feeling, ideas, talent or skill'.

Relations with voluntary associations — Trade union loyalties were not undermined; indeed, some students became full-time trade union officers and many other students (nearly 50%) would have preferred work in the Labour movement to any other. Although trade union membership remained high after the course, voluntary activity diminished in the group moving up the occupational scale. The number of students becoming less radical during the course was offset by the quantity becoming more radical. The overall result was a slight decline in voluntary political activity.

Cultural interests — Reading habits were strengthened and personal interests previously manifested were pursued more effectively. Students were impressed by the academic privileges offered by universities, to the extent that half of the Ruskin group of leavers applied for admission to a degree course. College attendance revealed interests, values and opportunities hitherto limited to 'the few' and most working-class students accepted this ethos.

Subjective social status and relationships — Influences from their working-class backgrounds persisted, although 23% regarded themselves as *very closely* identified with the working-class in 1957, compared to 50% before entering Ruskin. But students felt better equipped to meet middle-class and professional people and, indeed, the occupational status of best friends widened. There was evidence of greater self-confidence, to the degree that students identified with other social classes.

The enquiry does not suggest that the purposes of long-term residential adult education per se need fundamental re-examination but suggests that, *at that time,* the role of Ruskin College within the Labour movement could well have been re-examined and re-defined.

Coding: 1b(xv), 7c(v), KB833

THE DEVELOPMENT AND CHANGING ROLES OF THE ADULT
RESIDENTIAL COLLEGES IN BRITAIN by K. Rowe, M.A.(Ed)
thesis (2 vols), University of Keele 1970.

Aim
To trace the development and changing roles of the adult residential
colleges in Britain, dealing particularly with the period 1945-1967.

Method
The author surveys relevant published material and theses, and
visited various colleges or obtained information by post. The primary
statistical tables resulting from these enquiries are comprehensive,
clearly assembled and illustrated. Although the statistics cover the
period 1899-1967, the period 1945-1967 receives most attention.

Discussion
Residential colleges are of two types. The long-term colleges, which
are all independent foundations, offer, as their main educational
provision, courses of one or two years in a limited range of liberal
studies. Because they attract mature men and women, usually
between the ages of 25 and 40, who have for some reason been
unable to proceed to higher education at the normal age, they are
often regarded as 'colleges of the second chance'.

Short-term colleges are more difficult to define precisely, as they
can be confused with residential centres. The colleges are sponsored
by various organisations, their courses last for varying periods from a
weekend to two weeks, and there is always an academic head
responsible for devising and promoting a programme of work. The
residential centres are usually not open to the general public, but are
at the disposal of outside bodies who provide their own tutors. Some
have their own specialist staff, e.g. Ashridge Management College.

The first four chapters of the thesis are concerned with the general
historical background of adult education, the bearing of these trends
on residential adult education, and the development of short-term
and long-term residential colleges. The essential immediate post-war
problems, highlighted in 1954 by A. M. Hughes, were that, firstly,
the short-term colleges were not accepted by the general public as a
necessary and worthwhile part of the education system and,

secondly, that they failed to meet the variety of public demands, both in the vocational and non-vocational fields. But the difficulty of solving these problems was often due to inadequate staffing and financial support.

Chapter 5 reviews the pattern of residential adult education in the 1960s, to show the relationships of the diverse types of residential college: to one another, to the various bodies providing financial aid and to those bodies concerned with using their residential facilities. Chapters 6 and 7 deal particularly with the student body, staff, courses provided, the financial position and answers the question 'What do they offer and to whom?'. About 45,000 students attended maintained and assisted short-term colleges in 1967-68, of whom about 32,000 attended courses of less than four days. From a sample of seven courses at Burton Manor in 1951, 45% of the students left school between the ages of 16 and 18-years, 51% between the ages of 14 and 15.

In Chapter 8 the author considers some of the shortcomings and difficulties which many of these colleges face and try to overcome; for example, they largely serve the middle-class and the middle-aged, the need to plan courses 18 months in advance makes their programmes inflexible, the wardens and staff are pressed to use the accommodation continuously and are not given sufficient relief from that constant treadmill, and accommodation is often uninviting. All this the wardens know, but those responsible for the allocation of resources tend to ignore.

In the final Chapter, the author states the case for supporting the residential colleges, and suggests that the increase in industrial courses in co-operation with technical colleges and Industrial Training Boards, and the possibility of playing a vital role in the Open University structure of courses, may encourage further expansion.

Coding: 7c(v), 1b(xv), 2e, 2d, 3d, 4, 5d, 5l, 6, KB 828a

The Open University

THE RESPONSE TO THE OPEN UNIVERSITY — CONTINUITY AND DISCONTINUITY by N. E. McIntosh, prepared for the International Conference on The Implications of Mass Higher Education, University of Lancaster, 4-8 September 1972, published in *Higher Education* vol 2, no 2, March 1973 (12 pp).

Aim

a To consider the response of the general public in Britain to the arrival of the Open University

b To consider the response of those people who chose to start studying with the Open University

c To consider the response of those students who applied and provisionally registered to start their studies, but who decided not to carry on to final registration

Discussion

Firstly, the author argues that there are internal and external pressures to conform to existing systems, for example, the pilot experiment to admit 250 'qualified' — in the university-entrance sense — 18-year-olds in 1974. On the other hand, if an institution has the flexibility to meet new social demands then, in a way, it remains a 'new' institution as distinct from a novel institution.

Mrs McIntosh points out that one of the factors limiting the types of students applying to the Open University in the first year was that about 90% of those who left school early did not know that the University was genuinely 'open'. Thus, the system of enrolment of 'first come, first served, naturally took applicants from the better-informed and consequently this sample would show some skewness towards the middle classes. The quotas set for region, occupation and course choice only ameliorated the basic problem of 'informed' applicants. For example, scientists and engineers doubled their percentage of applications from 5.9% in the first 10,000 to 12.4% in the last 10,000, whilst the proportion of teachers fell from 43.4% to 23.8%.

In 1971, 40,817 applied, 35.9% of whom were teachers; a total of 25,000 were allocated places, 34.3% of whom were teachers. In

1972, a total of 34,222 applied, 21,065 were allocated places, 29.9% were teachers. In 1973, 32,046 applied of which 29.5% were teachers. Applications for 1973 were 62.6% men, 37.1% women; in the arts the proportions of male to female students were approximately equal but in technology the proportions were about 16:1. An important change in the first two years was that the proportion of those born in 1946 and later rose from 10% to 21%.

The author's third point is that about 20% of the first year's entry withdrew before 'final' registration. The highest proportion of any individual occupational group to withdraw was from skilled manual workers.

Thus, in 1971, of 24,220 registered, 81% finally registered, *of which* 81% took an examination or examinations, 74% passed one or two. 16,186 continued into 1972 courses, of which 24%, or 3,823 were to take or retake one or two foundation courses, 14% or 2,231 were to take foundation *and* second level courses and 62% or 10,132 students, were to take second level courses. The drop-out rate was of the order of 8,000 of the provisionally registered students, i.e. 33%, and 19% of finally-registered students, but of course some may rejoin the University when individual circumstances permit.

Coding: 7c(ii), 5k, 2a, 4, 3c

Adult education and technical training

THE RELATIONSHIP BETWEEN PRODUCTIVE INDUSTRY AND TECHNICAL EDUCATION IN MANCHESTER FROM ABOUT 1870-1939 by J. Dawkins, M.Ed. thesis, University of Manchester 1959.

Aim
To find out how technical education developed in one of the great industrial areas in Britain, and how it was related to the needs and demands of industry.

Discussion
The Manchester area is difficult to define; consequently, the author

refers to towns such as Salford which provided important evidence of educational activities of direct relevance to the city of Manchester itself. Similarly, productive industry covers an extensive field, so that certain large industries, such as engineering, were investigated on the grounds that they provided the most comprehensive information.

The thesis is in five sections, dealing in order with: technical education in 1870; elementary education evolving into technical instruction between 1870 and 1889; the leadership of the Council in developing technical education from 1889 to 1900; the development of day-release and day-continuation from 1900-1918; and finally, the inter-war years 1918-1939.

Findings

In 1939, as in 1870, technical education was still essentially a part-time evening study undertaken by a small proportion of people in industry. This is not to say that the period under review had not seen many significant changes in technical education, nor in the extent to which productive industry increased its contacts with the local authorities. The College of Technology received financial aid from industry for buildings after the First World War and gifts in kind, such as machinery, were also received, whilst various industrialists served on governing bodies and advisory committees. By 1939 industry was represented on certain examining bodies, such as the Union of Lancashire and Cheshire Institutes.

But there is plenty of evidence to show that industry did not do all that it might; on the other hand, there is also evidence to show that the local authority placed technical education after primary and secondary education when it came to allocating money. Of course, Manchester was over-identified with the textile industry, and day-release or any other extra cost would not be favoured by an industry in decline. Indeed, it was only when new, expanding industries, such as chemicals, developed in Manchester that a general ambience of confidence was created, and a more generous spirit to the long-term benefits of day-release emerged. Thus, even as late as 1956 the Principal of the College of Science and Technology (as it became) found it necessary to remark 'We shall have to persuade its (industry's) leaders to play their part in what is, in very truth, a co-operative enterprise'.

Coding: 1c(ii), 1b(iv), 1b(viii), 1b(xiii), 1c(xi)

AN EXAMINATION OF COURSES CONDUCTED BY THE SOUTH BIRMINGHAM TECHNICAL COLLEGE FOR THE TRAINING OF TRAINING OFFICERS by A. M. Hayes, M.Sc. thesis, University of Aston in Birmingham 1969. (Available on loan on microfilm only)

Aim
To examine the courses held, from October 1965 to June 1967, for the training of training officers, conducted by the South Birmingham Technical College, as a result of the Industrial Training Act 1964.

Method
42 training officers were interviewed approximately one year after they had completed the course; 5 of these were further interviewed a year later. The purpose of the interviews was to find out from training officers and, when possible, from management, what training developments had taken place in each organisation and how much of this could be linked with work on the course.

Discussion
The author illustrates the kind of person appointed as a training officer, how each reacted to different parts of the course, and what changes each was able to introduce upon his return to his company. Consequently, Chapter 1 deals with the importance of the training officer and his classification. Out of 42 officers attending 5 courses, 5 had graduate qualifications; 9 had HNC; 4 had ONC; 2 had GCE 'O' or 'A' levels; 1 had City & Guilds and 15 had no educational qualifications whatever.

Chapter 2 describes the conditions obtaining in the South Birmingham Technical College and on the Training Officers Courses. The contents of the courses are examined in detail in Chapter 3, whilst Chapter 4 is devoted to detailed case studies of the 5 officers chosen for the second interview, their opinions, experiences, etc. The project work of two officers, submitted as part of their course, is examined in detail in Chapter 5. The appendices include comparisons with other colleges, information about the industries which support the courses, and a sample programme.

Findings

The training officer with little background experience in training and with limited educational qualifications was able to obtain positive benefits from attending a course such as that provided by the South Birmingham Technical College. In contrast, the more highly qualified training officer did not obtain as much benefit from the course. The importance of this point is that the Central Training Council advocated high educational standards for all training officers, but despite this recommendation, those officers without any educational qualifications at all were able, as a result of their course, to develop considerably their companies' training in all fields, operative, apprenticeship, supervisory and general. Indeed, it is of interest that the enthusiasm of those appointed as training officers who were not educationally qualified far outweighed any educational disadvantages, and their achievements were considerable.

The author considers that the personal qualities of motivation and enthusiasm for training are the best qualifications for becoming a training officer. Nevertheless, perhaps the organisers of Technical College courses should have given greater consideration to the different levels of educational qualifications held by training officers.

Coding: 7c(xviii), 2a, 4

THE INDUSTRIAL TRAINING ACT 1964: SUNDERLAND — A SAMPLE STUDY by R. Winders, M.Ed. thesis, University of Durham 1969.

Aim

To examine the developments from the Industrial Training Act 1964 with particular reference to the changes in the further education system, taking Sunderland as a sample geographical area.

Method

Review of statistical returns, industrial training board materials, college record cards, reports of the local Youth Employment Service and questionnaires to all Sunderland engineering firms with more than 20 employees.

Discussion

The Industrial Training Act 1964 was introduced in order to ensure that, in future, all levels of personnel in industry would be adequately trained and appropriately educated. The Act granted to the Minister of Labour (later the Secretary of State for Employment and Productivity) the power to establish a Central Training Council and separate Industrial Training Boards for each branch of industry and commerce. Each board is authorised to raise a levy from employers within its scope and to pay grants to employers who undertake to provide training and associated education to the standard determined by the Board. The educational content is the responsibility of the Department of Education and Science through the Colleges of Further Education and of the examining bodies.

The first three chapters describe the situation in 1964, suggest the criteria by which developments may be evaluated, analyse briefly the evolution of training and technical education in Britain and review the Act itself in some detail.

Sunderland was chosen as an sample area because it reflects both the coalfield tradition and new growth, basic shipbuilding and conveyor-belt assembly, employing mainly women, typical of post-war light industry, and the retail distribution industry. Also exemplified in acute form are the national problems of unemployment and industrial change.

Progress was made before the Industrial Training Act; day release students increased by 277% from 1951-1961, to a total of 2,586, sandwich courses were started (190 students in 1961) and evening-only students increased 63% to 4,054 during the same period. Between 1962 and 1967 evening-only student numbers declined by about 1,800, day-release increased by about 1,000 and full-time and sandwich course students continued to increase.

The next four chapters consider in detail the work of the Shipbuilding Industry Training Board, the Engineering Industry Training Board (almost 5,000 women in Sunderland are employed in this industry, twice as many as in any other manufacturing industry) and Commercial and Clerical Training. Chapters 8 and 9 review and assess progress from 1964-1968.

Findings

In general, the Act creates a structure adequate enough to meet needs, but a strengthening of its administration is required at both central and local levels to ensure that all employees in all industries are suitably trained and educated.

However, it is still true that a continuing education of girls is sadly neglected, that there is a lack of development in day-release for the 15-17 age group.

Coding: 7c(xviii), 2a

VOCATIONAL EDUCATION AND TRAINING IN NORTHAMP-TONSHIRE 1850-1956 by D.M. Brooks, M.Ed. thesis, University of Leicester 1970.
[Copy of original research (not thesis) available in 16 sections in Northampton Reference Library and library of the College of Technology, Northampton]

Aim
To study vocational education and training, dealing particularly with two main branches, technical education and apprenticeship schemes.

Discussion
Six types of employment were singled out for special attention; these were agriculture, the boot, shoe and leather trade, the building trade, the printing trade, the carriage trade and the engineering industry. Through these studies the author traces the relationship between industrial training and technical education. He examines the extent to which young people were catered for in both respects, the sources of initiatives from which new developments emerged and he describes how local provisions varied from, or reflected, national trends. The role of voluntary bodies and their relation to statutory organisation is one of the recurrent themes of the thesis.

Chapters 1 to 3 describe developments up to the passing of the Technical Instruction Bill of 1889. Chapters 4 and 5 discuss the effects of this Act, noting that the Committee on the Position of Natural Science in the Educational System of Great Britain, the Thomson Committee, reported that in 1914, only about 7% of Britain's labour force was in receipt of some form of technical education.

Chapter 6 deals with the period 1918 to 1944 and is appropriately entitled 'The Half-conscious Striving of a Highly Industrialised Society'. Although attitudes changed in this period, industry was concerned, firstly, with the problem of economic survival in conditions of world economic disarray and secondly, with national survival. The overall picture throughout this period is one of a slow, but increasing, awareness by industry of the need for technical education for employees, and of the value of liaison with a good technical institute. But the lack of vision in this period was depressing; for example, in 1928 pre-technical classes for the 14-16 age group which included recreational subjects were axed. In 1935 the classes were revived, but in such a revised form that H.M. Inspectorate's report was highly critical; the LEAs ignored this report and it was not until 1938 that sufficient flexibility was introduced into the scheme to attract increasing enrolments.

Chapter 7 deals with the post-war expansion of technical education, but records the lack of a similar development of the County Colleges envisaged in the Education Act of 1944.

Conclusions
The whole picture of the period shows a gradual convergence of technical education and various branches of industry towards a unity of purpose.

Perhaps the principal interest of this study lies in the discussion of the lost opportunities which were the result of a lack of liaison between technical education and industry and between secondary education and the adult education movement.

Coding: 1b(xiii)

TECHNICAL EDUCATION AND THE LONDON COUNTY COUNCIL 1918-1939 by D. W. Thoms, D.Phil. thesis, Brunel University 1972.

Aim
The thesis is concerned with the process of course innovation and development in technical education in the period 1918-1939, both as

a historical study and as useful study of the relationship between curriculum management and manpower planning.

Discussion
The author starts by describing the general provision for technical education outside London, and by outlining the framework of technical education within the London County Council area, between 1918 and 1939. In the LCC area there were five major groups providing technical education: the aided polytechnics, other aided institutions, maintained technical institutes, evening institutes and day-continuation schools. Within this classification there was, of course, a vast variety of provision, but in technical institutes courses were of two types, the minor courses, of the less academic type, and the major courses, of a more advanced nature. The evening schools offered a wide variety of courses, both in technical and liberal subjects; the day-continuation schools were principally concerned with vocational education for the 14-18 age group. Chapters 3-6 deal respectively with evening instruction in the London Technical Institutes, day and evening instruction in the London Polytechnics, the London Monotechnics and the London Junior Technical Schools.

The second part of the thesis analyses the background to course innovation and assesses the reasons for the success of certain courses and the comparative failure of others. Since the topic is potentially so vast, the author limits himself to an identification of major factors, rather than a detailed consideration of each.

Findings
The period between the wars is sometimes regarded as one of stagnation and of false economies; in fact, considerable progress was made. The author argues that the process of course innovation and development in technical education resulted from a highly complex interaction of forces in which other aspects of the educational structure, including administrative, as well as teaching institutions, played a vital role. Emphasis has been given to the influence of senior administrative officers, such as Robert Blair, within the local education authority framework. Special mention is made of the work of the Board of Education, and of the limitations of the Board in failing to establish definite guidelines for course development in technical education. Important factors outside the educational

structure have also been considered, including the attitudes of parents and business management to formal technical training.

The point is made that the rapidly changing nature of employment increases the need for a flexible examination system. The author suggests that, for manpower planning at least, there should be effective research and identification of objectives by the DES, so that the technical education sector may respond to contemporary needs. He wonders whether the power exercised by professional institutions over curriculum and examinations is not at the expense of indicative planning and co-ordination by the DES.

The author particularly refers to the uneconomic aspects of evening study, especially the high level of student drop-out, and suggests that educational capital in the form of buildings could be more extensively used by lengthening the school year, rather than by use during the evenings.

The case for a better counselling service is cogently argued, as is the case for vocational courses of a broad nature for young adults. An interesting sidelight is cast on the power of the permanent civil service: the prejudice of the Principal Secretary to the Board of Education, L. A. Selby-Bigge, against compulsory day-continuation schools is quoted.

Coding: 1c(ii), 7b, 4, 6

THE IN-SERVICE EDUCATION OF MANAGERS AT UNIVERSITIES IN GREAT BRITAIN AND CANADA — WITH PARTICULAR REFERENCE TO THE UNIVERSITY OF MANCHESTER AND THE UNIVERSITY OF CALGARY by R. S. Chapman, D.Phil. thesis (2 vols), University of Manchester 1972.

Aim
To examine the continuing education, at universities, of those who are already managers in Great Britain and Canada. To review the government legislation affecting in-service management education; the background of British and Canadian managers; the management education provided by consultants, private institutions, industry and

others, and to review in-service courses in the University of
Manchester and the University of Calgary.

Method
Data was obtained from the students who attended courses, by
means of pre-course and post-course questionnaires. These included
information about the backgrounds of students, about their perception of changes in themselves in four knowledge and skills areas as a
result of attendance at the course, and about their assessment of the
attainment of objectives. Information was also gathered about course
instructors, and the aims and objectives of the course organisers were
ascertained.

Discussion
In 1965 it was estimated that about 17% of British managers had an
elementary education only, 15.5% secondary education (excluding
Grammar Schools), 55.5% had attended a Grammar School and 12%
had attended Independent Schools. Of the 35% who held a university
degree, 24% had graduated from Oxford or Cambridge and 80% held
a degree in science or technology. The Industrial Training Boards, set
up by the Industrial Training Act of 1964, generally found management training to be neglected.

The author reviewed the various institutions offering management
courses at university level: 'In Great Britain, the Open University is
practically made-to-order for management education'. He selected
Manchester University for special study because Manchester provides
a typical British manufacturing area, the city contained one of the
two government-endowed business schools, the university had an
extra-mural department which was active in the business course
area, and had residential facilities at Holly Royde.

The author evaluated university management courses, and
included in his consideration the theory of evaluation, case studies of
ten in-service management courses, and student self-evaluation.

About half of the first volume and the whole of the second
volume consist of appendices giving detailed and comprehensive data
and accounts of specific aspects of the problem; or example, from
tables 1.11, 1.12 and 1.13, we learn that the mean number of
organisations in which students had worked was 2.0, that the mean
number of jobs held in their working life was 6.2, and that the

maximum number of years spent in any one job was, on average, 5.7 years.

Findings
The author recommends the British Industrial Training Act as a prototype for Canadian legislators. Only 28% of top managers and 23% of directors in Britain had ever undertaken any management training. More than 30 universities in Britain offered degree studies in some aspect of business management, and all of these offered in-service management education through their extra-mural departments.

Teaching methods were basically four: the lecture, the group syndicate, recommendation of relevant reading matter, and communication practice in writing and speaking. Modern technology, he suggests, should be used more extensively, and shorter, three-day residential courses may attract managers from the small organisations.

Coding: 7c(i), 5b, 2a, 2b, 7c(ii), 7c(v)

Education in HM Forces, Merchant Navy

THE DEVELOPMENT OF ADULT EDUCATION IN THE ARMY — WITH SPECIAL REFERENCE TO THE ORGANISATION OF CIVILIAN AID IN ARMY EDUCATION SINCE 1914 by J. D. MacGregor, D.Phil. thesis (2 vols), University of Leeds 1954.

Aim
To examine adult education in the Army from 1767 to 1953.

Discussion
Until relatively recently, since the introduction of highly technical and specialised weapons, the Army was not considered by the civilian as an intellectual profession. Indeed, we find the Headmaster of Winchester, writing to the father of the late Field Marshal Earl Wavell to express regret that his son was joining the Army. 'I do not

think', he wrote, 'that you need take this extreme step, since I believe that your son has sufficient brains to make his way in other walks of life.' But the Army reflects the technology of the society that depends upon its protection and consequently, as the demands for literacy, numeracy and so on have developed in our society at large, so have the Army's needs for these accomplishments also developed.

Volume 1 examines the development of vocational training and liberal adult education from 1767 to 1945, but the main emphasis is on the work of the Army Education Corps in the second world war, and on the role of army education in preparing soldiers to return to civilian life. This volume includes an account of the contribution of the voluntary bodies, such as the Workers' Educational Association, to adult education during the period 1939-1945.

In the second volume, the author assesses the role of army education in the second world war, the role of the Forces' Educational Broadcasts, and army education from 1947-1952, when most soldiers were national service conscripts. He deals particularly with the suggestion, voiced by S. G. Raybould in 1942, that it was doubtful if army organisation was compatible with genuine education.

The author also describes fully the negotiations which led, from 1949, to the setting up of some 24 Universities' Forces Committees. These committees essentially existed to provide educational facilities to the Services when the Services themselves asked for help. The replies of the universities when these proposals were first mooted are of some interest; Liverpool, for example, was particularly insistent on the question of 'standards' and took the view that it was not the function of the Extra-Mural Department to organise or administer educational services which were not of university standard. Details of university-organised short courses of lectures, full-time courses, tutorial education and classes from 1949 to 1953 are given in appendices.

Coding: 1b(xvii), 1b(ix), KB864

AUDIO-VISUAL AIDS IN THE EDUCATION OF SEAFARERS WITH APPLICATION TO PARTICULAR PROGRAMMES by W. E. A. Carver, M.Phil. thesis, University of Sussex 1967.

Aim
To describe the testing and development of some programmed texts, incorporating audio or visual aids, for the use of seafarers studying by correspondence at sea.

Method
Four programmes were constructed, pilot-tested and revised. Tables give the results of the pre-test scores, post-test scores, improvement indices and retention-test scores for various sample groups of students.

Discussion
Correspondence courses are an essential and inevitable part of all Merchant Navy training schemes, but such courses may be enlivened and made more effective if programmed learning and audio-visual techniques of instruction are also used.

In 1967 the British Merchant Navy was composed of 112,915 men, of whom 40,588 were officers, 5,339 cadets and 64,343 ratings. Of this total, between 20-30% are on leave or studying so that, at any one time, about 85,000 are at sea, giving 5,000-7,000 correspondence students at sea, just over half of whom are Deck Cadets studying for the Second Mate's Certificate.

In 1966 the College of the Sea provided 537 courses taken by 445 students, but mathematics, ranging from elementary arithmetic to Advanced level GCE, accounted for almost half the enrolments. Just over 50% of the mathematics enrolments are made before the student is 20 years old, 80% of them before the age of 25. It is difficult to assess the drop-out of students accurately, but in the case of the College of the Sea it appears that about one-fifth send in work regularly after one year.

The development of four programmes is described, each incorporating some aid other than drawings; the 'ship stability' programme included 2 loop films, 'navigation' included a cardboard cut-out model, assembled by the student himself and used for subsequent parts of the programme, 'morse code' was associated with a tape recording and 'chartwork' used overlaid transparencies to illustrate the build-up of a problem. The programmes themselves are included in the appendices, and a separate portfolio contains the 'aids'.

The author emphasises the crucial role of the tutor and, in arguing the case for the use of more technology, reiterates the need to encourage composite courses of correspondence, residence and so on, rather than simple extensions of correspondence tuition.

Conclusions
More and better use of these aids should be made for seafarers at sea. That part of the seafarers' training which takes place at sea should be re-organised to make the economic provision of teaching aids on board ship more feasible. Nautical colleges should establish units to write programmes and to develop audio-visual aids for correspondence courses. (In fact, the first such Programmed Learning Unit started work at the Plymouth College of Technology in September 1967).

Care should be taken to ensure that the use of programmed learning does not isolate the correspondence student at sea from his tutors and the programmes used should be so designed that the students see them as strictly relevant to their needs. Without this motivational condition, programmes will not be used effectively in the unsupervised conditions experienced on board a ship.

Coding: 7c(xiii), 5j, 5k, 5m(xix), 2a, 5a, cf. KB876

THE GENERAL EDUCATION SCHEME IN THE ROYAL AIR FORCE by R. S. Walker, M.Ed. thesis, University of Dundee 1970.

Aim
To describe and assess one aspect of the educational service of the Royal Air Force, that is, the General Education Scheme.

Discussion
The General Education Scheme is an attempt to cover the educational needs of men and women in the RAF in a broad cultural

way. The author describes the history and development of the GES and delineates its implementation at station level. More Education Centres are being provided on stations, to include, besides classrooms, library, study room etc, an Information Room. This latter usually contains up-to-date information about current affairs, servicemen's careers in the RAF, re-settlement into civilian life and the recreational amenities on the station and in the local area.

In the Royal Air Force there are two service educational examinations, the RAF Education Test and the General Certificate of Education. The University of Cambridge Local Examination Syndicate has made special arrangements for servicemen who wish to take any GCE subject. Promotion at various levels depends on passing, or gaining exemption from, the educational examinations.

Education in the Services usually follows the best practices of adult education; in fact, most classes are conducted with a greater degree of informality than is often the case in civilian life. Most Education Officers are, for example, not particularly worried whether their students attend classes in uniform or civilian clothes. Methodological approaches in the RAF have to take into account that 'students' are frequently posted; the needs of national defence take precedence. Thus, experiments in the use and assessment of multi-media approaches are continuous.

The provision of information and advice to officers and airmen on re-settlement in civilian life is an integral part of the GES. This counselling service is reviewed and described. Similarly described are the miscellaneous educational services, the employment of civilian lecturers, the library services and the co-operation between the Services and the local education authorities.

Although specialist officers are responsible for the provision of training for airmen in their appropriate trades, the *organisation* of trade training is the task of the education staff. Commanders at every level are responsible for ensuring that their airmen receive training, and for deciding which of their airmen are to be trained in each particular field. This tripartite organisation is fully described in the context of continuation trade training.

The thesis includes, in the appendices, the syllabuses for the RAF Education Tests Parts I and II.

Coding: 2a, 1b(xvii), 6, 4, 5a, 5f, 8c

THE ROYAL ARMY EDUCATIONAL CORPS by J. E. Moran, M.Ed. thesis, University of Liverpool 1970.

Aim

To review the work of the Army Education Corps from 1920 to 1970.

Discussion

Since the Corps was founded in 1920 it has undergone many changes, most of which have been influenced not only by financial and economic considerations, but also by the changing aims of education in general and of the Army in particular.

The thesis starts with a brief incursion into the past, including the Army Corps of Schoolmasters and its immediate progeny, the Army Education Corps. It deals with training, roles and responsibilities and how these have developed in recent years.

Chapter 2 provides some preliminary information about the Royal Army Educational Corps; necessary qualifications of new entrants, training, both military and specialist Corps training; present-day responsibilities of the Corps ranging from remedial education to the supplying of educational stores, the types of commissions offered and the career structures of the Corps officers.

In Chapter 3 the author describes the present-day organisation and administration of education in the British Army. It includes an account of the latest developments of the Service Children's Education Authority, the Army Education Centres, the Institute of Army Education, the School of Preliminary Education, the Higher Education Centre in Germany, Resettlement Centres and Junior Soldiers' Units.

Chapter 4 deals with three topics, the Forces Correspondence Course Scheme, the British Army News Service and Junior Officers' Education in Germany. In Chapter 5 the author considers, in general terms, the Army School of Education and, in particular, the Overseas English Wing and Teaching of English as a Second Language. The Army School of Instructional Technology is the subject of Chapter 6, and special mention is made of the application of the behavioural sciences to learning processes.

The Army's attempts to cope with weaknesses in oral and written

English language are considered; consequently, the thesis includes an account of the use of ita with adults. Similarly, the thesis deals with the Corps' contribution to research in turbulence in servicemen's children and in handicapped children of servicemen.

Findings
The thesis is a comprehensive and up-to-date review of the RAEC; the principal finding is that a two-way system of communication between Army and civilian authorities in the field of education both exists and is mutually beneficial. For example, the Army's 'systems approach' techniques are applicable, with modification, to industrial undertakings and the army's experiments with multi-media systems of instruction have attracted the interest of civilian educators.

Coding: 7c(xxi), 3d, 5a, 5i, 5j, 5k, 4, 2c, 1b(xvii), KB870

Adult education for women and women's organisations

WOMEN'S SOCIAL OPPORTUNITIES AND ATTITUDES BEFORE AND AFTER CHILDBIRTH by W. M. Woodward, Ph.D. thesis, University of London 1956.

Aim
To assess the effects on the mother's social activities of a first pregnancy and to consider the influence on these social activities of the availability of a baby sitter; to assess the mother's attitude towards social activity, the social aspects of her husband-wife relationship and her willingness to spend short intervals away from the child.

Method
Interviews were conducted in 3 ante-natal and 7 infant welfare clinics; 186 women who were either expecting their first child or who had a child aged not more than 5 years, were selected as the sample population for interview and analysis.

Discussion
Since desire for social activities outside the home may be affected by the new relation with a child, the thesis starts with a review of studies of parent-child relations. In fact few pregnancies are fully accepted; there is a trend towards greater acceptance during pregnancy and after childbirth. Some cases of extreme over-protection — a complete absorption by the mother in the child — lead to a decreased desire for social activities outside the home, but milder forms of over-protection are more general, so that the mother-child relationship is usually but one element in accounting for the decreased social life of the mother.

Chapters 2 and 3 describe the design and method of the investigation and the characteristics of the sample; for example, the occupations of husbands, the occupation of the sample subjects, living accommodation and so on. In fact 51.1% of the husbands were in manual occupations, about 5% in the higher professional class, and about 41% in the clerical class. Of the women, there were no representatives in the higher professional occupations, 58% were clerical workers, 11% factory workers. 53% lived in a house or flat with their husband only; the rest shared accommodation with relatives, friends or lodgers.

Findings
Half the sample had no friends (as distinct from acquaintances, cf. Halmos 1952), but this was chiefly because of moving to a new district. Meeting other mothers-to-be in clinics, etc widened the field of acquaintances but rarely led to closer friendships.

59% had retired or would be retiring from paid employment as a result of the first pregnancy; about half of the total sample said they missed the company of work friends, but of those who had recently left work, three-quarters missed the social contacts there. 33% wished to have work outside the home; the older the child the more they wished to go back to work.

There was a decrease in the frequency of visits to entertainments; only 18% of mothers went out once a week, compared to 51% of those pregnant. The major change was with the first child and a second child made little difference to the frequency of visits. The major forms of entertainment were cinema, theatre and dancing. The place of entertainment was nearer the home after childbirth than either before or in pregnancy.

103

Reading and knitting were the most frequently mentioned interests in the sample, and about 38% of the sample wished to retain their interests. Those with social interests had a stronger desire to retain them than those with individual interests.

72% of the total sample knew someone who would babysit, but 44% of mothers of two children had no baby sitter, compared to 23% of the mothers with one child. Only 52% of mothers who lived away both from relatives and friends had a baby sitter. Visits to entertainments varied directly with the availability of a baby sitter.

Attitude towards social activity does not change between first pregnancy and after first childbirth. Nearly all subjects preferred to mix with familiar people rather than to extend their acquaintances. The conclusion was that attitude towards social activity is more a function of personality than of external events such as the birth of a child.

About 13% of mothers went out to evening social activities separately from their husbands, the overwhelming majority to entertainments. About 68% preferred to go to entertainments with their husbands, and 75% preferred to go on holiday with their husband (and children) only.

Coding: 2d

THE POSITION AND OPPORTUNITIES OF YOUNG MOTHERS — PROGRESS OR RETROGRESSION by H. Gavron, Ph.D. thesis, University of London 1964.

Aim
To study the difficulties confronting young mothers in the contemporary family, based on a comparative study of working-class and middle-class families.

Method
'Non-directive' personal interviews were conducted with 48 working-class mothers who were born after 1930, were married with at least one child below 5 years of age. The sample was drawn from the

practice lists of the Caversham Centre, a group practice in Kentish Town, London. 35 middle-class housewives were selected from a doctor's list in West Hampstead, and a further 13 were selected from the London lists of the 'Housebound Wives' register. This study is principally qualitative rather than quantitative.

Discussion
The first section is concerned with the methodology, summarised above. The second section provides an account of the historical changes in the last 150 years, principally noting that the status of women vis-a-vis men has improved, that the number of roles which women can perform in society have increased and have become more varied, and that women have experienced an extension in the freedom of choice between roles.

Findings
The third and the concluding section of the thesis are concerned with the findings of the survey. Five important facts emerged. Some of the mothers, particularly in the working-classes, considered themselves to be leading isolated lives. The role of 'mother' took precedence over all other roles; children were the central focus. The majority did not feel entirely at home in this role; mothers of both classes found themselves unprepared for the responsibilities of motherhood and for the restrictions it imposed on their lives.

Mothers in both classes relied on their husbands' support in facing their problems, but whereas the middle-class husband gave his support by co-operating with his wife in *extending her interests outside the home* and the children, the working-class husband gave his support by devoting his leisure to *sharing* his wife's roles *within* the home and participating regularly in all the household chores. Finally, 90% of the total sample was planning to work when the children were older.

There are other vivid snatches of illustrative facts; 47.9% of the working-class mothers considered that they had had an unhappy childhood; the 1961 St. Pancras (in which Kentish Town is located) survey revealed that only 35.1% of all households in the area had piped hot and cold water, fixed bath and water-closet (45% average for all London). 52% of the middle-class husbands never went out without their wives, and 30% of those who did go out without their wives also baby-sat for their wives regularly once a week.

Of the joys of motherhood, one young woman reported 'I felt such a failure as a mother, not knowing whether the baby was warm enough, or fed enough, or why it was crying. I began to doubt that I could ever do anything properly again'.

The author suggests that the situation should be improved by a re-analysis of the education of girls, a re-examination of the roles of women as workers, and by the re-direction of mothers and young children back into the main stream of society with the use of community associations, clubs, etc which include mother and young child in the situation.

Coding: 2d, 2b, 1c(iii)

THE NORTH OF ENGLAND COUNCIL FOR PROMOTING THE HIGHER EDUCATION OF WOMEN 1867-1875/76 by S. C. Lemoine, M.Ed. thesis, University of Manchester 1968.

Aim
To consider the contribution of the North of England Council for promoting the higher education of women from 1867-1875/76, as revealed in their *Reports*; to consider the contribution of the Council to the origin and development of the University Extension Movement by 1873 and to examine a particular example of a movement and demand for higher education by women in the decades of the 1860s and 1870s.

Method
The thesis is based upon nine Reports of the North of England Council, autographed 'Anne J. Clough', held by the Librarian of Newnham College, Cambridge. The xeroxed copy held by Manchester University includes material from the Fawcett Library, London.

Discussion
The author begins the thesis by considering the social and economic condition of middle-class women in relation to their circumstances. Mrs Josephine Butler, writing in 1869, considered that 'the present

distress (of women) must to some degree be reckoned among the phenomena of a transition period of society'. Transition is the theme of this chapter, for the author demonstrates that, in spite of severe disabilities, particularly in legal status, women had begun to assert their individual personality and, in the case of certain Privy Council 'qualified teachers', had begun to improve their economic position.

It is argued in Chapter 2 that the demand for female education, the work of Miss Buss, Miss Beale and Miss Wolstenholme in improving the secondary education of girls, and the enthusiasm of Miss Anne Clough, were responsible to a large extent for the University Extension Movement from 1873. Miss Clough's original letter of application for a lecture hall in December 1866 and her accompanying 'Prospectus' for James Stuart's early lectures of 1867 are preserved in the archives of the Liverpool Royal Institution.

Chapters 3 to 6 and their appendices consider consecutively the nine meetings of the North of England Council, held between November 1867 and June 1874. The Reports reveal the essential difference of principle between those educationalists centring around Miss Anne Clough and the North of England Council and the feminist activities of Miss Emily Davies in London. The former desired both to extend higher education to those excluded from it — women and working men — and to reform many aspects of the tertiary studies then available to young men, whilst the London group sought educational equality between the sexes on the sole principle that women should undertake, without alteration, the tertiary studies then available for men.

The North of England Council persuaded the Local Syndicate of the University of Cambridge to administer an examination for women in October 1868. The development of this 'local examination'. for women (re-named the Cambridge Higher Local Examination in 1873) is described and specimen papers are provided in the appendices. In addition, the general development of the University Extension Movement in the 1870s is analysed.

Finally, the decline of the North of England Council is explained. Stuart, who had lectured to women and working men from 1867, continued to be associated with the Council until its demise.

The North of England Council had, in its function as co-ordinator, led to the emancipation of many women from the confines of their homes: it led directly to the founding of a new Cambridge College, and to the development of University Extension lectures; it was administratively concerned with the North of England yet it influenced national education, and it demonstrated the Victorian capacity for voluntary action.

The personal charm and professionalism of Anne Clough comes across; for example, from an article in Macmillan's Magazine 1866 (Appendix II): 'The professor should also be expected to test the attainments of his class as he went on, and not merely to instruct' and 'A few dry facts are taught, but the life and spirit are too often left out, and there is a monotony in girls' education which is very dulling to the intellect'. After her exertions their horizons expanded.

Coding: 1c(iii), 1b(ix), 1b(v), 1b(iii)

AN EXAMINATION OF THE ROLE OF THE TOWNSWOMEN'S GUILD conducted by E. J. Miller and G. V. Gwynne, Consultants' Report, Tavistock Institute of Human Relations, 1971. [As is the usual practice, the National Executive Committee of the Towns-women's Guild reserves the right to retain the confidentiality of certain parts of the full report.]

Aim

To examine the organisation of the Townswomen's Guild movement, to see whether it is suited to the pattern of modern women's lives and flexible enough to change with the changing pattern of society.

Method

The consultants concentrated on three areas: London and the Home Counties, Yorkshire and Scotland. In each area they met one group of Federation and Guild officers, and two to four groups, each consisting of 12 Guild members — not current officers — usually from a single Guild. Individual interviews with National officers and with paid National Union officials took place. Parts of the meetings of the Central Council and the National Council were attended and documents concerning the movement were studied. After each group meeting, an individual questionnaire was answered by participating members: 112 questionnaires being completed.

Discussion

The aspect of the Townswomen's Guild that showed itself most clearly was the culture of dependency and conformity. Yet, though the movement values respectability and conservatism (with a small 'c'), it has outspoken radical elements at both national and grass roots levels. It has difficulty in attracting younger members, yet in some flourishing Guilds the members are predominantly in their thirties. The movement ultimately means different things to different members, and thus the problem of making legitimate generalisations is very great indeed.

The primary motivation for seeking membership was revealed as one of escape from the home, either from the restricted horizons of the family circle or from a home where the central duties of motherhood were completed. The consultants thought that the great majority of the members wanted entertainment or fun; consequently, the educational activities became a 'front' price to be paid for legitimacy.

This provision of a refuge partly explains the culture of conformity and dependency, and accounts for the exclusion of certain types of activity which would otherwise seem highly relevant. For example, for mothers worried about their adolescent children's problems, the only way the T.G. helps the members to cope with these difficulties is by giving a temporary respite from them. Does this set of values and code of conduct make the Guild unattractive to many women?

Few women independently sought out the Guild; Guild membership tends to build on existing friendships, thus helping to ensure that newcomers will be compatible with current members. The consultants question whether the Guild is accessible to the woman who is really isolated and friendless. Similarly, the consultants question whether the Guild provides for personal development, either through acquiring specific skills and new interests, or through attaining greater social competence and pose. Perhaps the cream rises in any jug!

The Guild also has a function for some women of providing them with the belief that 'women can do as much as men, given the opportunity'. The consultants found that this function was of no great moment for most women. Some members would like the Guild to be more concerned in practical 'good works'.

The attitude of members to officers was one of apparent respect and obedience, together with some concealed hostility; officers sit on a platform facing rows of members, and there were also signs that it is not always easy for a willing member to take office. Guild members were often ignorant of the work of the National Union; indeed, there seemed little sense of belonging to a national movement. Views about the Federation were more clearcut — the general view was that the Federation was somewhat unresponsive to members' needs. However, the consultants found that officers of the Guild, Federation and National Union shared a common culture and shared common objectives. But they considered that all officers have a vested interest in the hierarchical structure of representation, since it is this that confers their status.

A major problem seen by the consultants is that the hierarchy of Committees and Councils is ceasing to be effective in its primary function as a means of managing the affairs of the movement; if it fails in this, it is unlikely that it can fulfil its secondary function, as a means of personal development. Instead the structure is in danger of becoming an end in itself, a device for conferring status on officers and differentiating them from ordinary members. In this situation, the changing needs of the movement and its members may be sacrificed to the maintenance of the structural status quo.

Findings

The consultants considered that the movement was trying to use one form of organisation to perform three different tasks as follows:

a to provide social and recreational activities for women — a task best performed by an autonomous club with some means of keeping out unwanted members;

b to provide educational facilities for women — a task which also seemed to require an autonomous local body which, however, might find it useful to create a 'National Association for the Education of Women', through which pressure could be brought to persuade the educational bodies to lay on courses especially suited for women's needs;

c to mobilise and present women's views on issues of local, national and international importance — the political task. The consultants thought of a single 'National Union of Women' as an ideal, but doubted the viability of such an organisation in contemporary Britain.

Thus, the consultants suggest that women who attend the Guild as a social club may rationally object to committee business imposed on them by affiliation to a national body; women who join for educational reasons may share these feelings.

As for the National Union as a political force or pressure group, the consultants found that members felt less and less deeply about political issues and, in any case, the organisation was so slow that its deliberations were often overtaken by legislation. Consequently, the dilemma is that the National Executive Committee of the National Union feel a need to take the lead in innovation, partly because, at national level, outside bodies look to the NUTG to express the women's viewpoint, whilst the leadership of the Townswomen's Guild that most members have joined properly belongs to the individual Guilds.

The consultants suggested various alternative future developments, including some pilot experimental schemes. They emphasise a continuing need to develop effective consultation and the need to take active steps to stimulate debate at the grass roots of the movement. Indeed, it must be placed on record that, when the proposal for this research was placed before the Central Council of the National Union, although the project was expected to reveal the critical issues on problems facing the movement, nonetheless, the vote in favour of commissioning consultants was overwhelming.

Coding: 7b(xii), 2a, 2b

Education for retirement

CLUBS FOR ELDERLY PERSONS by G. G. Worthington, M.A. thesis, University of Liverpool 1956.

Aim
To evaluate the effectiveness of clubs for elderly people by studying the aims and objectives, membership and attendance, facilities, fees and finance and programmes of such clubs in the City of Liverpool.

Method
Members and leaders completed questionnaires and information

obtained from them added to the author's own observations. The method of evaluating club work is that of a practising social worker rather than that of a student of the theoretical processes of group organisation and dynamics. A sample of 25 clubs was chosen; 367 people completed returns (110 men and 257 women).

Discussion

The growth in numbers of clubs began in 1946 at the end of the war, although a good number of clubs were started from 1940 onwards. Some did exist before 1940; for example, Eleanor Rathbone inspired 4 in Liverpool in 1927. Clubs have been sponsored by many types of organisations, including the National Old Age Pensioners' Association, the National Federation of Old Age Pension Associations, the Liverpool Personal Service Society, the Women's Voluntary Service (now WRVS), and the Community Associations.

The aims of clubs are essentially to enable the elderly to continue *to live in their own homes,* but to get them out of their homes and into the community so far as health will allow. They are recreational centres where friendships are facilitated; they give individuals the benefits of serving, belonging to, and sharing, within a group. Often they provide the mental stimulus which older people particularly need to offset physical infirmities. They provide fun, amusement and spiritual uplift; they also provide pressure groups to remind society of their needs and rights.

Most members were drawn from the working classes; in the sample about 22% were skilled workers, foremen and semi-professional; nearly one-half were under 70 years and a third were solely 'housewives'; 62% of the male sample had been members of trades unions. About 47% of the total sample belonged to more than one pensioners' club, which suggested both that clubs are valued and that there is a need for more day-centres rather than more weekly clubs. 63% of the sample walked to the club in which they were interviewed; 32% used public transport regularly.

Club programmes usually have three elements: entertainment which caters for passive desires, competitive games which provide an outlet, and creative expressive activities. All these activities are described in detail, ranging from chess or draughts to group singing; surprisingly, sketching and drawing were not listed as an actual activity. Religion and music are vital forces in the lives of elderly people; 50% of the sample attended church, 56% listed listening to music as an outside activity, and since the range of outside activities is so much greater than the range of club activities, the author suggests that club leaders often underestimate their members' interests and argues that the educational content is too low.

In Chapter 6 the author considers the clubs' service to individual members, sick-visiting, chiropody services, gifts. Regrettably, some welfare organisations still use the clubs for hand-outs rather than as centres for companionship and so on; the need is for individuals to be directed to the proper place for help rather than to be given gifts of old clothes by the well-meaning. Perhaps the most important omission, in the author's view, is the lack of contacts between youth clubs and clubs for the elderly; each has individuals who could offer a service to the other.

Activities depend greatly on facilities, fees and finance; these are described in Chapters 7 and 8; their adequacy is questioned, and recommendations for improvements suggested.

The leadership of clubs is democratically elected, and the thesis quotes individual examples of splendid service to, and leadership of, clubs. Nonetheless, the author considers that the elderly need professional help; Cleveland, Ohio, for example, has one trained worker to every sixteen clubs to assist the voluntary leadership.

Findings

Members were younger than the author had been led to believe and had wider interests than club programmes suggested; not enough emphasis is laid on the continuing development of old people's minds — they do not stop thinking on the date of retirement. Indeed, is not social deterioration in the elderly like that of the unemployed worker — both groups think they have no future.

In Liverpool, 15,000 persons participated in a club programme; attendance figures are high and membership is held for long periods; all this is a considerable achievement. But with professionally-trained assistance, there could be an even greater contribution to old people's welfare through clubs. Programmes could be improved. The author suggests that each area should have a full-time, trained worker with overall responsibility for working with all old people's clubs. Furthermore, clubs should have the support of advisory committees to knit them into the work of the community at large.

Coding: 1c(v), 2a, 2b, 6, 8b, 7c(xxi), 5b, 1c(iii)

The library service

THE SOURCE AND USE OF BOOKS IN ADULT CLASSES by B. Luckham, Research Paper No. 5, Public Libraries and Adult Education Committee for the North West, 1967 (8 pp). Available from The Library Association, 7 Ridgmount Street, London WC1E 7AE

Aim
To investigate the source and use of books in adult classes in the Manchester University Extra-Mural area.

Method
By contact with 186 secretaries of responsible-body-organised classes and 115 responses from the random sample of 143 students who had attended at least two-thirds of their class meetings in 1966/67. 111 drop-outs also were contacted, for comparative statistics.

Discussion
Adult students can obtain books from several sources, but nevertheless concern is regularly expressed about the sufficiency of supply. In 1964/65, out of 401 total classes, about 38% were without any book supply for the class; 40% of WEA-organised classes were without any book supply for classes; 9% of Joint Committee (WEA with extra-mural board) and about 8% of extra-mural-board-organised classes were also so placed. Public libraries supplied about 19% of classes with books. 13 out of 186 class secretaries reported that they had received no list of recommended books. The deficiency in the supply of class books was concentrated largely in classes for short courses, and in social studies, science and politics classes.

The Extra-Mural Department book boxes included, as a priority, titles recommended by the tutor for his class. If a book was not available in the Department Library Stock (of approximately 20,000 volumes) then a purchase would be made, or a request would be placed with the National Central Library (which provided about 600 volumes per annum). The Manchester City Library also arranged bulk loans. Nevertheless, despite these varied sources, only about 50-66% of the titles requested could be supplied, but of the books supplied, the overwhelming consensus of opinion was one of satisfaction.

Were the books supplied used? From the statistical returns, the author concludes that more than one-third of the books appeared to have stayed in the boxes, and about one-third of the students did not borrow the books supplied. There was, however, a wider and more intensive use of books with classes of longer duration, and about one-half of the students in the average longer-course took one book. Nonetheless, ·there was considerable variation in the proportions of students borrowing books in different classes, and in a handful of classes *every* student borrowed a book.

Student borrowing does not seem to depend in any way on which organisation runs the course, WEA or University; the evidence suggests that individual tutor encouragement and interest is probably the principal reason for variations in student borrowing rates.

54% of the 115 students who responded to the questionnaire claimed to have borrowed books from a public library on the relevant subject during the period of their course, borrowing 1.5 books on average. However, of the 61 drop-outs (who left their classes after the first or second meeting) who replied, 33 said that they had borrowed public library books on the subject of the course they had originally selected, borrowing 2.6 books on average. This figure suggests that completers who borrowed 3.1 books from *all* sources borrow but slightly more than drop-outs, the difference being due to completers borrowing from the book box. But the difference between completers and drop-outs is so small as to suggest that interest levels in book borrowing is the same for both groups. 36% of the 15 students who 'completed' the course claimed to have bought relevant books during the period of the course, an average of about 2.4 books each.

Findings

On balance it appears that students do little reading in quantity and that they borrow more books from other sources than from book boxes. Only one-quarter of the students replying in 1966/67 held that the book box was essential; nearly all thought of it as no more than desirable. In fact student purchases of books are the most important source of supply; indeed, the author estimates that students spent six times as much on books per year as the Department of Extra-Mural Studies, and that they spent the equivalent of two-thirds of the total cost of fees.

The author suggests various alternatives, ranging from the discontinuation of the book supply to students to the retention of the present system. He suggests that book use is a declining feature of adult education, and that the methods of providing books should not be based on out-of-date assumptions.

Coding: 7c(xiv), 5c, 7c(i), 7c(iii)

THE ATTITUDES OF CHARTERED LIBRARIANS IN NORTH-WEST ENGLAND TOWARDS ADULT EDUCATION by E. R. Reid-Smith, M.Ed. thesis, University of Manchester 1968. [See also 'Measurement of Librarians' Attitudes towards Adult Education' published in *Research in Librarianship*; Vol 2, No. 11, pages 141-153]

Aim
To ascertain the opinions of librarians in libraries in Lancashire and Cheshire towards various aspects of adult educational activity; to discover the actual provision in the public libraries; to gather information of the actual personal participation of chartered librarians in library extension activities and in outside adult education; to test a hypothesis of scalability.

Method
After pre-tests designed to remove ambiguous and inapplicable statements, sheets containing several such items were posted to chartered librarians as follows:
a Survey 'A' of 45 quotations, completed by 81 people;
b Survey 'B' of the same 45 quotations, but with 10 of them divided into phrases to express ideas, completed by 33 people;
c Survey 'C' of 23 statements given and completed by 82 chartered librarians (32 chiefs and 50 assistants) and by 92 students in a School of Librarianship.
Responses were dichotomised to obtain reproducibility for various categories of respondents to various groups of items. Other questionnaires were given and personal visits were made.

Discussion

The thesis is written in five sections: an introduction, with a summary of aims and definitions of terms, a historical background both of England in general and of the North-West in particular, an account of the methods of investigation, an interpretation of results and a discussion of results.

A library is itself an organ which adult education bodies can use in the cause of creating and maintaining literacy; it is also true that the library can itself use other techniques and media than books to extend its services to the people. Consequently, there is a close partnership between librarians and members of other adult educational bodies, and the attitude of librarians towards their partners may be an important factor in the effectiveness of the service.

Examples of the librarian as animateur are given, such as that of the Lancashire County Librarian who, in the late 1920s, helped with the formation of study circles, both in connection with the National Home Reading Union scheme and with the BBC's programmes of talks and lectures.

Findings

Of 38 chief librarians questioned, 8 stated that they had no experience of participation in external adult education; 23 of the remaining 30 indicated that they had (previously or currently) been an ordinary member of one of the outside adult education classes organised by the WEA, the university extra-mural departments or by a local education authority. 19 chief librarians reported that they held active posts in external adult educational and cultural societies.

Of 52 assistant librarians responding, 31 recorded no contact at all with adult educational bodies. 5 assistants reported some committee or organising connection with external adult education bodies. It is worthy of note that at least three assistants regretted that they could not attend classes because of having to work late twice each week. Is it a matter, therefore, of attitudes?

85.1% of respondents to Opinionaire A thought that 'The public library should be recognised as forming part of the national educational machinery' but comments showed that this did not mean administratively. In general most librarians in the North-West were favourable in their attitude to their possible role as educators, but a substantial minority were mildly opposed to such an idea.

37 of the 38 chief librarians approved the allowance of extra tickets to individuals on request; 36 agreed that the provision of lectures and talks on books was a proper service; only 14 approved the provision of film shows for entertainment. 22 signified an approval of jazz music but only 6 approved of teenage pop. 28 approved of live music on library premises and 35 of the 38 approved in principle of the lending of originals or reproductions of paintings and drawing but only 4 had put the idea into operation, whilst 26 agreed with the lending of films and filmstrips and again only 4 had collections for this purpose. 26 approved of play-reading groups within the library.

32 chief librarians thought that libraries should make block loans to classes held outside library premises, and 24 reported that they were already doing so. 22 approved in principle of the provision of radios and television in the library for the reception of educational programmes only. 79% of librarians considered their libraries to be suitable meeting places for tutors and students of the 'University of the Air' (the Open University).

On the whole, students were less decided than chartered staff — presumably the proper modesty of the inexperienced. On the other hand, assistant librarians had clearer ideas of the objectives of the librarian as an educator than did the chiefs. The chartered staff tended to be more favourable towards relations with the external bodies than towards the librarian as an educator.

Some of these attitudes could be ascribed to comtemporary practical considerations; for example, the building may simply be too small to allow for lectures, etc or the provision of a record library may be possible but only at the expense of new books. 'The first priority must be a first-rate book and information service. Only then should we try to extend to other media.'

Coding: 7c(xv), 7c(i), 7c(iii), 7c(ii), 1b(iv)

THE LIBRARY IN SOCIETY — A STUDY OF THE PUBLIC LIBRARY IN AN URBAN SETTING by B. Luckham, Research project sponsored by the Public Libraries and Adult Education Committee of the North-West, published by The Library Association, London 1971 (181 pp).

Aim
To review the role of the public library in society.

Method
Primarily by interviews of, and questionnaires completed by, members and non-members in selected libraries in North-West England.

Discussion
Professor Thomas Kelly, in his Introduction, writes 'Most librarians, I fancy, will say that the general picture (given in this volume) is pretty much what they expected, but that it is more detailed and in greater depth. It is of interest, for example, that Mr Luckham not only tabulates the percentage of borrowers taking away the various categories of fiction and non-fiction, but also seeks to establish (a) how far these choices were deliberate or random, and (b) what other sources of books borrowers were using.' A summary cannot, perforce, include the very details which make the study particularly valuable as a source of reference, and regrettably must be confined to indicating the principal statistics.

The author reminds us that the library is a social and cultural focus, as well as a source of book loans and consultation. In 1964, 49% of 562 United Kingdom library authorities provided lectures, film shows, gramophone recitals, general exhibitions, film-making facilities etc, (at least 18 non-book services in total). In 1957-58 about 28.8% of the total population in England and Wales were library members: in the areas of Chester and Eccles, chosen for investigation in 1966, the respective figures were 29.4% and 27.8%.

From his enquiries the author found that 27% of males were members, 22.5% of females. The greatest proportions of members by age groups were 28% in the 20-34 year cohort and 31% in the 35-54 year cohort. 26% of members ended their full-time education before

119

the age of 15; another 35% terminated their full-time education between 16 and 18 years.

48% of members were in the managerial or higher professional socio-economic groups, 34% had attended grammar/public schools, 34% were estimated to be in the top decile by intelligence grouping.

There was an increasing propensity for a person to belong to a library if a greater proportion of eligible residents in the home were members too. Parental influence was the major encouragement to join libraries; about 50% of members named parental influence, 38% of members suggested teacher influence, 31% could not recall any influence. Membership of libraries correlated with type of property occupied; the better and more modern the housing, the higher the proportion of the residents that were members.

Surprisingly, 96% and 94% of members and non-members respectively took a national Sunday paper, but when the local weekly paper clientele is examined, the figures diverge to become 74% and 53% respectively. Library members were interested in both the local and the cosmopolitan.

From Chapter 3 to the end of the volume, more detailed statistics are provided to suggest answers to such questions as: Who are the users? How often do they use the library? When do people visit libraries? What type of books are borrowed? How are books selected?

The author considered the image of the library; 27% of members and 44% of non-members thought the buildings to be dismal. Adult class use of library accommodation was examined; respondents were asked where they would expect classes on particular topics to be held. Only 30% of members felt that a public library was the expected venue for literature classes.

The librarian's role and perception of adult education was investigated. 61% of chief public librarians had studied in some adult education course, compared to 36% of all adults; 42% of the 'chiefs' had studied in WEA/Extra-Mural courses compared to 12% of persons in all professions and managerial occupations.

In the final chapter the author considers the arguments for conservation and for change. Precise methodological details are given in the appendices and a portrait of the two towns of Chester and Eccles is included.

Coding: 7c(xv), 7c(iii), 7c(i), 2b, 2a, 8c, KB970

A HISTORY OF PUBLIC LIBRARIES IN GREAT˙ BRITAIN
1845-1965 by Thomas Kelly, Professor of Adult Education, University of Liverpool. Published by the Library Association, 1973 (543 pp) (Available from National Institute of Adult Education Library).

Aim
To provide an account of the creation of the public library service.

Discussion
Before the Public Libraries and Museums Act of 1964 there was no compulsion on any local authority to make library provision. Until then, the provision of a library service was essentially a voluntary activity requiring, in its earlier phases, the specific consent of the rate-payers. The heart of library history, therefore, is not solely to be found in such general aspects as the growth of library legislation but rather more in the localised history of the hundreds of individual libraries which together make up the library service. For this reason Professor Kelly reinforces the general narrative of the period up to 1919 with case studies of selected libraries, large and small. For the later period, because of the very large number of library authorities involved, the author has not continued with this method although, nevertheless, the narrative continues to be based firmly on the work and experience of individual libraries.

It may be argued that the library service both contributes to, and benefits from, the strength of the adult education movement. The author deals, therefore, with the role of libraries as specialist providers of books and also describes their extension activities; frequently he instances examples of their co-operation with, and support of, other sectors of the adult education movement.

This volume is divided into four books, the first of which deals with the period 1845-1886 and describes the origins of the first Public Libraries Act and the foundation of the Municipal Library Service. Case studies of the individual libraries are given, and the organisation and use of libraries is evaluated. Writing of the Parliamentary Returns for 1876 and 1877, the author notes that readers from working and lower middle classes are recorded in considerable numbers and infinite variety, and that everywhere there is at least a sprinkling of readers from the higher classes.

Book 2, dealing with the period 1887-1918, begins with a section entitled 'The Age of Carnegie'. The largest single factor in persuading local authorities to undertake the burden of library provision was the availability of substantial grants in aid, not, as suggested by the Select Committee of 1849, from the government, but from private funds, principally from Andrew Carnegie. Case studies once more illustrate the pattern of growth during this period. But these years were also notable for two other revolutions within the library itself, the 'Open Access Revolution' and the 'Dewey Decimal Revolution'. These changes are described in the context of an evaluation of library use and organisation during this time.

Book 3, 1919-1939, describes the birth of the county libraries, the Mitchell (1924) and Kenyon (1927) Reports, the further developments in the organisation and use of libraries, the National Libraries and the beginnings of inter-library co-operation. Significantly, in 1938 Edward Sydney, writing in the *Year Book of Education*, declared that the library should be 'the headquarters of all local cultural activities', whilst Eric Leyland in his book *The wider public library* envisaged the possibility that the library may evolve into a cultural centre 'built up with the Public Library as a nucleus, a Cultural Centre would include a library . . .'.

The final book, covering the period 1939-1965, includes a description of the library service in wartime, the McColvin Report of 1942, the post-war years, the emergence of the 'affluent society' and the Roberts Report and its consequences. The major concern to librarians in the early sixties was not a fear of television and radio nor of the other new technologies; on the contrary, most of these developments were seen as a means of providing a greater variety of services, whilst retaining the provision of books as the essential core. Rather there was a sense of unease about the allocation of resources. Were the libraries attracting a fair share of the nation's output of graduates? Were the libraries attracting a sufficient share of the national wealth to expand the library service and thus take advantage of new techniques and opportunities?

Appendices are provided, giving details of, for example, book-stocks, issues and population at selected dates, together with a select bibliography. More than forty-five evocative plates and illustrations complete the volume.

Coding: 1b(xxv), 7c(i), 7c(xix), 7c(iii)

Adult education and the mass media

THE HISTORY OF BROADCASTING IN THE UNITED KINGDOM by Asa Briggs, published by Oxford University Press. Volume 1 — *The birth of broadcasting,* published 1961, 425 pp; Volume 2 — *The golden age of wireless,* published 1965, 663 pp; Volume 3 — *The war of words,* published 1970, 765 pp.

Aim
A history of broadcasting in the United Kingdom; dealing principally with the British Broadcasting Company 1922-27 and the British Broadcasting Corporation 1927-1945.

Discussion
(Though the whole output of the BBC may be said to influence adult attitudes and consequently impinge upon adult education, we have taken the view that the programme output may be broadly classified under four headings: entertainment, information, educative and educational. Whilst accepting that the divisions are arbitrary, that the educational may be sometimes entertaining or that the entertaining is often educational, the summary below is concerned with those parts of the original text which seem to deal especially with educational or educative aspects of adult education.)

Pages 230-283 of Volume 1 discuss broadcasting as a 'public service', and the contents of the programmes, given that ideal. The author describes the initiation of the system of Advisory Committees, for example, the Central Educational Advisory Committee appointed in August 1924; their role as a formal channel of public influence on BBC affairs and their weaknesses. He argues that the conception of broadcasting as a 'public service' did not reach deep enough, nor perhaps democratically, into the subsoil of the community to ensure that 'the people' felt that the BBC was theirs. At the same time, the author explores the particular historical context in which the BBC operated.

Even by 1926 the foundations for two important contributions to adult education had been laid; music and drama broadcasts. 141 'plays' were broadcast between August 1924 and September 1925, 10% of which were of a classical nature. Almost from its inception

123

the BBC established itself as a patron in certain branches of 'entertainment', notably opera, to the extent of helping financially the British National Opera Company in 1923 and 1924.

Sir John Reith desired to make broadcasting 'educational' in the broadest sense. He believed, for example, that a debate on unemployment would be 'of the greatest interest' and would express the 'public service character of broadcasting', but he was often frustrated by his political masters. The fear of public controversy and until 1928 an official ban imposed upon it were facts of life that the BBC, in its infancy, simply had to accept, even though the officers of the Corporation continually pressed for greater freedom.

Volume 2, *The golden age of wireless,* encompasses the period from 1st January 1927, when the British Broadcasting Corporation took over the work of the British Broadcasting Company, to the outbreak of the Second World War. Sir John Reith, Managing Director of the old Company was given the title of Director-General. There was no sudden break or change; rather there was an extension and enrichment of the activity of broadcasting based in many cases on the foundations laid between 1922 and 1927.

Pages 185-227 deal with educational and religious programmes. Education, per se, was represented by many gifted professionals; for example, H. A. Fisher, who had devised the Education Act of 1918, was a Governor of the BBC from 1935-1939 and Sir Henry Hadow was Chairman of the BBC Committee which produced the Report *New ventures in broadcasting* in March 1928. J. C. Stobart, a former HMI who became one of the first educators of standing to respond to the new medium, wrote a memorandum outlining a plan for a new type of University 'The Wireless University' in October *1926* (vide the Open University *1971*).

An experiment in schools broadcasting was undertaken in Kent in June 1926, and in 1927 Mary Somerville was briefed to visit schools and judge for herself the effectiveness of the broadcasts. By 1929 about 2,400 schools listened regularly to the BBC schools service. But the service provided by the BBC outran the financial resources of many local education authorities, so that, even by 1935, the BBC could do no more than salute those authorities who were prepared to embark upon ambitious plans of wireless installation. Thus, schools broadcasting was firmly established; but what about the adult education service?

The BBC's efforts in adult education were less successful than with the schools, although for a time they produced what looked like spectacular results (page 218). Adult education talks had been first broadcast in 1924, and in April 1927 L. S. Lambert joined the BBC specifically to arrange such programmes. A representative Central Council for Adult Education was created in November 1928 and by 1930 there were over a thousand listening groups. 'All concerned with adult education should remember that a new ally has suddenly come into the field' commented the WEA Journal in 1931. In the same year a high point was reached when a series of BBC adult educational programmes was broadcast under the title 'The changing world'. But it has always been difficult to maintain momentum in adult education; for every wave of excitement there is a surfeit of grey routine.

The BBC's contribution to 'adult education' as narrowly defined gradually waned because the more professional BBC effort in the provinces was diverted towards schools broadcasting; the multitude of traditional adult education providers were not so easy to contact as a few Directors of Education; the providers themselves were cautious — 'The BBC study group cannot take the place of sustained class work' — and, finally, the place of adult education in the BBC's central organisation was never secure. Consequently, though the BBC had undertaken a pioneer experiment in adult education, it was not itself an adult education authority, and it did not wish to interfere with local education authorities. The work of adult education itself involved complex psychological and social issues and the BBC operated in the context of a society in which there was an undercurrent of resistance. 'We can imagine no more unsuitable medium for adult education than a state-owned service which enters the homes of people of every age . . . and rank of society'. (Glasgow Evening Citizen, 12 January 1927).

Volume 3, *The war of words,* describes the role and contribution of the BBC during the Second World War. Many teachers and tutors had joined the armed forces, and hence much school and adult education depended on the national broadcasting service. For many schoolchildren of that period, the only source of dramatic and musical experience was the BBC; for many adults, both civilian and uniformed, the BBC was also the main source of informed debate and comment.

But this volume is about a nation at war; inevitably education took second place to the other duties of a national broadcasting service with world-wide responsibilities, but, for example, the audience for radio drama actually doubled between 1939 and 1945. The account is mainly of the BBC's service to Britain's embattled citizens and to occupied Europe. The idealogical war against the bestiality of the Nazi regime, the overseas service and the political problems of the Corporation are all described in detail.

It is a matter of justifiable pride that, although fine distinctions between propaganda and pure information were often difficult to sustain, intellectual and moral standards were maintained, and the pertinent questions continued to be asked; for example, the author quotes J. W. Welch in 1942: 'Will our war-time broadcasts bear the scrutiny of an impartial Christian mind when peace has given us disengagement from theatened interests and has set our work in a wider context?'

Coding: 1c(x), 1b(xvi), KB456

THE DETERMINATION OF COMMUNITY ATTITUDES TO MENTAL ILLNESS by C. M. U. Maclean, D.Phil. thesis, University of Edinburgh 1967.

Aim
To investigate community attitude to the mentally ill and to ex-mental patients.

Method
An analysis of the results of 373 interviews of adults living in Edinburgh, conducted in 1966, using the short form of the Maudsley Personality Inventory, obtaining 47 statements of attitude and opinion regarding mental illness, using sympathy and social scales together with the results of a questionnaire submitted to Scottish psychiatric consultants.

Discussion
The first part of this study consists of a review of the literature on the determination of community attitudes to mental illness. Beginning with theoretical and sociological considerations, the subject is

pursued through the involvement of special groups of health workers, to the viewpoint of close relatives and eventually to the community at large. This section includes a review of the work of Nunnally (1957, 1958 and 1961) of the Institute of Communications Research in Illinois University, who found that, in general, the public seemed free of the worst misconceptions which the mass media were portraying, and that the lay public were closer to the point of view of the experts than either group were to the concepts portrayed in the media.

Findings

The results show that the Edinburgh population is generally familiar with this topic and is prepared to discuss it frankly. Although many traces of old stereotypes of mental illness still remain, and, whilst the public has not yet completely adopted the prevailing psychiatric viewpoint, there is evidence of a relatively greater sympathy and tolerance among the younger and better educated sections of the community. This may mean that still further acceptance of psychiatric diagnoses and treatments is to be anticipated in the future. At the same time personality factors, such as neuroticism and a high regard for self-reliance, determine the extent of the sympathy and tolerance people feel towards the mentally ill.

The picture of mental illness projected by the mass media in Britain seems to be educating rather than alarming the public, but there is still room for improvement in certain specific directions.

Coding: 1c(x), 5h, 5m(xiv)

THE PROVINCIAL PRESS AND THE COMMUNITY by I. Jackson, M.A. thesis (2 vols), University of Birmingham 1968. [Also published, in condensed and slightly modified form, as *The provincial press and the community*, Manchester University Press, 1971]

Aim

To consider the varying functions that the provincial press performs in contemporary society and to illustrate the kinds of content, both typical and untypical.

Method
This consists of a detailed examination of provincial newspapers with coverage of over 50% of local households, excluding the provincial morning press.

Discussion
The author states the basic principles of his analysis of the provincial press, namely, reference to its traditions and conventions, to the differences between local and national newspapers, to the frequency of publication, the nature of the readership and to social and cultural changes. The editorial concept of the readership, the influence of local institutions and community leaders, the editorial view of the paper's social role, the character of its circulation and of its competitive situation and of its ownership are also considered.

After a brief outline of their historical development, the author investigates each feature of the local press in detail. Chapters 2 to 8 deal respectively with news, the leading column, correspondence, features, advertising, attitudes to culture and attitudes to national politics.

It is argued that in the 1830s perhaps three-quarters of the operatives in the North could read and therefore the influence of the local press was considerable, even at that early date. In 1964 working-class readers outnumbered middle-class readers, so that, taking the average of three regions, Yorkshire, the Midlands and the South, there were approximately 2.6 working-class readers (C2, D & E) for every one middle-class reader (A, B & C1). But the evening newspaper attracted approximately the same percentage from each class and the proportion of readers increased as one moved from North to South, and as one moved from the DE social groups to the AB groups. As an example of the typical educational experience of readers, 77% of Midlands evening newspaper readers completed their education at 15 years or earlier.

The tone and content of local newspapers was determined by the interests and prejudices of the majority readership, although all, to some degree, attempted to cater for minority interests.

Advertising usually accounted, in the mid-1960s, for two-thirds or more of an evening newspaper's gross income and normally took 50-70% of the total space available.

Although up to three-quarters of provincial evening newspapers seemed willing to foster local cultural activities, most of them, however, appeared to derive their cultural attitudes from the puritan, Arnoldian tradition.

Findings
The provincial evening newspaper was predominantly local in its content, and concerned with the local mass-readership. The community 'good' was, in practice, closely identified with the good of local institutions and local commerce. It was an essentially conservative communications medium, upholding family and institutional life, accepting the Protestant ethic and capitalist assumptions. The author suggests that some features of this conservatism need to be challenged at local level through the restoration of competitive situations.

Coding: 7c(xxi)

AN ANALYSIS OF THE SOCIAL CONTENT OF POPULAR DRAMA 1955-1965 by J. S. R. Goodlad, Ph.D. thesis, University of London 1970.

Aim
To examine the possible functions of drama in society through a review of:
— literature on the functions of myths and ritual with which drama is associated in its origins;
— theories of roles which use the terminology of drama to describe social interaction;
— criticism which interprets drama in social terms;
— commentary on the nature and effects of mass communication.

Method
The experimental part of the thesis analyses the social content of 114 self-contained plays performed in England between 1955 and 1965; 76 popular television plays were selected from BBC Audience Research information and 38 London West End stage plays were chosen by estimated audience figures.

Discussion

The first five chapters deal with: the association of drama with ritual; the theories of roles; literary theories about the functions of drama in society; the nature and effects of mass communication; and the systematic study of drama on television and in the theatre.

In Chapter 6 the social content of popular dramas between 1955 and 1965 is analysed by the following dimensions: themes; goals/motives of central characters; play types; setting; endings. The author considers in Chapter 7 a theory of the functions of drama in society.

Findings

Morality and/or love themes were found in 79% of the plays. Morality themes dealt with transgressions against society, of which the commonest were motivated by a desire for power, money, revenge and sex. Nearly half the morality plays involved murder. The typical format was detective-story/thriller with a clear cut 'just' ending. Plays with love themes typically dealt with problems of monogamy, were comedies, and ended happily.

The author proposes, in conclusion, two sociological hypotheses:
1 that people watch drama to organise and confirm their knowledge of socially-approved behaviour; as an expressive element of culture, popular drama probably functions as a monitor of prevailing morality;
2 that as instrumental aspects of culture, drama and its functional equivalents, directly or through mediating processes of social intercourse, disseminate, and probably determine, the moral values upon which the prevailing social structure depends.

Coding: 1c(x), 2b, 7c(xix), 3d

Participation in adult education

Composition of students in adult education

A SOCIO-PSYCHOLOGICAL SURVEY OF THE STUDENT MEMBERSHIP OF ADULT EDUCATION CLASSES IN LEEDS AND CHANGES IN THE ADULT EDUCATION STUDENT POPULATION SINCE 1945 by I. Hanna, M.A. thesis, University of Leeds 1964.

Aim

To study the socio-psychological characteristics of students in adult education classes in Leeds 1945-1963, and to compare their characteristics with those discovered of students in evening institutes in Leeds in 1962-1963.

Method

Data was collected by personal questionnaire from students in adult education classes at the Swarthmore Educational Centre and the University of Leeds, together with a few other smaller class centres. A second, rather similar questionnaire was distributed to students in the Leeds County Education Committee recreational classes, conducted at its evening institutes. Other bodies and organisations were surveyed by direct observation, interviews with members and so on. The results of these surveys were compared to the results of the parallel Leeds Evening Institute Survey of 1962/63.

Discussion

Demographically, Leeds is representative of the West Riding conurbation; population increased very little owing to emigration, particularly of women, to the South of England. Leeds may be divided into three distinct areas, if a juror index is used (which indicated, at this time, higher valuation of domestic residence). Half the population lived in areas with a juror index of less than 6% jurors to residents on the electoral role, one-quarter lived in a J.6% to J.12% area and the remaining quarter lived in a wealthy area of index J.13% and over.

Recreational evening institutes were, during this period, the most rapidly expanding type of further education, increasing their membership from 4,864 in 1951/52 to 9,740 in 1962/63. Their appeal was mainly to women, who composed about 70% of membership, and to students from the higher J.% group, that is, 49% of total students. Consequently, the subjects offered would be of interest to that type of student, i.e. languages, arts, music and drama — those which appeal to the better educated.

In Chapter 4 the author traces the origins of the major institutions which provided adult education in Leeds; the Mechanics' Institutes, the voluntary organisations, the University Extension Movement. He then deals with existing, contemporary providers; the numbers in classes held in Swarthmore, in classes under the auspices of the Workers' Educational Association and in the Department of Extra-Mural Studies extension classes. New types of adult education courses are also considered; for example, the point is made that such as the University Extension technical and professional refresher courses and the advanced liberal courses were distinct post-1945 developments.

Leeds; in 1958 some 79 separate voluntary organisations or clubs were providing facilities. The work of these, and some other bodies, such as the British Council, the YMCA, and the Leeds Industrial Co-operative Society Education Department are described in Chapter 5 in considerable detail.

After a comprehensive review of pioneering research, *Learn and live,* by W. E. Williams and A. E. Heath 1936, *Tutorial class students,* by S. G. Raybould 1946/7, *Who were the students?* by W. E. Styler 1950, the WEA Working Party Survey 1959, and *Education in the adult population,* by J. Trenaman, the author describes precisely the construction of his 1961/62 questionnaire, the method of sampling and the principles adopted for various classifications.

Chapters 8 and 9 give, in detail, the results of the analysis of 860 student enrolment completed questionnaires and of the 20% sample of the 2,471 who returned and completed the Leeds Evening Institute Survey questionnaire.

Findings

The student population in the author's sample is unrepresentative of the adult population; men are usually married, mainly in the young-middle-aged range, women are usually young and single. Students tend to be younger than the general population, with more under 49 years and very few over retiring age. The better-educated, holders of better levels of jobs or skills, those who live in better residential areas — these form the majority of students. 50% are trained to professional levels, 10% in the less-skilled half of the population and the youngest students come from the poorest areas of Leeds. Adult education is a method of social upgrading and personal self-improvement. Male students enrol more in science and social studies, female students tend to enrol in liberal studies and arts.

The extension classes form the only male-dominated group; here young-middle-aged married men form the majority. These students are the most active in voluntary societies, professional associations and white collar unions. In the LEA classes, language students are the youngest of all, and are better educated than arts students, but they come from the poorer areas of Leeds. The Joint Committee (University Extension and WEA) students have a majority of minimum-legal-age-education leavers, manual workers and trade unionists. The voluntary bodies and WEA show the widest distribution of student ages and provide the greatest amount of recreational education.

Comparing the adult education findings above with the evening institute, 25% of evening institute students are aged 15-24 years, compared to about 14% of the adult education population. From ages 25-44 years and 55-65+ years, adult education has a greater percentage of the student body than the institutes. Women are in greater preponderance in institutes than in adult education as a whole, and normally are married. However, institutes had twice the percentage of manual workers than adult education claims; indeed, 47% of institute members left school at 15 and under, compared to 28% of adult education, and it seems that institutes attract both the young and middle-aged women of lesser education but of better-off families.

Thus, enrolments in adult education classes have increased since 1945, though population has been stable. Yet those with minimum formal educational experience and low economic status remain outsiders; could it be that the major institutions, with their present forms of curricula, methods and publicity, have lost their missionary zeal?

Coding: 2a, 2b, 4, 5a, 1a, KB1439

A STUDY OF FACTORS AFFECTING MEMBERSHIP AND PARTICIPATION IN VOLUNTARY LEISURE ASSOCIATIONS by J. W. F. Arriens, Ph.D. thesis, Unviersity of Cambridge 1968

Aim
a To examine the effects of basic demographic and socio-economic variables on *both* membership and participation in selected voluntary associations
b To examine the degree to which the family situation and the work situation for associational activity constrains participation
c To explain skews in membership according to age and socio-economic status by reference to family and work situation

Method
The introduction to this thesis discusses in considerable detail the motives and objectives of previous studies, the research methodology of these studies and factors associated with membership and participation in voluntary associations.

Because of the requirement of comparative data throughout the *whole* community, Harlow New Town, Essex, where basic demographic and socio-economic information is regularly assembled, was selected as the research locality. Four associations, covering a wide occupational range, were surveyed; an angling society, a choral society, a photographic society and a sports-centre with respective memberships in 1967 of 86, 129, 41 and 2,040. The survey is detailed, the statistical checks to establish control criteria are exhaustive and the tables of collected data are comprehensive.

Findings

There was a skew towards males among sports-centre members and, similarly, towards females in the choral society, compared with the demographic characteristics of Harlow. The photographic and angling societies were predominantly male. Persons aged 65 and over were under-represented. There were no married male members of the choral society between 20 and 29; married angling society members (all male) were slightly over-represented between the ages of 45 and 54. Married women were more affected in their participation by their families than were men, but the evidence suggests that the family situation is a much more significant determinant of membership and participation in voluntary associations than has hitherto been recognised. With the exception of married male choral society members, between 20% and 40% of married members considered their family situation had a significant effect on their participation, and this could explain certain skews in membership according to demographic factors.

In each of the four associations there are distinct relationships between socio-economic status and the sort of persons with whom participation usually takes place; for example, low socio-economic status members found it difficult to participate in partnership-games, such as squash. Lower social status females in the choral society seemed to need a friend to act as a sponsor in order to join. Overall, the importance of other members of the nuclear family for participation was inversely related to socio-economic status. Status divisions have persisted in new towns, despite the planned intentions.

In every association there was a marked relationship between the ease of participation and the length and regularity of the working week; particular difficulties were recorded for weekly hours in excess of 45 hours. In 1967 the average working week among wage earners was 46 hours. The lack of working-class participation is, therefore, not entirely a cultural matter; there are underlying social and economic structural factors.

Similarly, working-class wives are more often obliged to work and more often have larger families, but although voluntary participation and membership of the working classes is currently under-represented, the continued reduction of working hours and the control of family size may lead, in the long run, to an amelioration of some of the conditions which constrain working-class membership and participation.

Coding: 2a, 2b, 5m(xii), 5m(xiv), 5m(xix)

LEARNING AND LEISURE IN MIDDLE AND LATER LIFE by
Enid Hutchinson, published by the Pre-Retirement Association in
association with the National Institute of Adult Education and the
National Old People's Welfare Council 1970 (56 pp).

Aims
To consider the problems of the older half of the population,
particularly the relation between the leisure time interests of middle
life and retirement activities.

Method
The author, who has a long and distinguished personal experience of
and association with adult education, applies her insight to the
information provided by a major research project carried out by the
NIAE called *Provision for adult education,* published in March 1970.

Discussion
The NIAE conducted two surveys, one of a sample from the general
population and one of a sample of students in adult education
classes, called respectively 'the general population sample' and 'the
student population sample'. In 'the general population sample' the
people aged 45 and over amounted to 56% of the total interviewed,
47% of whom were male. The author considers three sub-divisions of
this group, the middle-aged, 45-54 years of age, the late middle-aged
or pre-retirement group, aged 55-64, and the elderly or retired, 65
years and over. Men over 65 formed 25% of the total male
population; 85% of them went to elementary school only and they
were already middle-aged when the 1944 Education Act was passed.
33% of the men over 45 were in the pre-retirement group; 87% of
these were still employed and 80% had completed their full-time
education in elementary schools. 39% of the men were in the
middle-aged group, 72% of whom completed their full-time
education at an elementary school. Of the women interviewed, 33%
were elderly, 31% later-middle-aged and 36% middle-aged; 46%, 22%
and 10% of the respective groups were widowed or separated from
their husbands.

The author deals with the leisure activities of both men and women in detail but two crucial points emerge; firstly, that men tend to shed, rather than add, to the interests they share with others as they grow older and secondly, that women more often find themselves having to face later life alone.

Of 'the student sample population', 22% were between 45 and 54, 18% between 55 and 64 and 7% 65 years and over. There were more women than men enrolled in more vocational classes and 66% of the students were drawn from the three top social classes. The student sample shows that they have wide interests outside the home as well as an enjoyment of home-based pleasures, that they had known more early education and had received a bonus in social advancement and retirement interests.

The author considers the reasons for joining classes and highlights the importance of providing classes at preferred times and in places within travelling distance of students' homes. 'How important it is to be well off, and hale enough, to have and to drive a car, if life is not to close in on you in retirement.'

Appraisal and Proposals
The author pinpoints four basic needs: the need for less restrictive policies for adult education, the need for an adult education officer in each area with a central responsibility for the oversight of needs, the need for well-equipped, all-purpose centres conveniently situated in relation to a mixed population, and the need to open these centres during the day as well as the evening.

As a recommendation, the author suggests that the middle-aged should be involved more closely with the needs of the elderly. 37% of women over 65 years in the general survey lived alone; 75% of men and 83% of women lived in one or two-person households; are they to rely solely on the casual and uncertain contact of friends and family?

Coding: 2a, 2b, 2d, 51, 7b, 7c(xxi), KB1075

LABOUR MOBILITY AND HOSPITAL MANAGEMENT — A STUDY IN MANPOWER RESEARCH by B. L. Donald, D.Phil. thesis, University of Southampton 1971. [Summary provided by the University of Southampton; no loan copy is available, but a reference copy is held in Southampton.]

Aim
Throughout this research into the adjustment to labour scarcity of hospitals, their managements have grown more concerned with shortages but have failed as in the past to produce radical initiatives. The aim has, therefore, been to demonstrate the use of information on mobility as a control and stimulus for manpower decisions. Exemplification of contemporary industrial manpower planning for the complex organisation of hospitals has been attempted. The key is the mobility which characterises hospital employment.

Method
The employment has been examined of a workforce of over 11,000 currently deployed in sixty hospitals of the Wessex Regional Hospital Board; joint sponsors with the Department of Health and Social Security. A pilot study to develop research methods produced recommendations for improved manpower management *including the training of mature women as registered nurses.* Preliminary analysis of data from universal pay records revealed the structure and deployment of the occupations and key problems including part-time working, stability and wastage. Universal questionnaires facilitated an analysis of some characteristics of local hospital labour markets. Interviews of a stratified random sample of the workforce were used to support an analysis of the direction, frequency and extent of mobility in geographical, occupational and employment terms, both in and out of hospitals. Thus the major organisational, social, economic and psychological constraints on mobility have been examined as aspects of labour shortages.

Findings
While conservative improvements in adjustment to scarcity are proposed initially, the analysis suggests adjustment is inhibited by the normative aspects of professional forms of organisation in which the requisite and the restrictive are confused. Radical experiments

are suggested, particularly for the organisation of nursing in chronic hospitals, but their acceptance may well be inhibited by the characteristics of hospital organisation studied separately (J. D. Kyle, Ph.D. thesis, Southampton 1971). An experiment in manpower analysis is proposed meanwhile to counteract these inhibitions.

Coding: 2a, 1c(iii)

CHARACTERISTICS AND OPINIONS OF PART-TIME GCE STUDENTS IN MANCHESTER COLLEGES OF FURTHER EDUCATION by A. Shaw, M.Ed. thesis, University of Manchester 1972.

Aim
To collect information on characteristics and opinions of male and female part-time day or part-time evening students, taking GCE 'O' or 'A' level examinations at five colleges of further education in Manchester in summer 1971.

Method
Three pilot studies were made in 1971, using students in colleges *outside* Manchester. 519, out of survey population of 746 students, taking GCE in summer 1971 in five colleges of further education *within* Manchester completed questionnaires. Structured interviews were conducted with the heads of departments in which most of the part-time GCE students were enrolled.

Discussion
Part-time General Certificate of Education courses were introduced into further education establishments in the 1950s, and gradually developed until, by 1970, enrolments had almost reached 200,000 and part-time GCE students represented 6.5% of all part-time enrolments in November 1970.

Throughout the history of British adult education, there are examples of people who have attempted to follow courses and obtain qualifications normally associated with an earlier stage of life. Part-time GCE courses in colleges of further education may be seen, therefore, to represent this phenomenon in our contemporary situation. The thesis is consequently concerned with a section of the education system where a number of interesting areas of overlap, conflict and uncertainty exist, such as the provision of courses and examinations normally associated with schools, the problem of 'general' versus 'vocational' education and the place of these courses and examinations in the general field of adult education.

The thesis consists of four sections, the first describing the introduction and development of GCE courses in the further education system in England and Wales from 1950 to 1970 and, in detail, the national situation in 1970-71. This section includes an account of students' personal and educational backgrounds and course records. For example, overall figures mask interesting and intriguing differences. In 1970, *over half the evening only part-time students* in colleges were female, whereas *only one quarter of part-time day students* were female, but the students taking GCE showed the opposite characteristics; about 55% of part-time day enrolments for GCE courses in 1970 and about 45% of evening enrolments were female.

In the second section the author considers part-time GCE courses in Manchester colleges of further education, the student characteristics and opinions, the student objectives and the student evaluation of the colleges' provision. In general the students were young adults, trying to obtain GCE qualifications for career purposes. The overall impression is one of general satisfaction with the provision but there were two main causes of dissatisfaction, namely the lack of the provision of an information and careers guidance service and the attempts of the college to involve students in courses with a broader content and in college life in general.

The students' study records, their 'wastage' and examination records, and the factors associated with examination performance is the subject of the third section. About 66% of all part-time students enrolled failed to complete the course, but there are marked variations between sub-groups; for example, 20% of day students failed to complete, compared to 70% of evening students. Furthermore, about 40% of part-time students failed all the subjects in which they sat examinations. This 'would present a dismal picture if it were not seen within the general educational framework where only a minority proceed successfully to take each hurdle in the examination race'. The trend was toward 'success breeding success' but there were many exceptions.

Findings
The fourth section, which deals with the conclusions, contains a part entitled 'practical applications of some of the conclusions reached'. These principal practical recommendations may be put in question form. Is enough information and guidance given? Is the GCE examination constructed for school use appropriate for adult assessment? Do those reforming the school examinations system take any account of the probable use of these examinations by adults? Whilst retaining the principle of the open college, is there a case for a more thorough diagnostic procedure to cut down wastage? Is there enough use of teaching machines or educational technology, to provide a service which will attract individuals with special responsibilities, such as housewives with young children? Are college extra-curricula activities sufficiently publicised to attract students? Is there enough co-ordination between individual colleges to provide a comprehensive local service?

Coding: 2b, 1c(ii), 2a

LEISURE AND LEARNING IN VOLUNTARY ORGANISATIONS
by B. Elsey, M.A. thesis, University of Liverpool 1972.

Aim
a To investigate the relationship between leisure activities, the voluntary organisations and their members on the one hand, and learning on the other
b To study the structure of voluntary organisations, particularly their ability to provide opportunities for self-expression through leisure activities
c To identify the sociological groups from which members are drawn
d To review the role of voluntary organisations in the adult education movement

Method
Twenty voluntary organisations in Birkenhead, a town suffering from structural unemployment, were surveyed; secretaries were interviewed and 74% of the total membership, or 350 members, returned self-completing questionnaires.

141

The meanings of leisure and the psychological and sociological implications of the learning process are discussed in some detail, as is the relationship between formal and informal education.

Discussion

In 1969 the infant mortality rate per thousand births in England and Wales was 18, but the figure for Birkenhead was 29, illustrating the extent of social deprivation. 61.5% of Birkenhead's active adult population is composed of manual and less-skilled workers, and although about 4% of the total adult population attend educational and recreational meetings, only a minority of working-class adults participate in voluntary organisations. Newsom children tend to become Newsom parents and continue to be indifferent to any organised activity with an educational content, however casual and informal. Adults of all classes, the non-participant majority, depend on home, family or neighbourhood as the principal centre and source of leisure activity.

52% of members were male, 55.5% over the age of 55 years. 20% terminated their full-time education at 17 but 43% left school at the earliest legal date, although 27% had further apprentice training. 30% who attended leisure meetings also attended practical evening classes, particularly the later school-leavers.

Overall, 56% of members were in the 'upper' social classes I, II and III (non-manual), but 57% of members were in the 'median' groups III (non-manual) and III (manual). 59% were employed, 12.5% retired, and, although Birkenhead had an above-average unemployment rate, only 1% of members were unemployed.

Learning is spasmodic, protracted and undifferentiated but, nevertheless, still a continuum of activity, of learning new things and practising or modifying old skills and knowledge. Learning is an incidental, but not unintentional, benefit of membership and the voluntary organistion is midway between the predominantly social and diversionary meeting, such as watching a football match, and the more specialised focus of the evening class.

The number of official meetings varied from 100 per year to 10 per year; some were held in purpose-built accommodation, some were attended by teachers or instructors but many extra meetings took place unofficially. In fact, 82% of those surveyed met each other outside formal meetings, 58% in other members' homes. Only 6 organisations used audio-visual aids.

Members accept that leisure activity has a learning content, but 'learning something new' was the fourth reason for participating, following 'to enjoy the company of others' (79%), 'to meet friends' (67%), 'to share interests with others' (65%).

Findings
The informality of the voluntary association enhances the learning process for members, and minority though they may be, they gain something in this type of organisation and thus, to a significant proportion of the adult population, the voluntary organisation is an alternative to formal education, and a means of breaching class barriers. Consequently, the LEAs may justifiably increase their support on solely educational grounds.

Coding 2a, 7c(xxi), 5a, 3d, 3c, KB1390

Attitudes, motives and behavioural patterns

LEARN AND LIVE — THE CONSUMER'S VIEW OF ADULT EDUCATION by W. E. Williams and A. E. Heath, published by Methuen & Co. 1936 (271 pp). Available at the National Institute of Adult Education Library.

Aim
To reveal one kind of education, that of adults, in the round by presenting a symposium of the consumer's opinion.

Method
A collection of testimonies on adult education, some of which resulted from an enquiry into the returned opinions of 128 Ruskin College students and 410 tutorial class students.

Discussion
[All other summaries in this volume are of texts written since 1945; *Learn and live* is the sole exception to this general rule, and it is included because the original is a paradigm of research in adult

education, because the human qualities revealed by the authors are timeless and, by no means least, because the faith expressed and exposed has inspired many of the men and women who have been concerned with adult education since it was written.

In this instance, the usual method of summarising seemed to be inadequate; hence the following text consists of quotations from the original book.]

Chapter 1 — 'For Livelihood or Living?: What are the motives which impel working men and women to seek further education? To broaden the outlook on life; life is more than a bread-and-butter existence. The development of individual personality — which has possibly been arrested — and then the development of the ideal of service to the community.

One of the by-products of adult education is definitely the vocational one; and there seems no justice or virtue in attempting to eliminate it so long as we fail to provide free and equal access to secondary and to university education. If a man or woman wants to take advantage of the facilities of a cultural education to better himself vocationally — why not? So long as the facilities are not diverted from their staple purpose, such fortuitous opportunities should be there for anyone who can use them for a different purpose.

Why I joined my first class? 'I held a position of trust and I wished to make myself equal to it' and 'I drifted in as it were', or 'I badly needed something to relieve the monotony of my work which was making me very nervous'.

What are some of the defects of non-vocational learning? 'Its chief defect is its failure to create 'value' in one's ordinary occupation' and 'The main defect is that one *feels* educated. But the world asks "What are you doing for a living?" and the answer is "I am a labourer": one feels the social gap more keenly'.

Should adult education be more closely related to working life? 'No. It is working conditions that want bringing up, not adult education bringing down to it', and 'No, we know our jobs right enough, we need to know more of what makes life worth living'. If adult education fulfils its real function, it will of necessity be closely related to the working life of the student because it will change his outlook on his work and its value to society, just as it will surely form his national outlook on life generally. This testimony may remind many of us who are too ready to dogmatise about the adult student's needs, how diverse those needs actually are — and therefore how elastic our provision for them must be.

Chapter 2 — 'Difficulties, what the adult student has to put up with'. Shift-work and overtime, home conditions of study, orphans, first-born and fathers of families — family obligations of one kind or another are commonly quoted by students as a special difficulty in the way of successful study. 'Employer dubbed me "a clever b------" and the WEA a political organisation'.

Chapter 3 — 'The Discovery of Happiness' — Has education made you less happy, or more? 'I can enjoy myself among different people. I have widened my circle of friendship and feel more sympathetic in outlook', or 'Less happy, I think, because it makes one realise the appalling ignorance around one, and the ignorance of the people who govern', and 'In spite of all that — had I to live my time over again, I should take up adult education again.'

Chapter 4 — 'Guide, Philosopher and Friend' — the relation of student and tutor. 'He opened my eyes' has a depth of conviction and authenticity which penury of language cannot conceal; and that a testimony is no less weighty for being cast in Salvation Army idiom. 'On the first evening the tutor said casually, after answering somebody's question, "Life is, after all, a shedding of illusions. We start with Santa Claus". That made me think'. Or to quote another student, 'My first tutor knew so little about the subject he set out to teach that I felt compelled to talk, and in doing so did assert my personality'. But has poor Henry Dubb once more had to suffer the feudal charity of Superior Persons, ask the authors.

Chapter 5 — 'Creative Work' — in the literary line; work in the arts and crafts — artists by accident. 'Have made over a dozen violins and two cellos in my spare time', or 'Invented a steam pressure reducing valve which is an improvement', or 'Numerous suggestions have been adopted by the GPO Suggestions Committee'. The authors comment, 'our belief is in a system of further education which gives working men and women the chance to share in that human collaboration which we call progress.

Chapter 6 — 'Family Repercussions' — Has your engaging in adult educational activities had any personal consequences in your relations to your own family? 'It has made it possible for me to inspire my two youngest sisters to keep up their education' says one student, but another reports 'We lost touch with each other . . . our [speaking of his wife] intellectual lives are separate — now there is little or nothing in common. Experiences of education have also been the first begetters of a new and fuller family harmony; and what began as an individual possession has become a collective one.

Chapter 7 — 'Our Second Chance' — not for themselves alone — that is to say in the experience of adult education, they have discovered how much they missed as children — how little they were prepared in early life for the more satisfying uses of leisure. One of the results of adult education is to make parents regard their children as their own second chance.

Chapter 8 — 'The Best is Yet To Be' — defects in the methods of adult teaching — some, not all, tutors 'boss' the class too much — many more would take advantage of adult education if it were not for the bogey of having to do written work. Administrative defects of adult education — 'the movement is as sect-ridden as non-conformity, and each sect would sooner dissolve than merge into the big movement we need' remarks a student. One defect of organisation which is strongly criticised is the movement's failure to recognise the need for comfortable premises for its work. Perhaps the biggest volume of criticism directed against the organisation of the movement is an account of its failure to capture young people.

Appendix I — origin, development and methods of the enquiry; Appendix II — statistical summaries; Appendix III — what a University Tutorial Class is and what Ruskin College is.

'We all assume too much the ignorance of the generality of our contemporaries; this is sheer bluff on our part. We bluff ourselves with the belief that we are better than they and we bluff them into believing we are abnormal' warns one student replying to the authors' questionnaire.

Coding: 2b, 1b(x), 1b(ix), 1b(xv), 3b, KB1432

THE MEASUREMENT OF ADULT INTERESTS by T. H. Coates, D.Phil. thesis, University of London 1950.

Aim
To study the measurement of adult interests, which are postulated to be directly related to attitudes; to attempt to measure four values —

the valuation of religion, beauty, truth and social-mindedness; and the two dichotomies of manifestation, the verbal-active and the gregarious-isolated.

Method

The methodological approach is based on Thorndike's *Adult interests,* published in 1936, and the work of P. E. Vernon and G. W. Allport on the study of values. A pilot, self-administered questionnaire in trial form was given to a mixed sample of various adult education groups in England and Wales, and 119 replies were received.

The main questionnaire consisted of 76 re-scored papers of the trial run, together with 242 completed replies of the main questionnaire, giving a sample total of 318 responses from four groups in adult education and two groups of university students for comparison purposes. 119 were in extra-mural-department-conducted classes, 59 in LEA evening institute classes, 20 in long-term residential colleges, 19 in non-residential centres. 59 were returned by post-graduate university students of education and 42 by university students concerned with child study. 167 were men, 151 women. The extra-mural students in the sample were drawn from London, Leicester and the West Riding of Yorkshire, and the evening institute students from London and Leicester.

Discussion

The subject matter of the thesis demands a careful definition of terms, a survey of the methodological implications of such investigations and a considerable amount of statistical testing for degrees of reliability, etc. Consequently, the author considers the growth of interest study, the links between interests and values, the selection of categories for measurement, the establishment of provisional norms, reliability and interpretation, inter-correlations and further item analysis and the problems arising out of the Thurstone or the Likert scaling methods.

Findings

The measurement of adult interests, though difficult, is approachable. Interest and attitude measurement are essentially the same, and any measurement of degree of objective interest is a measurement of subjective attitude. Particular interests have been held to be related to values through concepts, and it is suggested that the most useful approach to the measurement of adult interests is to begin at a very general level by measuring broad values. The questionnaire, measuring religious, àesthetic, theoretical and social values, and the modes of manifestation, verbal-active and gregarious-isolated, is shown to have sufficiently high degrees of reliability, particularly in the religious aspect, to make it useful in further research.

From the data, as measured in both the preference and opinionaire sections, men were more devoted to truth and women to beauty; in the opinionaire section, women seemed to be more religious than men. There was no significant sex difference on the verbal-active or gregarious-isolated scales.

So far as evening institute and university extra-mural class groups are concerned, the feature is the similarity of the results; if the samples are representative, there is much less difference in the values of these groups than heretofore assumed. However, extra-mural students scored more on the social opinionaire. The questionnaire distinguished between the postgraduate 'handpicked' university students and the group of university students preparing for kindergarten teaching in a child study course. The former group was found to be significantly more theoretical.

Comparison of the university students with the extra-mural and evening institute groups shows only one striking difference: that the university students are much more aesthetic in their preferences and opinions. The inference is that appreciation of beauty may be a by-product of an extended education. This is particularly interesting because the postgraduate group, predominantly male, scored almost the same on aesthetic scales as the child study group, almost all female, so that when both sexes have an extended education, the sex difference on the aesthetic value revealed in the general group is modified.

The residential college group, as revealed by the questionnaire, seemed to be a group of serious young men, somewhat less religious than the general group, inclined to be theoretical and placing social-mindedness in a pronounced first place. Younger men were found to be more socially-minded than older men.

An attempt was made to gauge the effect of locality, and although London and Leicester students scored higher on the scale of aesthetic values than West Riding students, differences in the programmes offered could mean that those West Riding students enrolled had experienced shorter full-time education than those in the more Southern regions.

From 196 student responses, attempts were made to study the reasons for discarding interests. It is argued that 26% of the 277 lost interests were due to a change of concept — e.g. loss of interest in aircraft — 'I saw what damage they did during the war'. Neglecting reasons such as age and change in circumstances, 176 cases remained, and the author argues that 62% fitted into the hypothesis that interests are related to values through concepts (prima facie evidence). Consequently, the key to generating new interests is, firstly, to ascertain a person's values, then to decide what concepts will be adequate to link the desirable interest to the dominant values and, subsequently, to provide the educational experiences which make it possible for these new concepts to be formed.

Adult tutors will wish to derive a person's values, that is, to use some development of the questionnaires offered in the thesis, and to derive broad conceptual attitudes by measuring present interests. Upon this knowledge of current interests, and broad and dominant values, the tutors can then decide the style, the method of teaching, and the content of the programme.

The study does not include devices to make a direct, quantitative assessment of concepts; indeed, the author explicitly argues for further research and development in this area.

Coding: 2b, 3d, KB1316

SOME PSYCHOLOGICAL ASPECTS OF SOCIAL STRATIFI-CATION — A STUDY OF OPINION AND ATTITUDE by F. M. Martin, D.Phil. thesis, University of London 1952.

Aim

To examine popular conceptions of the nature of the social stratification system, together with certain related beliefs and attitudes, and to consider the influence of such conceptions and beliefs within, and between, social classes.

Method
862 interview responses (the interview schedule is included as an appendix) were used to classify the subjects into five categories, as follows: 133 managers and professional groups who assessed themselves as middle-class; 210 members of supervisory and technical and clerical grades who assessed themselves as middle-class and 108 of these grades who regarded themselves as working-class; 111 manual workers who described themselves as middle-class and 300 manual workers who identified themselves as working-class.

Discussion
The author considers the theories of Lloyd Warner, Alison Davis, Winslow Jones and Richard Centers. He then describes the design and execution of the survey, the construction of occupational and subjectives indices, the characteristics of various social classes or the differential social perspectives. Criteria of status are established and various patterns of aspiration are examined; for example, aspirations for daughters. The hierarchy of power is considered as part of a study of the conceptions of power and the exercise of class interest in the 1950 election is considered.

Findings
About 66% of the professional group think of their class in occupational terms; 75% of them define the working-class by similar standards. 85% believe education is a class determinant; 33% think of income as an equally important determinant. 86% are confident of assessing the social standing of persons by, primarily, speech. 25% thought that they were in a better position to help their children than their own parents had been.

The salaried group who considered themselves middle-class thought very much along the lines of the professional and managerial group. The main difference between those in this section who assessed themselves as middle-class and those who assessed themselves as working-class lay in their ratings of occupations. The latter defined the middle-class much more rigorously to include only professional and managerial occupations. For the whole group, improved opportunities are seen primarily as educational opportunities.

Three-quarters of the manual workers define themselves as working-class by occupation. In all the manual groups, education was given an important rating; about 70% claimed to judge social status by speech, dress and bearing. About 66% of the total group wished their children to continue their education beyond the age of 15, but only 11% considered that education should continue up to or beyond the age of 20.

Coding: 2b, 3a

AN ENQUIRY INTO THE INTERESTS AND ATTITUDES TOWARDS CONTINUED EDUCATION OF YOUTHS IN CERTAIN DAY-RELEASE CLASSES IN NOTTINGHAM AND LIVERPOOL by F. Elliott, M.Ed. thesis, University of Nottingham 1952.

Aim
a To survey briefly the historical growth of day-release classes
b To survey by questionnaire the attitudes and interests of young adults to day-release
c To make recommendations for the curriculum and organisation of a County College

Method
A survey was conducted by questionnaire presented to 547 young men and 126 girls in Nottingham, and to a control group of 157 young men and 146 girls in Liverpool. All were attending day-release classes in the period 1948-1950, and many also attended evening classes, either voluntarily or as a condition for day-release.

Discussion
Of 976 questioned, 808 had attended Secondary Modern Schools. Most students' attitude to their secondary school lay between the answer 'did not mind it' and slightly above the 'rather liked it'. Most students 'rather liked' day-release, although the ex-secondary Grammar School male students were the least enthusiastic. Many students felt that their secondary school had not prepared them for entry into industry and that day-release classes were helpful. Nevertheless, many students complained that day-release courses were *not* sufficiently vocational; the demand for increased practical work was

151

continuosuly reiterated. A large number of students found the manipulation of pen or pencil a very difficult operation, and this may have been the cause of their dislike of note-taking. The length of time spent at day-release classes did not affect the subjects studied at evening classes. Occupation was consistently the chief factor governing the evening class subject-choice.

Findings
On the basis of interests and attitudes expressed by this sample, physical recreation would be the most popular section of a curriculum for young adults; games, dancing and swimming were far more popular than physical training. Practical crafts and vocational subjects followed in popularity, and there was a fear of subjects which had not been previously taught at a secondary level.

The author argues that the principal aims of County Colleges should be to continue general education, to pay due regard to the vocational bias of courses, to help adolescents find satisfactory employment, to help improve students' knowledge of English and mathematics, to provide facilities for students to follow their hobbies and to train students in applying knowledge in practical situations. He argues for small classes, informal teaching methods, a teaching-day of about six hours, and for close co-operation with the Youth Enployment Service.

Many students sufficiently keen to attend day-release classes often lack the skills to gain from a continuative adult education service which may emphasise the literary mode: 'everybody ort to no' as one student wrote, is phonetically understandable, even if difficult to decipher.

Coding: 1b(xiii), 2b, 2c, 6, 5a, 5c

A SURVEY OF SOME OF THE PROBLEMS OF VOCATIONAL EDUCATION IN PART-TIME DAY-RELEASE CLASSES by F. Jones, M.Ed. thesis, University of Nottingham 1954.

Aim
a To review the historical development of part-time vocational education

b To study the attitudes and interests of students in part-time day-release
c To study some of the effects of examinations on part-time day-release
d To assess the abilities of students attending day-release classes

Discussion

The first three chapters comprise a historical survey of the development of vocational education in England, particularly the part played by the Royal Society of Arts, the Science and Art Department, the City and Guilds of London Institute, Evening Schools and Day Continuation Schools to 1951.

Two chapters deal with interests, attitudes and leisure-time activities of students; two questionnaires were completed, the first dealing with interests and attitudes by 180 students, the second dealing with leisure by a representative cross-section of 200 students. The final two chapters consider the problems of examining and of selecting students for day-release.

Findings

In 1920-21 there were, in the day-release category, 48,800 students in vocational classes and 3,200 in non-vocational classes; by 1950-51 the respective figures were 246,300 and 58,800. Clearly the function of day-release in 1950 was to carry on the vocational work of the evening continuation classes.

In 1948 the majority of young adolescents were ardent cinema fans; about 80-90% attended the cinema at least once a week.

As may be expected in adolescents concerned with their future, the majority of students evinced a strong interest in vocational subjects. Most students recorded a feeling of satisfaction brought about by achievement and progress in a particular subject but, in stressing the importance of targets, the author notes that objectives may be prescribed without recourse to examinations.

Such was the emphasis on vocational education in day-release studies that the author argues for an expansion of the services of the adult education movement to comprehend this student body and to redress the cultural balance.

Coding: 2b, 1b(xiii), 1b(ii), 6

SOCIAL FACTORS IN SCHOOL PROGRESS — A STUDY OF THE HOME ENVIRONMENT OF THE CHILD by Elizabeth D. Fraser, D.Phil. thesis, University of Aberdeen 1955. [also published as *Home environment and the school*, University of London Press, (latest edition 1973)].

Aim
a To determine whether school attainment is influenced by factors in the home to a greater degree than by intelligence
b To identify those aspects of the home environment which most influence school progress

Method
A sample of a representative group of 408 Aberdeen schoolchildren, aged between 12½ and 13½ at the time the enquiry began in 1949, was taken. Results of intelligence tests (IQ) and attainment tests (EQ) were available. Homes were visited and four major aspects of home environment were distinguished and sampled: the cultural, the economic or material, the motivational and the emotional. A scaled measure of the child's school progress, called his 'criterion score' was devised.

Discussion
This thesis includes much information about parental attitudes, of interest to adult education. The questionnaires asked for information on parents' cinema habits, reading habits (analysed in considerable detail), hobbies, newspapers bought and read, educational backgrounds, incomes and domestic living space. For example, in 106 homes out of 403, neither parent claimed to read anything more than the newspaper or a magazine story.

Findings
The principal result which emerged from both factor analysis and multiple correlation techniques was that, given each level of intelligence, a child's school progress is more closely related to factors in the home environment than to his intelligence score.

Coding: 2b

THE ATTITUDES AND INTERESTS OF GIRLS ATTENDING A DAY-CONTINUATION COLLEGE by A.M. Fessler, M.Ed. thesis, University of Nottingham 1955.

Aim
An investigation of attitudes towards, and interests in, aspects of school life, further education and leisure amongst girls aged 15-18 years attending a Day-Continuation College.

Method
Questionnaires and personal interviews were used to obtain the opinions of 504 Day-Continuation College students, and the results are presented in simple, ranked tables.

Discussion
More students claimed that they learnt a lot in their final year at school than that they learnt nothing, but nearly half claimed that they learned only a little that was new. This unsatisfactory verdict on the final year at school may affect their continuing education.

33.4% of all students attended evening classes, primarily for vocational reasons. Most students took evening classes seriously, but frequently regarded them as an unfortunate limitation on their leisure activities. Those of greater academic ability were the most interested in the Day-Continuation College. However, unfavourable comment was directed against things which could be altered, for example, unsuitable teaching methods and the repetition of subject matter taught at school, whereas favourable criticism centred on the essential function of further education, that is, the opportunity for continued study. There seemed to be a positive association between a lesson that is enjoyed and one from which much is learned; the most successful lessons were those in which both teacher and student participated, and popular lessons were those which required general, rather than special, abilities. 75% liked film strips, but 15% recorded that 'you don't have to work so hard as in another sort of lesson'. Many recorded that impressions of filmstrips were impermanent.

As the age of students increased, so did the tendency to dislike subjects regarded as useless, but there was an acceptance of 'useful but unpleasant' lessons. The girl worker-students attached great importance to their work which was, on the whole, neither intellectually demanding nor mentally stimulating. Consequently, mental exercise was something one left behind at school, so that the popular leisure interests were social, physical or emotional.

Findings
Results suggested predominantly favourable attitudes to school and further education, and a utilitarian attitude to curricula. Students appeared chiefly interested in topics of immediate concern to themselves, and used their leisure time for recreational rather than educational purposes.

The low level of leisure interests at this age emphasises the need both to incorporate into the curriculum of all types of further education leisure pursuits which will lead to a more balanced life and to accentuate cultural activities by, for example, providing extensive library facilities.

Coding: 2b, 4, 5f

AN INQUIRY INTO THE LEISURE INTERESTS OF THE PEOPLE OF READING by F. M. Taylor, Ph.D. thesis, University of Reading 1955.

Aim
To find out how much leisure people in Reading have, and the way in which factors such as sex, age, occupation, marital status and so on affect leisure activities pursued by individuals.

Method
The thesis is principally concerned with the manual, skilled and clerical workers. 654 individuals were interviewed in the family unit in 1951; leisure data was obtained by guided informal conversation.

Discussion
The thesis describes the historic development of leisure for the masses, and reviews the previous literature on the subject. As leisure activities often depend on local circumstances and opportunities, a historical and contemporary socio-economic picture of Reading is given in some detail.

The occupation composition of the working males in the sample was: 16.3% operatives, 41.3% skilled workers, 30.1% clerical, etc, 12% professional; about 18% of housewives did some outside work. As regards terminal, full-time educational age, 12% left under 12 years, 67.1% between 14 & 15 years, and 20.6% after 16 years of age. 56.4% were satisfied with their jobs and 38.8% expressed some dissatisfaction.

Many statistical tables summarise the variables of the enquiry; public entertainment, radio, cinema, games-watching, unorganised group activities such as talking to neighbours, individual activities such as reading and betting, other outdoor activities, organised activities are all analysed in this way. Tables show, for example, the percentage participation by sex and occupation in various forms of leisure activity.

The thesis abounds with detailed information; for example, 49.7% of the total of adults read books; 78% obtained their books from a library and of these 50% were from a public library, 31% from a chain library and 5% from a subscription library. 63% of those that left school at 18+ had 5 or more hours leisure per week, compared to 41% who left school at 13 or younger. But the period studied (thesis presented in 1955) seems somewhat remote when considering current patterns of the use of leisure; only 10% of the sample had television. Thus, games-watching is listed, appropriately for that time, as an outside activity.

Findings

The principal finding is that, even before the large-scale introduction of television into the home, the majority of people of Reading spent the greater part of their leisure in their individual homes and in unorganised group activity, rather than on provided amusements, commercially-directed individual activities or organised group activities. Secondly, the amount of participation and the frequency of participation in leisure activities is closely related to sex status, marital status and occupational status. Thirdly, activities which were cultivated most frequently, by the majority of the population, were mainly to be found among those which the greatest numbers said that they enjoyed best.

Coding: 2b

SOME DETERMINANTS OF ACADEMIC PERFORMANCE AMONGST ADULT STUDENTS by H. B. Miles, M.Sc. thesis, University of Wales 1956.

Aim
To reveal the influence of some of the factors governing the degree of success of mature adults as full-time students.

Method
A sample of 73 men and 48 women, aged between 26 and 45 years, was used; they were preparing, in three separate institutions, for the London University Diploma of Nurse Teachers. Scores were obtained for different aspects of cognitive ability (by tests), together with self-ratings of personality and the effects of factors such as anxieties relating to finance and family responsibility, attitude to student status, and difficulties in adjusting to new associates and a new environment (by questionnaires). Using the results of the Diploma examination as the criterion of academic success, the data was subjected to centroid analysis. The practical prediction of academic success was also examined by constructing group profiles of the upper and lower thirds (based on criterion performance) of over and under-achievers, and by computing regression coefficients for best prediction of the criterion.

Findings
Discernible trends in the factorial analyses suggest that for men, academic performance is determined less by intellectual factors than by emotive ones arising largely in connection with their circumstances in their married and paternal roles, and are associated particularly with anxieties over finance and family health. Amongst women, intellectual status is more frequently decisive. Age, accuracy and verbal skills are related to academic success in men and women, but more clearly in men.

The profiles and multiple correlations support these findings. Prediction by cognitive tests has practical possibilities in the case of women; a battery of verbal and non-verbal tests gives an R maximum of 0.61. Men are practicably almost unpredictable; for example, men in the upper and lower thirds are distinguished only by a comprehension test and by age. Over and under-achievers in nearly equal numbers accounted for more than one-third of the sample. Financial worry is the only criterion which is significantly greater for under-achievers than for either the normal group or the over-achievers, and should be taken into account when interviewing students for full-time courses.

Coding: 2b, 6

A STUDY OF THE EFFECTS OF TELEVISION UPON THE INTERESTS AND INITIATIVE OF ADULT VIEWERS IN GREATER LONDON by W. A. Belson, D.Phil. thesis (2 vols), University of London 1975. [published as *The impact of television,* Crosby Lockwood, 1967]

Aim
To test two principal hypotheses; firstly, that in the field of interests, television has led to a reduction in viewers' identifications and in the level and the diversity of behaviour associated with those identifications, and secondly, that television reduces initiative.

Method
There were three stages in this enquiry. Firstly, extensive interviews of a non-directive kind were held with about 112 viewers or non-viewers. The general views of 300 viewers and 100 non-viewers about the effects of television were obtained by letter. Secondly, a pilot survey was conducted to determine a weighted sample of 50 areas of interest. Thirdly, a full survey was conducted by questionnaire which gave usable returns from 440 viewers and 342 non-viewers. The author describes the full procedures for devising, using and processing the sample in Chapters 2-8, and this section includes his development of stable correlates of interest and initiative as a means of isolating the effects ascribable to television.

Discussion
In 1956, the BBC was the sole broadcasting authority in the UK. As a background to his study, the author describes the television audience, the geographical spread of television, the size and nature of

television programmes, the exposure to television programmes and related research in the post-war period. About 45% of families in the Midlands had a television set in 1955, 41% in South-East England but only 12% in Northern Ireland. In 1954/55, TV transmissions per week lasted about 42 hours, and were watched, on average by about 40% of adults each evening. Annual transmission time had increased from 1,705 hours in 1951 to 2,526 hours in 1956, but already the percentage share of light entertainment had risen, and the percentage share of drama, newsreel and documentary films had fallen.

Chapters 9-13 give the results and the interpretation of the findings, and offer some criticisms of the survey method. Volume 2 reviews generally-held theories about the effects of television which were derived from the preliminary interviews and contains samples of the questionnaire, etc.

Findings

Television has reduced viewers' interests and has reduced the frequency of occurrence of viewers' acts of initiative. Television's treatment of various topics has *not*, through those topics, made up this loss. However, the evidence suggests that the loss is of a temporary kind, reaching a maximum in the first or second years of viewing, and tending strongly towards recovery in the ensuing four years. Furthermore, there are considerable variations; some specific areas of interest deviate markedly from the general picture. Though there is a marked loss of identification in the first two years, then a slow recovery, the reduction of interest in things in which viewers were *intensely* interested seems to be permanent, whereas *mild* interests do not seem to be affected either seriously or permanently.

Similarly, the viewers' level of activity associated with interests fell sharply in the first and second years of viewing, and then slowly recovered. As regards diversity of activity, the loss again is in terms of the viewers' more intensely pursued interests. For instance, such interests as those which were taking place three times or more per fortnight never seem to recover to the pre-TV-viewing level. But those interests which take active form at least twice a fortnight seem to recover after six years' viewing. Interest in a topic featured in a TV programme has been known to rise markedly above the pre-TV level in the first year or 18·months of viewing, but, significantly, interest in such a topic is followed by a permanent loss of identification and interest to below the pre-TV level.

Of course, the effects of television may be complicated; for example, in this period there was a substantial increase in the attendance of viewers at art galleries. But could the gain in attendance be accompanied by a small loss in identification? Perhaps television reduced the level of identification (with paintings) of the total viewing public, most of whom were unlikely to attend exhibitions but who were mildly interested in paintings and, at the same time, stimulated attendance in that minority with a predisposition to attend. If so, is the price of promoting the attendance of the few, a loss of interest of the mass?

Coding: 1c(x), 2b, 5h, cf. KB465

ATTITUDES TO OPPORTUNITIES FOR FURTHER EDUCATION – IN RELATION TO EDUCATIONAL ENVIRONMENT AND BACKGROUND IN SAMPLES OF THE ADULT POPULATION by S. J. M. Trenaman, B. Litt. thesis, University of Oxford 1957.

Aim
To assess the individual attitudes to educational and cultural opportunities and to enquire into the environmental factors that appear to exercise the greatest influence upon them.

Method
The information required for the main study was obtained through three investigations: (a) the attitude to education test, (b) questions about educational activities and access to educational ideas, and (c) personal particulars. It will be appreciated that the investigation was conducted in an area of essentially qualitative and often subjective judgment by the person completing the questions. Numerical values were attached to subjective answers in various categories, and consequently, the author needed to devise a system of weights or utilise adaptations of previous systems to assess experiences as rich as those of, for example, education.

For that reason, six out of nine chapters, Chapters 3 to 8 inclusive, are to a large extent concerned with questions of statistical methodology, of reliability and so on. The statistical argument is characterised by qualities of thoroughness and clarity which may help the non-mathematically-trained reader to follow the text, but in establishing the authenticity of his conclusions the author has, perforce, used statistical arguments of some sophistication, and has assumed that the reader has an insight into mathematical logic.

Chapter 3 deals with the construction of the attitude test. The author considers the problem of the collection of statements, the alternatives, the sorting into Thurstone-scale positions, problems of subjective classification and the treatment of doubtful responses. He considers the selection of items for factor analysis, group factor analyses and bipolar analyses, and explains the use of a specially-designed scalogram board and the results of scalogram analysis.

Chapter 4 is concerned with the reliability and validity of the attitude to education test; the reliability of individual response, of test items, of population response, internal validity and the correlates of attitude. Chapter 5 describes the design of the questionnaire on educational environment; the adaptation of the questionnaires to the limitations of the general public, the five categories of educational opportunity — library membership, reference books, leisure-time cultural activities, reading of newspapers and magazines, and the reactions to educational broadcasts. The construction of a scale for broadcast reactions by factor analysis of item endorsement is described, as is the definition and categorisation of personal particulars.

Chapter 6 is about sampling in the pilot study and in the main study; the problems of sample stratification, of procedure and method in the pilot study, of the completion of questionnaires at home or elsewhere, of the composition and representativeness of the main sample. Chapter 7 gives the results of the enquiry into educational environment. The statistical basis of recording and analysing the data is detailed, and similarly, the results of the enquiry into the identification of attitudes to education is given in Chapter 8. Again, problems of analysis and interpretation are dealt with in detail.

The principal samples were taken as follows:
a To test and endorse 42 items of attitude statements, 200 completed questionnaires were obtained from three sources: 42 from members of the public attending groups at Broadcasting House, 108 by post from a systematic sample of people on the London electoral register, and 50 from members of households in the Oxford area.

b A pilot experiment was conducted by two samples of people, 70 and 77, drawn from the Greater London electoral registers, using the ward juror percentages for stratification.
c The main experiment consisted of a sample of 1,000 people selected in a similar way as in (b).

In both samples, the educational background questionnaire was completed at home, but the personal particulars questionnaire and the attitude test was completed by groups on the BBC premises.

Discussion
In Chapter 1, the author describes the educational problem which was to be investigated, the extent of further education and the growth and influence of the new means of communication which presented new educational opportunities. What is meant by attitudes is defined in Chapter 2; that is, an attitude is defined as a settled and persistent system of values in relation to some object of thought, permeating and prompting a person's reactions, judgments and behaviour.

The subjective classification chosen for attitude testing towards educational opportunities in Chapter 3 consisted of five broad categories: 'values' such as education and social responsibility, 'openness of mind' such as the importance of other people's views, 'appetite for learning', 'method' such as the importance of tuition and 'consequences' such as education for qualification. These categories were expressed in 16 item statements in the final 'attitude to education' list.

Though Chapter 4 to 8 noted in the section 'Method' above also include some statistical tables of results, Chapter 9 and the appendices contain the comprehensive account of conclusions and findings.

Findings
There is a common dimension of meaning underlying all attitudes towards education — the complex of ideas relate, in part, to a single scale on which any individual's position may roughly be determined. This attitude appears to be stable and persistent; formed in early childhood it appears to persist throughout adult life. Critical attitudes are accompanied by some acceptance of educational values — even the most hostile usually accept some educational values.

About one-third of the sample were found to have a declared

interest in educational opportunities, with about one-half of the total having a natural curiosity to extend their understanding. Early education is the basic determinant. The further education provision reinforces the basic educational pattern; only 13% of persons of elementary education have taken up further studies. Education attitudes are affected, independently, by (in order of importance): the hearing (or viewing) of spoken word broadcasts, an interest in the more serious newspaper items, and membership of a library.

Although certain values are, to some extent, shared all the way down the social scale, there is resistance to education at the lower levels, possibly because educational attitudes are compounded of deeper social attitudes. What, then, can be done? However much the institutions of further education redouble their efforts, they are not likely, in general, if the findings of the present study are to be believed, to overcome resistances in attitude which have their origins outside the educational field. Perhaps the most hopeful possibility is that those other independent influences upon attitude — broadcasting, the press and the public library service — could prepare the ground for extensions in the educational provision. The three are complementary, not competitive. Each has an inescapable responsibility either to use its opportunities for trivial or for cultural ends. Broadcasting in particular can most easily reproduce the remaining traces of popular culture and so help common people to build what is peculiarly their own.

Coding: 2b, 3c, 7c(xix)

AN INVESTIGATION, BY STATISTICAL METHODS, OF THE EFFECTIVE COMMUNICATION OF EDUCATIVE MATERIAL AND AN ASSESSMENT OF THE FACTORS MAKING FOR SUCH COMMUNICATION, WITH SPECIAL REFERENCE TO BROADCASTING by S. J. M. Trenaman, D.Phil. thesis, University of Oxford 1961. [See also published version: *Communication and comprehension,* by Joseph Trenaman, edited by E. M. Hutchinson, Longmans 1967 (212 pp).]

Aim
The investigation was divided into two stages. In one, a number of

characteristics of the recipient were considered, as they affected comprehension of a small but varied sample of educative materials, each of 20-minutes broadcasting duration, as they varied between equivalent versions in the three media of television, radio and the printed word. In the second stage, the factors within a wide selection of broadcast (television) programmes likely to make for increased comprehension were investigated, and the results related to those of the first stage.

Method

In stage one, seven different types of subject matter were represented in the test precis; five of them, dealing with gardening, archaeology, modern history, science and art, were presented in equivalent versions through the three media to matched samples of the population; another, on Africa, was presented in television and radio versions; the seventh, an extract from 'The Archers' about treatment in mental hospitals, was used only in the radio version.

The test precis were presented in pairs to a total of 1,020 adults, meeting in groups of about 35 at a time. Systematic sampling was used from electoral registers of London boroughs stratified by juror-percentage. Comprehension tests, tests of previous knowledge and of attitudes to educative material, questions about interest, presentation preference and so on were administered. The reliability of the measures was considered, and the possibility of collusion between partners (usually relatives) sitting together was examined. The special arrangements made to project telerecordings so as to simulate the normal viewing screen, the results of a pilot study, and the biases in the sample are reported.

In stage two, the study was half replicate of a 2^7 factorial design, accommodating 64 programmes in 10 blocks of four programmes each, representing combinations of seven factors at high or low levels of value. The required combinations were obtained after an analysis of 484 programmes. Suitable programme qualities were suggested by previous studies and by television producers. The factors finally selected, after a pilot run had eliminated those for which reliable assessments could not be obtained, were:

- interestingness of the subject matter
- verbal difficulty (vocabulary difficulty plus sentence length)
- verbalisation rate
- number of major points

- concreteness or abstractness of the subject matter
- personifaction of the subject matter
- visual movement

The first ten minutes of each programme was projected; comprehension was tested as in stage one. The sample was 703 adults recruited as for stage one.

Findings

To begin with stage one of the investigation, the recipient and the communication media in the analysis of variance of comprehension scores, differences between one programme and another, and differences between the occupation grades are very significant indeed, and account for far more variation than any differences between one medium and another. Occupation and education are highly correlated in this study and the occupation scale is also closely linked to intelligence measures. The television versions obtained slightly higher scores than the radio versions, and the latter were slightly more effective than the printed ones, but the differences were not large enough to apply to *any* programme.

Previous knowledge of the subject of the programme or article was found to correlate with comprehension at about 0.6, the knowledge gained from the programme (i.e. beyond what was already known) was even more closely associated with comprehension.

Interest and comprehension show different relationships for individuals and for groups. As between programmes, the *mean* levels of interest correlate highly with comprehension, and previously declared interest is a fairly reliable prediction of group comprehension scores. Previous interest and post-exposure interest, working from group means, correlate at 0.86. The connection between individual expressions of interest and comprehension is much weaker, producing correlations of about 0.25.

Significantly more confidence was expressed in the television versions than in the radio or printed versions. Attitudes to sources of education were measured on a prepared scale. In contrast to the interest findings, they were significantly and constantly associated with the individual's comprehension, but not with group levels of comprehension.

In stage two, the factors within educative programmes making for effective communication, the findings were that analysis of variance showed that concreteness of the subject matter was outstandingly significant at all levels of occupation, and that personification became important at the lower levels. Further regression analyses explored the effects of some of the factors measured on finer scales, and included dramatisation as an additional factor. Concreteness was still dominant, but both personification and dramatisation were highly significant among less-skilled workers. These three factors above all accounted for more than half the variance at all but the top occupational levels. Vocabulary difficulty (excluding sentence length) has lesser significance, and an above-average number of major points actually improved comprehension, but not indefinitely. Normal variation in the rate of speaking does not affect comprehension, nor does visual movement measured as a differential factor. Content factors are therefore seen to be much more significant than factors of expression or style.

The interactions of subjective and objective factors set serious limits on any prescription for effective communication. Distinctions could be made between (a) the top 20% of the population in education (professional and highly-skilled workers) who are accustomed to abstract concepts; (b) the next 25% (skilled workers) who need some personification but are interested in much documentary material; and (c) the remaining 50% of the population for whom concreteness of theme and dramatisation or personification are essential to effective communication.

Coding: 2b, 5h, 5c, 3d, 7c(xix), KB1145

THE SOCIAL STRUCTURE OF THE LIVERPOOL NEGRO COMMUNITY WITH SPECIAL REFERENCE TO THE FORMATION OF FORMAL ASSOCIATIONS by D. R. Manley, Ph.D. thesis, University of Liverpool 1959. Available on loan in microfilm form. [Also incorporated in *A report on race relations in Liverpool*, edited by T. S. Simey and J. B. Mays, University of Liverpool, which includes contributions by H. Maddox of the Department of Social Science, University of Liverpool.]

Aim
To examine the social structure of the negro population of Liver-

pool; particularly, to study their attempts to adjust to a new environment, to study their internal social group structure and to elicit, if possible, generalisations about how migrants from one culture react to another.

Method
The principal period of research centred around the years 1952-1953. Information was collected from a variety of documentary sources. Formal interviews were conducted with officials likely to come into contact with the minority group, such as teachers, and with 15 coloured full-time students. Further informal interviews were conducted with the minority community. Participant observation was, in this case, a highly relevant research procedure.

Discussion
Negroes in Britain may be generally divided into two groups; those who arrived at the time of the First World War and those who arrived during and since the Second World War. The negro community is not homogeneous; it is composed of several sub-groups, of which the largest single group is from the West Indies, but all sub-groups share a single characteristic – they are a minority of the general population.

Chapter 1 deals with the complexity of majority-minority relations, and reviews previous research. Having described the research procedures in Chapter 2, which precluded the use of refined sampling techniques because of the need to establish contact with a community which is particularly sensitive, the author describes the social and historical background of the negro community in Liverpool. This is important, for often the negro problems are not related to the general conditions of the district in which they live. Consequently, if the coloured family is unstable, this is ascribed to race – but in that district the social conditions may be such that all families are unstable, whatever their origins. It is worth noting that 33% of the total population on Merseyside are in the category 'semi-skilled' and 'unskilled' workers, but 75% of the coloured population are in this category.

Chapter 4 reviews the factors influencing assimilation and adjustment, specifically negro-white relations. The author suggests that about 33% of the British population are tolerant, 33% mildly prejudiced and 33% extremely prejudiced. In general, relations can be complex; a negro may have excellent individual relations with a landlord but find himself rejected if he becomes friendly with a member of the landlord's family. Negro attitudes to white, anglo-coloured and immigrant women are the subject of a section on 'home and family life'. In essence, the problem is that most negro immigrants are male; thus white wives have three problems, understanding their negro husbands' culture, dealing with their own families, and integrating into the negro community.

In Chapter 6 the author considers the negro community; not a homogeneous entity but a group of individuals with a wide variety of personal characteristics. Given the personal heterogeneity of the negro group, they, like any other community, have formed formal associations, and these are described in Chapters 7, 8 and 9. The hopes, failures and successes of the various associations are described in detail, but of particular interest is an account of Stanley House, the Community Centre founded in 1946 intended primarily for negroes. Its struggle illustrates the desire of the negro to improve his own status, the disappointments for those seeking closer negro-white associations, for, in practice, most of the white members were women or friends of coloured people. Furthermore, the history of the centre illustrates the desire of the negro to avoid setting up a totally negro 'Little Harlem'.

Finally, from the studies of individual associations, the author examines in general the characteristics and role of negro associations. He argues that leaders of such associations might help the negro community to adjust to their host community; he re-emphasises that the negro community is not united but fragmented, their main difficulty being to organise sufficiently to promote greater assimilation.

Coding: 2b, 1b(xxvii), 7c(iv)

WORKERS' EDUCATION — A PSYCHOLOGICAL SURVEY by I. R. Haldane, Ph.D. thesis, University of London 1962.

Aim
To consider the results of a survey, in 1959, at the London Working Men's College, which investigated students' educational motives and

attitudes and the stereotype of a 'working man's' college as factors affecting enrolment.

Method

10 non-directive interviews and group discussions were conducted as a pilot survey: the main survey was by questionnaire, and by the interview of 242 current students, 41 past students and 50 students from the Mary Ward Settlement, the North West Polytechnic and the Quintin School. Factor analysis was used.

Discussion

The first part of the thesis outlines the historical background of adult education in general, and the London Working Men's College (WMC), with particular reference to social and political developments. The survey results are then presented. Some methodological problems are discussed, including the concept of social class, for example, the Young and Willmott 1960 finding in Woodford that, in a predominantly middle-class suburb, 48% of manual workers interviewed considered themselves to be 'middle-class'.

Findings

The name 'Working Men's College' is shown to suggest a dreary institution, catering for the trade-training of students from the lowest socio-economic strata. The real situation differs in almost all respects; WMC contains a disproportionate number of students from higher occupational and intelligence levels, and the majority (53%) of students consider that they belong to the middle-class. But a greater number of students at WMC than at the other institutions felt that they shared a working-class allegiance.

Of the 43% of students who thought of themselves as working-class, 60% left school aged 14 or under, 50% had no educational qualifications and 51% (compared to 47% of those who thought themselves to be middle-class) earned £10 or less per week. Between 1/3 and 1/2 of the students who belonged to the strata which are generally associated with the working-class felt that they were middle-class.

Educational aim was shown to be related to age, occupation, education and economic stratum. Vocationally-orientated students are, on average, younger, poorer, less-educationally qualified and from less-skilled jobs than non-vocationally-orientated students.

Students from these lower strata who assess themselves as 'middle-class' seem more vocationally-orientated than similar students who assess themselves as 'working-class'.

The strengths and weaknesses of WMC are examined; the reason why the majority of past-students did not re-enrol at WMC was not because of disappointment with their experiences there, but because they developed other interests which appealed more than evening classes. These interests were often related to their course of study at the WMC and so, in a way, they had achieved their goals. The non-admission of women and the high average age of students were subjects of unfavourable comment.

83% of the current students at WMC thought WMC better than other places 'for non-vocational study', 75% because of ease of access, 71% for understanding life, 62% for 'pleasant building', 41% for 'good tuition', 92% for 'canteen', 84% for 'discussing things', 93% for 'friendly tutors', 86% for 'lower fees'. Statistical tables provide further detailed information.

The author suggests that the vocational/non-vocational controversy is of diminishing importance — the subject matter is often the same although the aim for studying may differ; there is no boundary. He concludes that more attention should be paid to the needs of individuals rather than to providing adult educational facilities for any one social class.

Coding: 2b, 2a, 3c, 1b(vii), KB667a

A STUDY OF THE EXTENT TO WHICH THE PUPILS OF SECONDARY MODERN SCHOOLS ARE PREPARED FOR THE KINDS OF FURTHER EDUCATION AVAILABLE TO THEM by R. G. Ablett, M.A.(Ed) thesis, University of Southampton 1963.

Aim

To review the conditions of secondary modern schooling, especially as it is related to further education, to review the pupils' studies, to assess their educational abilities and to examine what opportunities exist in further education for them.

Discussion

The evidence suggests that there seems to be a large number of pupils leaving school at 15 years, and entering society with no clear decisions about their futures, and without having completed an education that prepares them for employment or leisure. But 70% of the secondary school population are secondary modern school pupils, and thus there is a considerable variation in the abilities of the children.

After a review of the previous research and an experimental investigation of considerable statistical sophistication, the author suggests four conclusions. These are that secondary modern schools attempt the familiar study of subjects without showing any high standards of achievement; that higher standards in orthodox studies could be attained; that no special skills have been developed to characterise secondary modern schools per se; and that the most distinctive and stimulating work seemed to have taken place when some incentive, such as an external examination, was offered.

The author reviews the degree of co-operation between further education, employers and schools, and concludes, essentially, that few boys appeared to have acquired any notable measure of skill in dealing with ordinary problems, that few secondary modern schools had the resources to provide the range of courses required to deal with the wide range of ability of their pupils; that in further education, the abler secondary modern pupil has to continue his studies under the most unenlightened and difficult circumstances and the ordinary, less-able school leaver has very little opportunity to take courses of study or training suited to his personality and ability. The vocational guidance he receives is amateur and desultory.

Such, then, is the picture painted of the educational background of a large sector of the population entering the field of adult education, planned as part of a continuum of a life-long educational experience.

Coding: 2b, 2a, 6

FURTHER EDUCATION – AN ENQUIRY INTO LEISURE-TIME ACTIVITIES IN THE WOLVERHAMPTON AREA by A. J. Ingram, M.Ed. thesis, University of Leicester 1964.

Aim
To enquire into the leisure-time activities of people in the Wolverhampton area, with particular reference to the leisure-time activities which adults are to pursue directly, because of provision by the Wolverhampton Local Education Authority, or indirectly, through the voluntary bodies aided by the local authority.

Method
Questionnaires were issued to men and women attending day-time and evening classes in the evening-institute-type of subjects, at the Wolverhampton Adult Institute in the period 1959-1963. The students' ages ranged from 17 to 69 years; 1,365 responded. Questionnaires were also sent to the secretaries of certain voluntary bodies.

Discussion
Wolverhampton is an industrial centre; originally based on the heavy industries of coal and iron, it is now concerned with the production of electrical equipment, heavy-duty motor vehicles, rayon, iron and steel ware, tyres and machinery. Chapters 2 and 3 review the history of adult education in Wolverhampton. Although the Subscription Library and Literary and Scientific Society contributed much to further education, the present day facilities for leisure-time activities are not derived from them but spring rather from the Mechanics' Institute, the Working Men's College, the Art School, the Free Library and the Juvenile Instruction Centre. Consequently, the development of these is briefly described until September 1963, when the adult institute moved into premises vacated by the Technical High School.

Findings
Of the students attending the adult institute, 43% did not receive an education beyond elementary or secondary modern school; 33% went to grammar schools or to pre-war secondary schools, but not beyond; 24% went on to teacher or technical training or to

173

university. Students, more than half of whom had received an education beyond elementary or secondary modern school, were attracted to classes concerned with soft furnishing, tailoring, woodwork (women), woodwork (men), dancing, physical education (women) and languages. Dressmaking, typing and cookery attracted other students, more than half of whom had terminated their education at elementary or secondary modern school.

In Chapter 5 the reasons for joining classes are given, subject by subject, and the age distribution of the sample population is compared with the age distribution of the local total population. The reasons varied: 33% 'to learn a language to go abroad' (language classes), 31% 'because they just happen to like the subject' (craft classes), 37% 'because they wish to learn something for its own sake' (typing class); the two latter reasons were mentioned most frequently.

The returns on occupation and social class given in Chapter 6 are consistent with national enquiries; compared to the local population distribution, the professional classes are over-represented in the sample, and the partly-skilled and unskilled occupation are under-represented. Of the 1,365 students responding, 655, or 48.7%, were housewives. If social classes III and IV were added together, 70.7% of institute students were in this group compared to 72.6% of the Staffordshire (the local area) population.

How did students hear of courses? Details are given for subjects, but, overall, 61% heard of the institute through friends who were already members, 15% through press advertisement, 10% from the printed prospectus and 9.5% from other sources.

Accommodation and staffing are described in Chapter 8. The accommodation provided by the adult institute is supplemented by space and facilities in the various community centres which are nearer to the residential areas of the town. Details are given of the education and professional training of each member of staff. In general, the author comments, the investigation revealed the necessity for 'in-service' teacher training and attendance on courses. The author supports a balanced staff of both qualified teachers and craftsmen and women.

The local authority and the voluntary bodies are considered in Chapter 9. In 1961/62, there were 625 enrolments, 300 in WEA courses and 325 in extra-mural university classes, but there was, apparently, no research as to the social composition of students attending these classes. Details are provided about 40 societies, ranging from the French Circle to the Wulfum Cine Club.

The facilities for leisure-time activities through youth and community centres are briefly surveyed in Chapter 10. Of interest is the fact that the number of leaders employed by the LEA, or by LEA grant-aided voluntary organisations, nearly doubled, from 21 to 41, during the period 1960-1963.

Coding: 7c(iv), 2a, 2b, 7c(i), 7c(iii), 8, 4, 1b(xiv), 1c(vii), KB1382

THE EFFECT OF COMPULSORY PART-TIME DAY-RELEASE EDUCATION UPON THE ATTITUDES TOWARDS FURTHER EDUCATION OF EX-SECONDARY TECHNICAL AND MODERN SCHOOL BOYS by R. A. Abel, M.A. thesis, University of London 1964.

Aim

To ascertain the change in attitude, during one year, of 117 students taking Ordinary National Certificate (ONC) and City and Guilds (Craft) courses, who had attended *all* types of secondary schools and who were compelled to attend part-time day-release courses in engineering at technical colleges.

Method

By finding the difference in mean scores on a specially constructed attitude scale of the Likert-type, given at the beginning and end of their first year, students were divided into three categories, those whose attitude became more positive, those whose attitudes became more negative and those whose attitudes did not change. Information from a personal data questionnaire, a Works Condition's inventory, a vocational interest blank, a college attitude essay and ability tests, was analysed. Student progress reports and internal examination results were also used.

Discussion

The historic growth of part-time day-release education and recent research and literature, for example, that of E. C. Venables, J. Ross, M. P. Carter and S. F. Colgrove, are reviewed in the first section. The central core of further education in the early 1960s consisted of about 200,000 boys of 18 years or less in industrial courses pursued during the day. Many authorities on technical education considered the system as being less than satisfactory; for example, although many students received support from employers to attend colleges, few were actually rewarded for any achievement. The rest of the thesis describes in detail the author's plan of investigation, her analysis and interpretation of data and her conclusions.

Findings
The ONC students' attitude towards further education changed in a negative direction; the craft students' attitude remained stable. But more ONC students than craft students thought that the best way to qualify was by full-time study rather than day-release, and the former were not impressed by the technical colleges' claim to be a 'a second chance'.

Interestingly, most of the jobs of the students in the positive categories were obtained through the Youth Employment Service and, generally, there was a close connection between occupational interest, job held and attitude towards further education and, perhaps, continuing education.

Coding: 2b, 1b(xiii)

EXPLORING THE RANGE OF ADULT INTERESTS by John Robinson — A report of a BBC enquiry in 1964 (12 pp) included in *Progress in library science*, edited by R. L. Collison, published by Butterworths, 1965.

Aim
To explore the range of adult readership interests as part of a general investigation into adult interests.

Method

Extensive enquiries were conducted by four BBC Education Officers during six weeks of September and October 1964, in co-operation with the Further Education Liaison Officer. Evidence was collected through interviews and visits, and from 900 individual completed questionnaires. A wide range of contacts was reached, mainly in places of work (so not necessarily in touch with any educational group) in the North-West, South-West and Southern counties of England, in London and in Scotland.

Discussion

When the evidence was amalgamated, it seemed to harmonise very closely with the spectrum of adult attitudes discovered by Joseph Trenaman in 1955-57 and described in his book *Education in the adult population*. Very briefly, he concluded that about 10% of the adult population have 'a consistent interest in education', that another 40% or more are 'interested' and 'pro-educational' and that some 45% are 'resistant to new ideas and higher values'. The question to be answered, therefore, was how far had changes taken place since Trenaman's investigation.

By far the clearest and the most persistent pattern running through the evidence was that the great majority of adult interests, that is potential educational interests, do not arise from some academic or intellectual curiosity, but from the personal, practical needs of everyday life. Most people want to know why their children behave in the way they do: inter alia, they might well go far along a course correctly described as 'psychology'.

Most often these personal concerns are related to people's homes and families — home decoration, cookery, etc. This leads naturally to what is surely the most important of all these home interests: the interest in personal relationships and personal development within the family. Children's education came only a little behind practical hobbies in frequency of mention in the responses to the questionnaires.

New interests are evident; for example, those arising from the new family mobility, based on possession of a car, and the growth of interest in travel abroad. Another range of interests arises from people's work, including their expectations of new work and their apprehensions of retiring from work altogether. Vocational guidance is a widespread interest among young people and their parents and vocational help was also required by married women wishing to return to work. Similarly, the improvement of work skills attracted interest; for example, a course advertised 'Science for you' brought eight enrolments but the same basic course offered as 'Science for the Pharmacist' attracted over 100. Various aspects of industrial relations were mentioned frequently.

There were some less common interests — law, science, biography, architecture and oriental religions — which nonetheless attracted a significant minority. Some special audiences were revealed: the immigrant, the retired and the young adult. Similarly, some notable absences of certain lines of interest were discovered; there was no widespread interest in formal bodies of knowledge, nor in international affairs or politics generally, nor, indeed, in religion in a general sense.

Findings
In summary, a clear and consistent pattern of interests and attitudes, reaching across half the population, was revealed. The pattern that emerged suggested, not an inert society, but one that is exploring and developing and certainly presenting new opportunities for adult education.

The enquiry also suggested that there were new interests, and certainly new attitudes, amongst those already participating among the 10% enthusiasts and/or committed, implying the need for new approaches to educational interests and a break with certain academic traditions and educational orthodoxies.

Coding: 2b

A STUDY OF SOME OF THE ATTITUDES OF STUDENTS IN A DAY-CONTINUATION COLLEGE WITH PARTICULAR REFERENCE TO THEIR EDUCATIONAL, HOME AND FACTORY BACKGROUND by A. Isaacs, M.Ed. thesis, University of Birmingham 1965.

Aim
To discover why students, aged between 15 and 18 years, happened

to be apathetic to their studies (particularly social studies) at Bournville Day-Continuation College in the period 1957 to 1962.

Method
The study was confined to a group of about 100 young, male day-release students in a Day-Continuation College who were all employed in the Bournville Chocolate and Cocoa factory. A questionnaire was constructed to measure the correlation, by ranking, between attitudes to college and work, to college and school and to work and school. A further hypothesis, that there were differences in the three age groups surveyed, was also tested.

Discussion
The usual intelligence range of the students recruited from Secondary Modern Schools and sent for day-release was from about IQ80 to IQ105. The students showed no signs either of disliking the college nor of being resentful of their employers; they simply were bored and indifferent in the classroom. Why was this so? The author argues that there is insufficient research into the teaching of the less literate, and quotes the comments of both Dr P. Venables and of Mrs E. Venables published in the late 1950s and early 1960s.

Many students felt that instruction should be vocational, but how much regard should be paid to teaching the skills that will be made redundant by a change in technology? How far should there be a distinction between vocational and non-vocational education? What is the best course for students of average ability whose jobs have no clear or compelling vocational or social interest?

The author describes the method of measuring attitudes, the composition of the student sample, their educational background, family background, housing circumstances and their leisure patterns. The Bournville factory, the reasons why students chose to work there, the nature of their jobs and their attitudes to employers and unions are also described. An appendix gives full details of the questionnaire and of the information elicited.

Findings
For college and work there was a significant positive correlation in the case of the 15+ and 17+ age groups; for the 16+ age group the result was positive but not significant. For college and school, there was a significant positive correlation for the 17+ group only. Most

students were pleased to leave school, even though they were possibly hand-picked by their head teachers to work for this particular company.

The author suggests that Mrs E. Venables' concept 'that to understand student attitude to day-release, it is necessary to appreciate the nature of their relationships with the employer' has been confirmed. He argues that there is insufficient contact between school and day-release college and insufficient research into student motivation or into curriculum design in day-release institutions; for George, aged 17 years 10 months, helping to make corrugated paper on a machine with 'not much to do most of the time but look', much of life seems to be 'a waste of time'.

Coding: 2b, 4

THE DEVELOPMENT OF GOLF IN ENGLAND — AN ESSAY IN THE SOCIOLOGY OF LEISURE by K. Wadd, M.A. thesis, University of Leeds 1965.

Aim
To study golf as one branch of the games and sports solutions to the problem of leisure time.

Method
The thesis is essentially descriptive. A few basic statistics are used to illustrate the arguments.

Discussion
Golf is interesting for two reasons; firstly because of its increasing popularity, and secondly because of its association with a high social status. About 233,000 tickets were issued, ranging from season to day tickets, by golf clubs controlled by municipal authorities in 1962, compared with about 170,000 in 1958.

Golf effectively spread into England from Scotland in the 1860s and from 1880 to 1914 there was a 'boom' in the formation of clubs, most of which tended to own their own private courses and to be socially exclusive. Between the wars fewer private clubs were founded, but an increasing number of municipal courses were opened and artisan clubs formed.

There is some conflict over whether a modern golf club should be, primarily, a country club providing facilities for the middle-class family, or whether it should adhere to its traditional men's club pattern in which women are no more than tolerated.

Findings

Societies which cater for leisure, such as golf clubs, can be distinguished from other social organisations in that they are primarily expressive, existing for no other purpose beyond themselves, and as they can appeal only to the loyalty of members, their control is largely normative.

A golf club tends, more than other games and sports clubs, to cater for middle-aged and elderly people; it also tends to control more land and buildings than other such clubs, and consequently has developed more complex, differentiated organisation with some unique and interesting characteristics.

Coding: 2b, 3c

A COMPARATIVE STUDY OF WORK ATTITUDES OF MARRIED AND SINGLE WOMEN IN MANUAL AND CLERICAL OCCUPATIONS by A. S. Close, M.A. thesis, University of London 1966.

Aim

To study the work attitudes of 369 women employed by a large transport organisation in West Middlesex.

Method

A questionnaire was devised with multiple-choice items and space for individual comments to be added. Replies were coded and tabulated into four job groups: administrative/supervisory, clerical, operators and canteen attendants; and three marital status groups: single, married and others.

Discussion

In the decade 1951-1961, Britain's labour force increased by 1.8

million, 1.2 million of this increase being due to more married women working. *Consequently, as patterns of work change, so do leisure opportunities alter.*

Findings

Nearly half of the married and formerly-married women had children, of whom more than half were over 16 years of age, and more than three-quarters over the age of 11 years.

About 60% of the women 'on the whole liked their job'. There was little difference in attitude between married and single women, though higher-salaried staff liked their jobs considerably more than other categories, and feelings about jobs tended to be more favourable as the length of service increased.

Reasons why married women worked were related to their husbands' earnings: where these were low, the family's needs were most important; where earnings were high, the family's needs were mentioned much less than 'extra comforts' and 'because it is boring at home all day'. For some 56% of married women, their salaries provided extra comforts, but about 35% wanted the money for basic family needs. About 50% worked because their job was 'interesting' or 'staying at home was boring'. Surprisingly, 10% of the married women faced their husbands' disapproval by going out to work.

Coding: 2b

THE HUMAN ECOLOGY OF SUNDERLAND — A STUDY OF SOCIAL STRUCTURE AND ATTITUDES TOWARDS EDUCATION by B. T. Robson, Ph.D. thesis, University of Cambridge 1966. [published in revised form as *Urban analysis: a study of city structure*, Cambridge University Press, 1969]

Aim

To apply a geographical method of analysing the social structure of an urban area, particularly to examine the development of attitudes towards education of parents of boys about to sit the 11+ examination.

Hypothesis
That the neighbourhood, or the immediate physical and social environment in which people live, is an important source of some of the common forces which influence the development of attitudes towards education.

Method
A detailed historical survey of economic and social trends from about 1800 compares Sunderland with other towns in the United Kingdom, and a similarly detailed survey is made of residential patterns of urban growth within Sunderland itself. A multivariate component analysis of urban social structures is used to divide Sunderland into seven areas, for an examination of the sociological effects of areal differentiation within the town. Questionnaires were completed in 1963 by 188 parents of boys due to sit the 11+ examination in 1964.

Findings
Sunderland is predominantly working-class and dependent on a small range of heavy export-orientated industries, associated with ship-building. Attitudes are influenced by the physical legacy of poverty, by memories of the depression in the 1930s. In 1935, 40% of the male population were unemployed, and even in 1937 this figure had only fallen to 20%. The policy of council re-housing tends to select younger, larger families, leaving older, one or two person households to rent private accommodation in the older sections of the town where conditions are unfavourable.

Overall, there is a significant correlation between social class and educational aspiration, whether the families are ordered by class of the father, the mother (as judged by her pre-marital work) or by a combined score of both mother and father. But areal forces increase the favourableness of attitudes towards education in four out of seven areas. The largest deviation from the pattern of scores which would be expected, if social class alone determined the attitudes developed, occurred in a skilled working-class area. Thus, the neighbourhood in which the individual lives appears to bear some relationship to his attitudes towards education *over and above* the general pattern associated with class membership.

Neighbourhood characteristics may be an index to the self-image of the individual and the neighbourhood itself might be a factor in the kinds of pressures which are brought to bear on the individual to participate in any formal educational associations.

Coding: 2b

THE EDUCATIONAL ACHIEVEMENTS AND ASPIRATIONS OF TRADE UNIONISTS AT A STEEL WORKS SINCE 1944 by K. V. Russell, M.Ed. thesis, University of Leicester 1967.

Aim
a To find evidence for the following hypothesis in a comparison of full-time educational experience, school leaving age, economic competence (instanced by house ownership), age and political party membership, of trade union officers and members at a steel works.
b To consider also, a comparison of members' and officers' aspirations for non-manual employment, and their utilisation of further educational facilities.

Hypothesis
That manually employed trade union members, in selecting trade union officers, chose members according to distinguishing criteria.

Method
A medium-sized company, Round Oak Steel Works Ltd, Brierley Hill, Staffordshire, which had two thousand trade unionists, was selected for investigation in the period 1964-1966. After a pilot survey by questionnaire and interview of 28 branch officers of two manual branches of a union in Leicester, a suitable questionnaire was prepared and a stratified random sample of 60 men was chosen, to be compared with a sample of 95 trade union officers responsible for the organisation and management of their union. The author notes that there are few industrial unions in the United Kingdom and issues a warning regarding the smallness of the numbers surveyed.

Discussion
The thesis reviews the factors determining the degree of social mobility since 1944 and examines how far the greater educational

opportunities resulting from the 1944 Education Act have reduced the reserves of ability from which trade union officers are recruited. From a survey of 7 secondary modern schools between 1958 and 1962, 6 schools were described as 'inadequate' and one as 'seriously inadequate'. Children in the area had, in 1964, a one-in-ten chance of securing a place at a selective school.

When comparing trade union officers and members, there was no significant degree of difference in mean ages, in marital status, in the average size of family, nor in status category with about 50% of each being in Category III (1961 Census, Social Class).

A larger proportion of officers were purchasing their own homes but, of course, all officers must be over 21 years of age, and are normally more than 25 years old. About one-half of the officers claimed to have had non-academic success at school, having held positions such as form monitor or house captain, against about one-third of the members.

There was no difference between the educational background of officers and members, but a substantial number of officers, 53 of the 95, compensated for their education at non-selective secondary schools by participating in further educational activities of a vocational nature. Trade union officers exclusively used the WEA facilities, particularly the day schools, and trade union educational services. Their educational activity was solely related to the improvement of their promotion opportunities within the manual class, which was acceptable as the ultimate aspiration. In sharp contrast, only 19 out of 60 members participated in education after school.

The thesis includes a description of the formal and informal leadership roles of trade union officers and officials.

Coding: 2b, 2a, 7c(iii), 4, KB748

MARRIED WOMEN AND YOUNG WOMEN STUDENTS AT A DAY COLLEGE OF EDUCATION AND IN THEIR FIRST YEAR AS TEACHERS by D. Case M.Ed. thesis, University of Leicester 1967.

Aim
To examine whether married women and single women who had

decided to teach would be culturally/environmentally more aware than groups of non-teachers matched for age and background. To test the likelihood of role conflict occurring in association with the multiple-role occupancy of married woman, and to discover the principal facts of background, recruitment and guidance of day college of education students as compared with students from other colleges.

Method
After empirical pilot studies to sample groups, including WEA and extra-mural students and WI members, 350 personal interviews were conducted in connection with the selection of candidates. 235 questionnaires were issued and 220 were returned completed; 143 were sent to married women (about 77% of whom had been married for 11 years or more) and 92 to single women, covering annual intakes in 1961, 62 and 63. Personality, background, environmental awareness and attitude to teaching tests (after Gross, Mason and McEachern, 1958) were given. A separate questionnaire was issued to, and returned by, 247 probationary teachers (122 ex-day college and 125 other-than-day-college teachers).

Discussion
Questions of the employment of married women outside the home, the recruitment and training of married women teachers, the concepts of cultural/environmental awareness and role theory with role conflicts, are discussed in the first chapter. The following chapters deal with the methodology of the investigation, the personality of the teachers in each group, the cultural awareness of married women who choose to teach, the attitudes of each group to teaching and the problems experienced by each group during the probationary year.

Findings
One-third of the respondents in this enquiry had husbands in social class I, but the sample as a whole was widely spread over social classes I, II and III (vide Kelsall, 1963). 'Homework/study', 'washing/ironing' and 'food preparation' were the greatest burdens for the married woman at work; 'shopping' and 'care of the family' were considered to be of subsidiary concern. 50% of married women reported the positive interest of husbands, 20% said that work involvement had improved family relationships and 50% reported

that 'stimulated conversation' had resulted. Only 20% reported to have experienced a role conflict between 'student' and 'wife/mother'. 71.56% indicated 'evenings' as the most popular time for study and between about 74% and 89% of each group reported that television had 'a slight effect' or 'no effect' on study. Both married and single groups reported the heavy curtailment of social activities; 40% of married students said that they were 'worse off financially'.

Mature married students between 31 and 40 years seemed to be more culturally/environmentally aware than other women who had not chosen to teach, and married women generally compared favourably in this respect with final year university students (vide Richmond, 1963). The attitude of both groups towards teaching was the same, but single women expressed a majority wish to proceed to an external degree, whereas the married women, on balance, rejected this idea.

20% of the probationary teachers reported that their classes contained more than 40 children. Great reliance was placed upon head teachers for guidance; deputy-heads did not figure as an important source and no mention was made of the 'Inspectorate'. The author recommends closer co-operation between college of education, local authority and school during the teacher's probationary year.

The evidence generally underlines the determination and organisational qualities of the mature married women in the sample.

Coding: 2b, 2d, 6

WORK AND LEISURE — A STUDY OF THEIR INTERRELATION by S. R. Parker, Ph.D. thesis, University of London 1968. Accessible in the University of London Library; no loan copy available [also published as *The future of work and leisure,* Paladin, 1972]

Aim
To consider work and leisure as spheres of life, to conduct empirical enquiries in various types of relationships between work and leisure and to consider the theory and practice of these relationships.

Method

A series of pilot interviews were conducted with 200 men and women in ten occupations, selected from commerce and the local government services. The main survey was by means of postal, self-completing questionnaires; 250 people from each of four occupational groups were selected: that is, bank employees, youth employment and child care services employees and manual workers. The first three groups were contacted respectively through bank managers and the two professional associations, but in the case of the last group, the sample was drawn from manual workers living in Camden who agreed to complete a form after door-to-door calls.

In the bank employee sample, there were no married women; in the child care sample there was a low proportion of single men but a high proportion of single women; in the youth employment sample there was a high proportion of married women.

The main sample was supplemented by six case studies of various types of residential social workers, and by an analysis of the work-leisure activity patterns of local government councillors.

Discussion

The first section of the thesis is concerned with definitions of 'work' and 'leisure', and outline of the relation of work and leisure patterns, the social and individual functions of leisure, the content and meaning of work and leisure for various occupational groups and the relation of the meanings of work and leisure within the concept of a central life style. Part 2 consists of the author's report of his empirical enquiries. Particular mention is made of the common factors which enable residential social workers to have a life in which work and leisure are integrated, and the types of relationship between local councillors' work and council activities.

The results of the investigation are the bases for the examination of commonly held assumptions about work and leisure. Thus, in Part 3, the author considers the typology of work-leisure relationships, and the problems of extension, opposition and neutrality of each variable. Is there an answer to the problem of the confrontation of work and leisure? The theories of Friedlander and Friedmann are considered as possible answers. The author suggests that there are not two types of persons seeking fulfilment in *either* work *or* leisure. On the contrary, men and women in all societies need to have both work *and* leisure; that is, the opportunities for rewarding work and for varying kinds of leisure to complement that work.

Findings
The author discovered that some people found it difficult to estimate the amount of their leisure time, and that definitions of what constituted leisure varied considerably. Occupations seemed to determine the total amount of leisure time available, but marital status determined the distribution of leisure time between family, non-work friends and 'being by oneself'.

Bank and manual employees were reported as having about one hour a day more leisure than the others. Asked how they would use two extra hours' leisure per day, 41% of manual workers, 30% of child care officers, 29% of youth employment officers and 27% of bank employees opted primarily for home, garden and family-based pursuits.

Coding: 2b, KB1388

A FOLLOW-UP STUDY OF SCHOOL LEAVERS by P. A. Atkinson, M.Phil. thesis, University of Reading 1968.

Aim
To survey the results obtained in an investigation spread over three years, into the leisure-time activities of young people aged 15-18 years, in a town with a population of between 120,000 and 150,000 situated within commuting distance of London.

Method
215 school leavers mainly of the secondary modern streams, either answered questionnaires or were interviewed by students in 1960/61. Interviews were conducted from a sample of the original 215 in 1961/62 and 1962/63; 122 were actually interviewed in 1962, 113 in 1963.

Discussion
The research design and questionnaire is described in the opening chapters; thereafter each chapter covers one aspect of the enquiry,

that is, home and school backgrounds, work and earnings, further education, local facilities and youth organisations, leisure activities. A concluding synthesis and a discussion of the author's findings constitute the final chapter. The total effect is to give a picture of the social life of young people who have completed their full-time education and who are on the brink of the world of adult education.

Findings

The investigator discovered a certain amount of reticence among young people to answer questions which might carry the disapproval of authority, but in this case the difficulty was largely overcome. Generally, parents did not interfere unduly in the lives of their sons and daughters; few young people disputed parents' rulings or standards. 61% would have stayed on at school for a further year if a suitable course had been available, but 80% said they liked their work, even after two years' experience. 42% of those aged 17 were concerned with some aspect of further education.

Membership of youth organisations fell from 56% in 1961 to 34% in 1963, but several boys and girls joined adult organisations, especially those associated with their work. The large majority seldom listened to anything but pop music on the radio; the numbers that watched television declined from 80% in 1961 to 62% in 1963 — the 15-17 age group watched for about 13% of their leisure time (26% for adults according to Laurie). 80% went on holidays whilst at school, but by the time they were 17 only 67% went away.

In general, the group was 'even in its leisure, slow to be stirred' but although there was apparent apathy towards local facilities whose improvement could make leisure activities more interesting and rewarding, this group showed interest in a more widespread range of hobbies and a wider variety of subjects than might be expected. Regrettably, as Hancock and Wakeford found with the young workers interviewed in 1965, 'books are no part of their lives'.

Coding: 2b, 1c(vii)

NEEDS AND INTERESTS OF THE ADULT COMMUNITY IN THE UNITED KINGDOM — Reports by the Education Departments of the British Broadcasting Corporation and Independent Television Authority, presented at the 8th meeting of the European Broadcasting Union Study Group on Teaching by Television, Rome, June 1969 (94 pp). Copies held at Further Education Liaison Office, BBC, London W1A 1AA and the Education Office, IBA, 70 Brompton Road, London SW3.

Discussion
Part 1 (evidence submitted by the BBC)
Evidence of needs and interests
About 90 people professionally engaged in the field of further education or involved in activities mundane to further education were consulted about the further education needs of the United Kingdom. They identified national needs which included: a larger and better-trained cohort of teachers, more professional community workers and the encouragement of more members of the community to participate actively in their own community. In addition, they suggested certain problems which should receive the attention of the adult education section. These were: the problems of environmental planning, the generation gap, the role of women in society, the problem of respect for, and understanding of, immigrant communities in this country and of different peoples in the world, the question of industrial communication, the need for adult re-training, the need for a greater understanding of science and technology and the question of leisure activities.

There are, of course, the important needs of specific groups; for example, the problems of women at home, of the younger generation per se, of parents, of various occupational and professional groups, and so on. Personal needs are also analysed, such as the need for personal communication and self-expression.

How are these needs to be met? The authors offer many specific suggestions, perhaps the most important of which are a plea for closer co-operation between providers and for greater imagination in offering various combinations of teaching techniques.

Evidence of the interests of the adult population was collected. Interests derived from the home and family are most widespread, but those arising from work and careers are not inconsiderable.

The 16-20 age group
Part 1 includes a report of an enquiry into the specific needs and interests of the 16-20 age group which might be served by educational broadcasting, and on the likelihood that such broadcasts would be effectively used. This group is, the report suggests, divided by class, intellect and age, but united by emotion; consequently the emphasis is upon the need of this age group to develop mature personal relationships towards each other and towards other age groups. Television seems to be more important to this age group than radio, other than radio 'pop' music.

Given that there is much detailed information in this section, the authors warn that, firstly there seem to be general differences between the 16-17 age group, and between the 18, 19 and 20 year group and that, secondly, the latter group is in many ways an unknown tribe.

Part 2 (evidence submitted by the ITA, now the Independent Broadcasting Authority)
Evidence of viewers' preferences
This section consists of the results of research into the educational interests and preferences of the viewing public. In the following Table, 130 topics were placed in 15 groups and the percentage of 1,850 adults in homes with television who stated that they 'would definitely watch' at least one of the topics in a group is recorded

Group	Would definitely watch %	No. of topics in a group
1. Home & Family	82	26
(Safety in the Home)	44	1
2. The Sciences	64	16
3. History and Geography	59	10
(Travel)	42	1
4. Home Maintenance	56	3
5. The Arts	48	8
6. Law and Government	47	12
7. Hobbies	47	8
8. Theatre	45	4

9. Careers	44	13
(Education)	29	1
10. Current & World Affairs	42	3
11. Local Affairs	39	3
12. The Car	39	2
13. Religion, Philosophy &		
Human Sciences	35	6
14. Literature	27	5
15. Languages	13	6

(Sports and popular music were deleted because of imprecise respondent interpretation).

These conclusions emphasise the popularity of domestic subjects, and of the sciences. However, this general ranking of groups of topics conceals the fact that the different groups have interest and appeal to different sections of the public; for example, 71% would like languages to be 'fairly elementary', 29% 'more advanced', but division in the case of 'The Car' is respectively 53% and 47%. Moreover, if we take the example of 'Careers', 54% of men, 35% of women, 48% of age range 16-24 years, 51% of age range 25-44 years and 37% of those over 45 years would definitely watch'. There are similar variations in interests according to viewers'' social grades and terminal education ages. Preferences for topics also vary according to the viewers' own estimate of the average number of hours spent watching television each night.

If groups are subdivided into topics, then the percentage which would definitely watch shows a considerable range; for example, Group 1 ranges from 44% 'Safety in the Home' to 7% 'Tailoring'; 'Care of old People' at 32% ranks higher than 'Child Development', 'Child Psychology', 'Consumer Advice' or 'Motherhood'.

The Tables provided deal with all 15 groups in order; these and the other tables are of some consequence to all those interested in adult education because they ratify or correct expert opinion about the interests of the adult audience, they demonstrate respects in which these interests coincide with or diverge from the known interests of students involved with the field agencies of adult education, and they reveal what people consciously identify as their main interests.

Coding: 2b, 5h, 5b

THE IMPACT OF MOTORISED LEISURE ACTIVITIES ON THE COAST, WITH REFERENCE TO EAST CENTRAL SCOTLAND by J. K. Fitz-Henry, M.Sc. thesis, University of Edinburgh 1969.

Aim

To study the impact of motorised leisure activities on part of the coast of Scotland (the Firth of Forth), which is readily accessible to the tourist, weekend and day visitor.

Discussion

Leisure demands on the coastline are increasing. The phenomenal increase in the use of cars for motorised leisure activities and the resultant new forms of coastal recreational activity are part of the changing patterns of adult participation in recreative education. (Consequently, this thesis is briefly summarised as an example of research providing background information for adult educators.)

The chapter titles are as follows: the Evolution of Coastal Resource of East Central Scotland; the Growth Components of Motorised Leisure Activities; the Outlook for the Future; Planning for Coastal Recreation and Conservation in Britain; Planning for Coastal Recreation and Conservation in East Central Scotland; Planning for Coastal Recreation and Conservation in East Lothian.

Many hopes for the amelioration of countryside and coastal problems lie in the empowering of the Countryside Commission to call conferences and meetings, *to engage in education* and the provision of publicity and information. Of interest is *the need of coastal towns* to provide *indoor* recreational facilities for youth and for coach parties.

Coding: 2b, 5m(xiv)

WEST INDIAN ORGANISATIONS AND WEST INDIAN PARTICI-
PATION IN THE DENOMINATIONAL CHURCHES IN THE MOSS
SIDE AREA OF MANCHESTER by C. R. Kinder, B.Litt. thesis,
University of Oxford 1969.

Aim
To analyse the leisure-time social relationships of West Indian
immigrants, as illustrated by their associational and religious lives.

Method
The author was a Youth Club leader in the area in 1964, and has
been in Africa and Jamaica. As a white man, he had to achieve a
social relationship acceptable to members of the West Indian community. Essentially his role was that of participant-observer, and his
methods were adopted to meet the standards of courtesy as much as
the needs of scientific validity.

Discussion
In the leisure-time sphere of social life, the dominant society had
made few demands on the immigrant and he was free to opt for
whichever social relationships he chose. The author demonstrates
that in their religious and voluntary associational life the majority of
West Indians have opted to avoid social relationships with whites,
and have become 'encapsulated' within a West Indian community.

Two main reasons emerged for this 'encapsulation'. Firstly,
members of the same racial group preferred to identify closely with
each other, to the exclusion of the members of other racial groups.
Secondly, the West Indians perceived rejection at the hands of the
dominant society, which the author accounts for in terms of the
immigrants' expectations on arrival being unacceptable to the
dominant society. This realisation of rejection led to the development of hostility towards the dominant society.

The example of the denominational churches serves to illustrate
the West Indians' minimal institutional dispersal into the leisure-time
social structure of the dominant society. The author shows that for
those West Indians who did join the 'white' churches, the church did
act as a channel of communication with the dominant society,
whereas membership of a West Indian pentecostalist sect and
voluntary association did not facilitate the extension of a West

195

Indian's contacts into a wider set of social relationships in Manchester. Exceptions to this rule were found among those who played the role of leaders of the voluntary associations.

Furthermore, the author demonstrates that within the 'encapsulated' West Indian community, ethnicity, religion and social class were the dominant social factors which operated to mediate social relationships and to create the significant categories of social interaction.

The thesis contains clear maps and photographs of Moss Side to aid the reader who is not familiar with the area.

Coding: 2b, 1c(viii)

A STUDY OF SOME SOCIAL AND ACADEMIC FACTORS WHICH AFFECT MATURE STUDENTS IN A COLLEGE OF EDUCATION by R. J. Palmer, M.Ed thesis, University of Liverpool 1969.

Aim
a To investigate the problems encountered by mature students and the associated degree of worry
b To investigate the influence of sex, parenthood, age and previous experience on academic and teaching results obtained in the final certificate examination.

Method
A questionnaire was presented to 238 students of one day-college of education, and biographical data of third-year students in the same college was compared with final examination results in main subject, theory of education and practical teaching.

Discussion
The factors which possibly disrupt a student's progress and the literature concerned with such studies, for example, the studies of Zweig and Musgrove, are reviewed. Married women have to resolve the conflict between the demands of family and college; men who change career in mid-stream may experience a fear of failure and of loss of face. It may be that over-motivation produces poorer

performance, as suggested in the Yerkes-Didson hypothesis.

Surprisingly, there is little difference in the courses offered to mature and younger students in Colleges of Education, neither to remove stress situations specific to mature students nor to take advantage of their maturity and wider experience of life.

Findings

Nine major problems were identified from preliminary interviews with a small sample: (1) personal worries, (2) worry over academic work set by tutors, (3) specific classroom problems on school practice, (4) problems of relations with staff, (5) problems connected with their own children, (6) within marriage, (7) relating to college facilities, (8) associated with friends and neighbours, (9) regarding their own abilities in academic work. Questionnaires asked students to rank these problems and a five-point scale was devised for each individual statement, so that there were five degrees of 'worry', ranging from 'very much' to 'none'. The answers to these questions are contained in 157 tables in a comprehensive appendix.

College academic problems are the principal worry, regardless of entrance qualifications, but this worry reduces with the length of study. The mean level of worry connected with school practice also reduces with the year of study, though with less agreement with the mean. All three years record approximately the same level of worry for the 'personal academic' category. Women record higher levels of worry than men, but men, in the third year, are more concerned about school practice than women.

Married students do not record high mean levels of worry for marriage problems, but there is evidence of wide variations. However, married women worry more than both married men and single women about all aspects of college life. Single men worry more than married men about college work, and worry more than single women about teaching practice. Women record higher mean 'worry' levels than men for college academic problems at all ages, but both males and females in the 45+ age group worried less about the 'personal academic' than did their younger counterparts. Children at pre-school, infant and junior stages give most concern, particularly to mothers, though this area of worry was never ranked number one.

The correlations between various groups of mature students' anxiety rankings and final certificate examination results did not reach the degree of statistical significance to justify more than tentative comment and indicate a need for further research.

Coding: 2b, 4

THE APPORTIONMENT OF TIME BY COLLEGE STUDENTS by I. Ward, M.Ed thesis, University of Birmingham 1969.

Aim
To describe how 219 students in a College of Education apportioned their time during a period of five days in their second term at college.

Method
Information was obtained by means of diaries kept by students. After a pilot study, in the main investigation the diary divided the day into 20-minute units and into 7 activity divisions: namely, time-tabled work, private study, sport, cultural activities, socialising, personal commitments and relaxation. A fifty-point questionnaire was used to assess the study habits of students (adapted from 'Study Habits Inventory' by Mallison, Penfold & Sawaris).

Discussion
The planning of the diary form constitutes the major part of this thesis, the remainder being taken up by a review of the literature, the results and discussion of the conclusions.

Findings
The major factor influencing the amount of time spent in study by students is, quite simply, the demands set by the institution in terms of quantity and quality.

Secondary school background did not significantly affect the amount of study time reported by students, and neither did the sex of the students. An older group of students reported more working time than younger students, and students showing high marks in 'education' reported more working time than students scoring low marks.

The average apportionment of time for male students was, out of a total of 73.8 hours: timetable work 19.7 hours; work related to college course 12.7 hours; personal commitments 21.3 hours; socialising 14.3 hours; sport 1.9 hours; cultural activities 3.9 hours.

As to method of study, of total time: 49.4% was in writing essays; 19.1% in directed reading; 16.3% in practical work; 14.1% in taking notes and 0.8% in discussion. 68.7% studied in their own room, 10.2% in the library, 12.5% in the common room.

Coding: 2b, 5a

STUDENTS WHO ORIGINATE FROM THE WORKING CLASS —
SOME ASPECTS OF THEIR SCHOOLING, HOME BACKGROUND
AND EXPERIENCES SINCE COMING TO UNIVERSITY by
S.E. Earl, M.Ed. thesis, University of Aberdeen 1970.

Aim
To obtain a detailed account of the school experience and home background of working class students (originating from social classes IIIB, IV and V) and to see whether their development reflected the pattern reported for other persons upwardly mobile through education. (The thesis is included in this text as containing research findings on culturally upwardly mobile females, perhaps typical of many women who use the adult education service.)

Method
49 third-year female arts students constituted the sample. Three techniques were used: personal interview; 't' test of performance of female working-class students on entrance and in the third year (a verbal reasoning test, a motivation scale, work habits attitude scale and two personality inventories) which could be compared with other female students; and a questionnaire about experiences at university.

Discussion
The discussion consists essentially of a brief review of pertinent literature and detailed consideration of the scope and aims of the investigation, the design of the research and an assessment of the results.

Findings

The school experiences of the working class students at Aberdeen University reflect those reported in previous investigations of unwardly mobile pupils.

— Cultural interests in working class homes are more closely related to upward mobility than material affluence.

— The parents of upwardly mobile students can be distinguished by their encouragement of good performance at school and their favourable attitude towards further education.

— Working class students do not differ from non-working class students in study habits nor on ability and personality measures.

— Class of origin does not affect involvement in extra-curricular activities at university.

— Neither frequency of doubts about the wisdom of deciding to attend university nor frequency of criticisms of deficiencies in the university are related to class origin.

— Students who originate from the working class emphasise the utility of a degree.

Coding: 2b, 3c

A FOLLOW-UP STUDY OF DAY-RELEASE STUDENTS OF AGRICULTURE IN OXFORDSHIRE TECHNICAL COLLEGES by R. Pateman, M.Phil. thesis, University of Reading 1971.

Aim

To find out from the students themselves the extent to which they have been influenced by the experience of day-release agricultural education, particularly their experience before enrolling on day-release courses, their views on the content, teaching methods and timetabling of their courses, the value of the courses, their reasons for discontinuing the course, their subsequent employment and further education, and their views on further training needs.

Method

The methodology used in the study was a postal survey of all day-release students of agriculture, agricultural mechanics and seed trade subjects in Oxfordshire during the period 1956-1967, together with a total of 50 interviews of a random sample of students. A response rate of 62.2% was obtained to the postal questionnaire; i.e. 395 completed questionnaires.

Discussion
One of the most significant developments in agricultural education since the 1944 Education Act has been the growth of day-release courses. The author traces the main development of part-time agricultural education from 1845 to the present day, mentioning particularly the effects of the Reports of the Loveday Committee from 1945-1949, the Carrington Report 1953, the De la Warr Report 1958, the Crowther Report 1959, the Lampard Vachell Reports of 1960 and 1961, and the Pilkington Report of 1966. This is followed by a detailed examination of the development of the Oxfordshire system, and a discussion of the method of enquiry and analysis of returns.

Findings
Most courses are for the 15-18 year old farm worker, but 30% of students on agricultural courses in Oxfordshire are not in farming jobs; indeed, almost one-third of ex-students are in posts bearing no relation to farming or related trades. Most students enrol upon courses for vocational reasons, but the courses do not adequately cover the very diversified local pattern of agriculture. One-quarter of the students go on to full-time courses in agriculture, but 15% drop out before completing one year, and 50% do not obtain a formal qualification.

Few·non-academic courses are available and farmers do not value formal academic qualifications highly. Of the students still in farming, 65% either attend, or intend to attend, evening courses; the need for continuing education with a predominant vocational element is quite accepted.

Coding: 2b, 1c(ii)

CITIZEN PARTICIPATION IN REDEVELOPMENT, WITH SPECIAL REFERENCE TO NEWTON HEATH, MANCHESTER by C. T. Davies, M.Ed. thesis, University of Manchester 1971.

Aim

To study citizen participation in the planning process of urban renewal, paricularly in Newton Heath, a district in North-East Manchester, and one of the first areas in metropolitan Manchester to be developed in terms of the Town and Country Planning Act of 1968.

Method

After a pilot survey, three questionnaires (either self-completion or recorded by interviewer) were used: the participation in planning questionnaire; the Newton Heath 'Community' questionnaire; and the voluntary organisations questionnaire.

In the first of these enquiries, awareness of planning matters was gauged by using an adaptation of the Likert scale for rating attitudes. Replies were rated along a continuum from 'fully aware' to 'ignorant'. The questionnaire was first administered in 1970, before any effort had been made to involve people in the planning process. The same questionnaire was readministered in 1971. 5% random samples were taken in 2 polling districts, 125 and 122 respectively being finally interviewed in the participation in planning sample, first and second tests.

The second questionnaire was designed, not only to collect factual social data, but also general attitudes of residents towards their community and redevelopment. Interviews with 166 respondents drawn from the electoral registers of 3 polling districts took place in 1971. In the third investigation, 65 voluntary organisations were visited in 1971, interviews being held with at least one committee member of each organisation.

Four tests were applied to the collected data: the students t-test, F-ratio test, correlation measures and the chi-square test. Extensive appendices give not only summary tables of the comprehensive evidence collected, but detail precisely the methodology of the investigation, even to the inclusion of examples of calculations of all the various tests.

Discussion

The main body of the thesis is made up of four sections. Section 1 covers the general aspects of citizen participation in the planning process. Values implicit and explicit in the concept are examined, as are the functions and dysfunctions of participation and the typologies of participation in planning. After a short comparative study of citizen participation in North America, the author describes the evolution of the legislative framework for statutory participation, comments on its advantages and shortcomings, and refers to a few examples of citizen participation in England and Wales. This section ends with a review of the nature of citizen participation with respect to the city of Manchester.

In Section 2 the author gives a brief historical sketch of Newton Heath, offers a sociological analysis to determine whether or not a 'community' in fact exists in that area, examines the influence of formal voluntary organisations, an illustrates the importance of various religious institutions to the local community.

Section 3 is a case study of citizen participation in planning in Newton Heath, made up in two parts; firstly, a chronology of participatory activities in the area from 1966-1971 and, secondly, an evaluation of these activities. The final Section comprises an appreciation of the role of community development in town planning, a discussion of recent changes in the concept of community development, a consideration of the relationship of community development to participation in planning, and suggestions for improvements.

'Alienation', says the author, 'is having a widespread effect not only on people's happiness but on the whole ethos of community life'. But are people prepared to leave decisions to a remote figure? Is it possible to leave decisions to local councillors, only 15% of whom had had any further or higher education (source given)? Is it right to leave decisions to planners who are part of the intellectual section of the population, with a high education and esoteric tastes?

Redevelopment — which is certainly not peculiar to Manchester — often involves the withering of the soul of the old community. How do the voluntary associations react? What is the response of the religious organisation? Why is there an almost apathetic attitude to politics on the part of the people of Newton Heath? In addition to examining these and many other very human questions, the author provides fascinating statistical information, including readership of local newspapers, main reasons for wishing to remain in the area, net income per week, etc.

203

Findings
'In Newton Heath public participation in planning has been almost non-existent' and 'If, as is said, planning is indeed for people, then the legislators must provide the legal framework in which plans will truly reflect the values and aspirations of the people'.

Coding: 2b, 3c, 1b(xxvii), 7b

Problems of literacy

AN ENQUIRY INTO THE READING HABITS OF PART-TIME DAY RELEASE STUDENTS by J. Smedley, M.Ed. thesis, University of Manchester 1953.

Aim
A fact-finding survey to investigate the reading habits of students of the 15+ to 18+ age range who received part-time day-release education at works' schools and Colleges of Further Education.

Method
The report is based upon written questionnaire answers of 1,304 students who replied in the period November-December 1951. Four establishments co-operated: two works' schools, one works' college, and one technical college, respectively located in Lancashire, South Yorkshire, Nottinghamshire and Derbyshire.

Discussion
In 1950, 257,000 students were receiving day-release education and little was known of their leisure reading habits, although, for example, Rowntree, Lavers, Reed and Herford had conducted investigations.

The author surveys five facets of literacy; the quantity of reading, the quality of reading, the use of libraries, the actual publications read and newspaper reading patterns. A detailed comparison between sexes, ages, colleges and localities, measuring the quantity of reading is supplied in the form of a series of statistical charts. The 'quality of reading' questions depended on a rating method which was subjective and, consequently, the findings are tentative. One firm conclusion emerged, however; that 6% of the girls and 14% of the boys sampled admitted to reading material of a harmful (lascivious) nature. The other three aspects of the investigation are presented as a descriptive account of the patterns of student behaviour.

Findings

Repeatedly throughout the thesis, the author reports the failure of the students to move forward and accept an adult standard of reading, and the general picture presented by the enquiry is of a vast amount of time spent in reading inferior and ephemeral matter. Of the 17 year olds, 56%, 60% and 37% respectively never use a public library, never use a college library and never use any library. Girls tend to read more than boys and the amount of reading done between the ages of 15 and 18 does not vary materially.

It is argued that the responsibility for the low level of cultural enjoyment discovered (and confirmed) by this enquiry cannot be laid upon the schools. The creators of a vast, homogeneous market for trivial literature are not interested in the development of readers' susceptibilities nor is the growth of their powers of discrimination.

Coding: 2c, 5c

PROVISION FOR ADULT LITERACY IN ENGLAND by R. M. Haviland, dissertation, School of Education, University of Massachusetts 1973. (Abstract supplied by author) [Published in part as *Survey of provision for adult illiteracy in England,* School of Education, University of Reading, 1973].

Aim

Firstly, to establish a comprehensive list of the publicly and privately administered adult literacy programmes in England; secondly, to collect data about the adult literacy programmes and to analyse that data with a view toward indicating the major directions of the programmes as regards their administration, teaching methods and materials, tutor training and financing.

Method

By a library search of the published documents which treat the subject of adult literacy and provide information regarding the background of the problem; by the compiling of a comprehensive list of the adult literacy instruction programmes in England; and the collection and analysis of basic data about the adult literacy instruction programmes on the basis of information obtained via 239 completed and returned questionnaires sent to 384 listed literacy programmes.

Discussion

The background information reviewed in the study indicates that there exists in England a substantial number of people, perhaps as many as two million, who can be classified as either 'illiterate', that is, having a reading age of seven years or less, or 'semi-literate', that is, having a reading age of between seven and nine years of age. It further reveals that since 1960 the reading levels of school children aged eleven and fifteen, which improved from 1948 to 1960, are no longer improving and that the number of fifteen year olds in England's supported schools who are classified as 'illiterate' and 'semi-literate' is growing.

There are privately and publicly administered adult literacy instruction programmes in England which seek to assist adults who have reading difficulties. Since no comprehensive list of these programmes existed, a list of the individual programmes was compiled as part of this study. Information regarding the existence of literacy programmes was sought from education authorities, related organisations and interested individuals. In all a list of 384 programmes thought to provide adult literacy instruction was compiled.

Findings

1 The number of adult literacy instruction programmes has grown from less than ten in 1950 to more than 230 in 1973. Growth has been particularly rapid since 1967.
2 during 1972 at least 5,170 adults received literacy instruction for a period of six months or one school term.
3 There are approximately 1,900 tutors teaching adults. Of these half are teaching adults on the one to one ratio, and approximately one half are working as volunteers.

4 The largest number of programmes in the study provide two hours of instruction weekly. Few programmes provide more than six hours per week.

5 Classes for adult illiterates tend to be small, hardly ever more than fifteen students and more often between five and ten. The importance of individualised instruction is widely recognised and fifty programmes utilise it exclusively.

6 The tutors tend to depend on home produced materials for instruction but do use various books and reading schemes such as the SRA International Reading Laboratory and the Sound Sense Series. Tape recorders are the most commonly used audio-visual equipment.

7 The training of tutors specifically for adult literacy work is not common. Where it exists it usually consists of a few evening discussions about teaching problems.

8 The vast majority of the programmes are receiving the financial support of their local education authority or from the Home Office. The most pressing financial need of the programmes is for suitable teaching materials.

The study shows that there is an increasing awareness of the adult illiteracy problem at various levels in England but that the present provision is inadequate to deal effectively with the magnitude and complexity of the problem.

Coding: 2c, 2a, 5c, 5b, 8b, 4

Problems of attendance

WASTAGE AMONGST DAY-RELEASE AND EVENING CLASS STUDENTS AT THE TECHNICAL COLLEGE by J. Brown, M.Ed. thesis, University of Manchester 1954.

Aim
To investigate the reasons for the decline throughout the session in the numbers of students attending part-time evening classes in order to take Ordinary National and Higher National Certificate courses in the engineering Departments of the Oldham and Bolton Technical Colleges, during the period 1950-1952.

Method
The evidence was collected by the examination of attendance registers, questionnaires to 317 day-release students, 50 informal interviews with a group comprising part-time teachers, employment and education officers and employers, a ballot form to 266 evening-class only students, and interviews with 20 such students, and reference to examination results.

Discussion
The thesis is in eight sections, the first two of which review pertinent literature and outline the design of the research. Chapter 3 deals with student opinion of National Certificate part-time day courses — the typical young apprentice engineers. Four points emerge: two poor teachers in one department can affect every student in the department at some time; bad engineering workshop conditions have a marked effect on junior classes; the best students are able to link subjects into problem-solving topics; syllabuses tend to be overloaded.

Chapters 4 and 5 deal with the problems of the older, evening-class student. Single students complained that there was too little time for social activities, that text-books were expensive, and that there was a lack of facilities to study at home. Married students, 64%, mentioned home responsibilities as the main deterrent, and the older the married student, the more important this problem became. All older students mentioned 'a long way to travel' as a handicap.

Chapter 5 also includes the actual statistics of wastage of evening-class students and to this evidence is added, in Chapter 6, the reasons given by students for leaving their classes, when personally interviewed, together with 20 biographies describing the working life of each student. One, a machine operator, found that once the machine was set it required little attention, but as the noise level was high he could not talk to his mates. Thus he felt very tired at nights and wished to relax. When he found the third year of his course incomprehensible, he left — 'I just did not know what the bloke was talking about'.

Chapter 7 deals with the attitudes of local authority officers and part-time teachers,. and the other education problems of part-time students. Of part-time teachers, the impression is variable; to quote one 'the first year is difficult because you have to write out lessons, but then you just read them every year'. But other teachers are dedicated professionals, inspired by social motives. The attitudes of most employers are also variable, as were the views of local employment, welfare and education officers. Astonishingly, some of the latter were inclined to describe part-time day-release education as 'coddling the mediocre'! At the time when this thesis was researched, the Juvenile Employment Officers had no knowledge of technical education, so the author has omitted the results of his interviews with them.

Findings
About two-fifths of day-release students give up because of a loss of interest — mental wastage — half because they are attempting a course beyond their potential and about half because of the frustration of their daily jobs. Evening-class students appear to leave most frequently when they find themselves unable to progress; for example, repeated failure in the examination. One-third gave up, but two-thirds continued despite great difficulties. Married men found domestic responsibilities a great handicap; 40% of engineering students replied that they were simply too tired after a day's work to continue studying — and this figure is in close agreement with the percentage performing heavy work. However, in general, evening-class students were commended by teachers for diligence, punctuality and quality of work.

Coding: 2d, 2b, 8, 6

RECRUITMENT TO AND WASTAGE FROM ADULT TRAINING PROGRAMMES (WITH PARTICULAR REFERENCE TO NURSING) by J. M. MacGuire, D.Phil. thesis, University of London 1964.

Aims
To clarify ideas on the concepts of profession, professional education and training, the process of socialisation in the context of pro-

fessional training and employment and withdrawal from training. To survey particular circumstances in the nursing service and to consider the process of professional socialisation against the background of the structure of the employing institution.

Method

The study of recruitment and withdrawal patterns was undertaken in 5 general nursing training schools in the Oxford area between 1959 and 1964. Interviews were conducted in four stages during the career of student nurses. The survey started with 290 students. The interview schedule is given in an appendix.

Discussion

In 1961 about 11,000 women entered teacher-training in England and Wales, compared with about 18,000 women starting nursing-training. Whereas the development of professional education in general has been in the direction of separating professional training from professional practice, student nurses are recruited into an employment situation and not into an educational one. Their training is an institutional apprenticeship.

Hospitals are on-going communities, characterised by specific attitude constellations and, therefore, the training of student nurses can be regarded as a process of socialisation. The attitudes held by student nurses become more alike, within the group and to those of their seniors, during training. These changes are usually attributed directly to the process of training; but an alternative hypothesis is that student nurses with atypical attitudes at the point of entry withdraw, whilst those holding attitudes consistent with professional demands complete their training. Completion of training, on this view, is a function of anticipatory socialisation and thus the thesis is a study of a particular occupational personality.

Although the findings are specific to the training of nurses, the implications are of interest to tutors concerned with students whose occupational role is sometimes at variance with other roles he or she may wish to play in the context of the wider community.

Coding: 3d, 5a, 6, 4

Section 4

Theory of education

General education and social theory as applied to adults

THE RELATIONSHIP BETWEEN ADULT EDUCATION AND SOCIAL ATTITUDES IN ENGLISH INDUSTRIAL SOCIETY by E. J. King, Ph.D. thesis, University of London 1955.

Aim
To examine the general assumption of a direct connection between conventional adult education and healthy social attitudes.

Discussion
The post-war Labour government included a large number of men who attributed their general and political education to university tutorial classes organised by or for the Workers' Educational Association. It did not seem unreasonable to say that the traditional adult education of Britain had made them the men they were. The spread of democratic education for responsibility to all groups of our society could, it was supposed, be assured by somewhat similar means. Comparable lessons might be learned by similar methods and applied overseas; that is to say, methods believed to have been effective with certain men during half-a-century or so in one country were quietly supposed to have a general validity. But if this contention of certain working-class leaders were true, what of the 90% of the British population who never voluntarily undertook any form of adult education?

There are other problems. Can we assume that circumstances have changed so little that historical precedents are still applicable today? Can we consider social culture and, indeed, individual personality without giving special attention to the impact of industrialisation.

Pre-industrial societies maintained continuous education through-out life for all their members, at all levels and at all points of experience. Much of this was done by social, political and vocational rehearsal. Cultures were, thus, the syntheses of total education. Industrialisation, however, has occurred too fast and on too large a scale to be incorporated as a social instrument for education. The unprecedented power of industry and the degree of specialisation have disrupted the patterns of social education, so that men's lives have been shaped for industry. This, the author considers, is a reversal of the customary relationship. Healthy perceptions and attitudes have become increasingly difficult to sustain in a rapidly changing and complex industrial society.

Are the kinds of adult education with which we are familiar adequate? Is adult education aimed at the emancipated rather than being concerned with emancipation? We cannot rely on experiences based, not only on past historical circumstances, but on past educational theories; thus, a radical examination of purpose and method in adult education is necessary.

Industry itself must become part of the educative society for human beings; industrial situations are also social situations, and the educative possibilities of many social situations need to be explored. We may start by building education into industry by practical experiment accompanied by research; for example, through the machinery of joint consultation in industry. But whatever the expedient, the overall view of the educative work of society must be preserved and no activity should be excepted.

Coding: 3a, 5a, 2a, KB1363

ILLITERACY AND SOCIAL CHANGE — A COMPARATIVE SOCIO-PSYCHOLOGICAL STUDY OF CERTAIN WELSH, ENGLISH, RUSSIAN AND POLISH MOVEMENTS TO INCREASE POPULAR ENLIGHTENMENT IN THE 18th, 19th AND 20th CENTURIES by J. McLeish, D.Ph. thesis (2 vols), University of Leeds 1963. [also published, in part, as *Evangelical religion and popular education* Methuen, 1970]

Aim

To relate certain developments in adult education in Wales, England, Russia and Poland to the determining historical factors which gave rise to the evangelical, religious-political, nationalist and revolutionary movements in these respective countries, and to relate these developments to certain theories of social innovation.

Discussion

Part 1 of the thesis deals with illiteracy and social movements, the mass literacy campaign in Wales, religion, politics and popular education in England, popular enlightenment and the Polish peasant and illiteracy and the revolutionary movement in Russia.

Chapters 1, 2, 3 and the first part of Chapter 4 deal respectively with the personal contribution to mass literacy of Griffith Jones and Bridget Bevan in Wales from 1737-1775, of Hannah More in England, of Konarski in Poland and of P. V. Pavlov in Russia. The author thus studies four different societies: isolated Wales, industrialising England, the peasant inertia of Poland and the revolutionary movement in Russia struggling against a régime which, in June 1862, could issue a general order abolishing all special institutions which had arisen for the dissemination of reading amongst the common people.

The second part of Chapter 4 deals with the Soviet campaign against illiteracy from 1917-1939. 'Literacy', said Lenin in 1921, 'is not a political problem, but the very fundament without which it is impossible to speak about politics at all'. In 1932, at the peak of the campaign, approximately 14 million illiterates and near-literates were instructed, and even in 1939 nearly 7 million were under instruction.

In Part 2 of the thesis, the author moves to a consideration of theories of social change, for he argues that literacy is never conceived as an end in itself. The agents of popular enlightenment are interested in the fruits rather than the process, and in seeking change, the spreaders of literacy have met with some opposition from a vested interest in the status quo. Thus, he compares the dialectic of Marxism (Chapter 5) to the functionalism of Malinowski (Chapter 6), to the theories of Parsons and Smelser (Chapter 7) and to the contributions of the Freudian school of psychoanalysts, including Rattray Taylor's special development of the theory of parental identification.

In Volume 2, the Marxist model, the psychoanalytic model, the functionalist model and the social action model (Parsons) are each tested against the historical data. The author argues that each of the four theories fits the historical data more or less closely, but in some cases the fit is better than in others and, consequently, each provides a certain illumination in defined situations not give by the other theories.

Thus, he concludes that a new theory of social change must be formulated to overcome the weakness of the available theories. This is stated in the form of a 'set of rules', rather than of sociological laws, since at the present stage of development of sociological theory a great number of empirical studies are necessary. Experimental studies of group processes are needed to supplement historical investigations before an approach is possible to the formulation of laws of exceptionless validity from which predictions may be inferred.

Coding: 3a, 2c, 3c, KB1370

EDUCATION AND SOCIAL PURPOSE by K. E. Shaw, M.A. thesis, University of Bristol 1964.

Aim
To characterise the principal aspects of the work of six major contributors to the field of social philosophy and sociology, namely: Auguste Comte, Herbert Spencer, Ferdinand Tönnies, Emile Durkheim and Vilfredo Pareto.

Discussion
Each author offers an account of the major stages in social change within Western society, and proposes it in the form of law, model or analogy. In so doing, each discusses directly or by implication the nature of social facts, and how they are perceived and related to one another.

The author examines positivist theories of ethics and moral education, together with criticisms of the positivist position, and considers Henri Bergson's discussion of the place of intuition amongst mental operations and his criticism of intellectualism as an attempt to resolve some of the difficulties presented by the Comtian Positivist Doctrine, and its treatment by subsequent writers. The place and function of general theories of sociology and social philosophy within a Sociology of Education course are examined, and some of the conflicting views of the nature of sociological judgement, and how concepts, such as that of purpose, enter into judgements about society, are assessed.

The author concludes that such judgements cannot take the form of laws, but rather that the refined concepts to which they lead suggest new perceptions which assist society to accommodate change.

Coding: 3a

Philosophy of adult education

THE BEARING OF MODERN ANALYTICAL PHILOSOPHY ON EDUCATIONAL THEORY — A CRITICAL EXPLORATION OF THE LITERATURE 1942-1965 by A. Tubb, M.Ed. thesis, University of Durham 1966.

Aim
An exploration of recent post-war education theory and moral philosophy, including a discussion of the nature of history as an example of the nature of the conflicting approaches.

Discussion

The activities denoted by the terms 'modern analytical philosophy' and 'educational theory' are quite familiar to the majority of those whose work lies within the academic sphere. What is less certain is the extent to which it is known, firstly, that there exists a connection between these two activities, secondly, that modern analytical philosophy bears impressively on educational theory and thirdly, that the fact and the manner of this connection is something which has been demonstrated and developed quite recently in the intellectual life of the English-speaking community.

The thesis' starting point is the work of C. D. Hardie. In his pioneering work and in the present sustained contribution to educational thinking of many philosophers, together with the writings which steadily accumulated during the intervening years, there is ample evidence that the main division within pure analytical philosophy is reflected in the applied field. The rival 'positivistic' and 'linguistic' approaches are clearly discernible. In ethics, the early 'positivistic' position persists in the form of arguments for ultimately irreducible moral differences; but it is opposed by many educational philosophers, for example, by those taking a 'linguistic' view as expressed by R. S. Peters

The educational discourse displays these opposed emphases. The largely 'linguistic' elucidation of the role of definitions and other language elements given by I. Scheffler is criticised from a scientifically-orientated 'positivistic' standpoint, particularly in the contributions of G. R. Eastwood.

A central issue, that of the nature of educational theory, is similarly debated by representatives from each of the branches of analytical philosophy. The 'linguistic' P. H. Hirst argues that educational theory is a complex 'field' and not a distinct form of knowledge as a counter to the simpler 'means-ends' interpretation developed by such 'positivists' as D. J. O'Connor.

The importance of the above argument to practising tutors may be stated thus: 'Traditional methods of teaching, based upon unconsciously absorbed theory of a pre-scientific commonsensical kind, which is picked up at *best* by intelligent reflection on wide experience, are not appropriate for a mass society undergoing a knowledge explosion, no matter how well they may have worked in the past nor how well they may *seem* still to work when judged only by those same people who use them'.

Coding: 3b, 5m(vii)

THE IDEA OF EDUCATION FOR LEADERSHIP by J. L. Harrison, D.Phil. thesis, University of Manchester 1968.

Aim
a To describe the idea of education for leadership in Western Europe from the time of Plato to 1900 through a study of the theory and practice, and to identify its main modes and elements and their unity in form and purpose for successive periods of time
b To use as a method of description a variety of the different approaches allowed by the nature of the subject; focussing, for example, more on (say) curriculum than on methods of study; on general philosophical assumptions and climates of opinion than on sociological and economic determinants; on specific theory of education for leadership (Plato, the Jesuits) than on generally held, if loosely organised, ideas
c To discover what theoretical conclusions as to the desired nature of education for leadership seem to follow from the dominant principles of the idea as well as from non-educational facts of leadership

Method
A critical historical survey: Volume 1 covers the period from Plato to St. Augustine of Hippo; Volume 2 deals with the period from the early middle ages to the conspicuous influence of the Jesuits in sixteenth century education and to their suppression in 1773; volume 3 continues the account from 1640 to 1900.

Discussion
The chief determinants of the form and content of education for leadership are, on the one hand, the fundamental attitudes and beliefs, sensitivities and knowledges of an age, and on the other (although inter-relating with the first), the basic socio-economic structure and the way in which it is changing at the time. Individuals do slightly modify such forces, but are, in the main, the instruments of their cultures.

The idea of education for leadership that emerges is one of the education contemplated for the socio-political responsibilities of members of the ruling sectors. Secondary education provided for the knowledge, sensitivities and attitudes in terms of which leadership was conceived to function. Where higher education has been available, it has been structured after the secondary model with certain additions. Where secondary eduction was weak, so was the higher education. This secondary education was, in theory, always of a liberal-general nature.

Nevertheless, vocational, technical, practical and professional education are all legitimate aspects of a liberal-general education. In modern times, a general education without trained practical skill of direct reference to the world that leaders manipulate seems to be a contradiction in terms. It seems to be inevitable that the practical conditions of knowledge, adaptability and the right use of leisure should be incorporated in any education for leadership. It is equally true that it is a real function of education to distance itself, to some degree, from possibly ephemeral socio-economic actualities.

Education for leadership assumes that education ought to be for full men rather than for great ones; perhaps the leadership qualities to be cultivated should be collective and co-ordinative rather than charismatic.

Coding: 3b

Psychology of learning in adult education

THE EFFECT OF SIX MONTHS' INSTRUCTION IN SCHOOL SUBJECTS ON SOME MENTAL FACTORS OF ADULTS by W. B. Walls, M.Ed. thesis, University of Leeds 1945.

Aim
To discover whether six months' instruction in school subjects resulted in any improvement in the mental factors of many ex-elementary and a few ex-secondary young men who wished to train for aircrew in 1943-1944.

Method

Batteries of 19 tests, administered at the beginning and end of the course, were applied to 112 men, of an average age of 18 years, who studied for six months a curriculum consisting of mathematics, general science, mechanical drawing, geography, English and modern history. Tests were based on Thurston's Psychometric Monograph No. 1 the Spearman-Denison GVK test and Holzinger & Swineford's tests. Relatively detailed statistical correlation data is provided.

Findings

The adults, whose previous full-time education had ceased some years before the beginning of the six months' instruction period, had an initial educational standard approximately equivalent to that of the third form of a secondary school. By the end of the course there was a significant improvement in abilities involving the spatial factor, the verbal factor, the number factor, the arithmetical reasoning factor, the mental speed factor and the immediate memory factor. The fact of this improvement is a warning to psychologists who believe that an individual can be represented as so much g, k, v, n etc factors. A person's factorial composition can be changed in a relatively short space of time by suitable training environment. However, it is, of course, possible that the improvement recorded is not due to a change in group factors but is rather the result of a change in the men's attitude and general behaviour towards tests. The thesis also surveys some early 20th century psychological theories, such as those of Thorndike and Burt, and includes some discussion of the problem of 'transfer'.

Coding: 3d, 2b

THE PART PLAYED BY KINAESTHETIC EXPERIENCE IN PERCEPTION AND THINKING by W. Strzalkowski, D.Phil. thesis (2 vols), University of Oxford 1946.

Aim

To show that mental processes are due to the primordial experience which people have when they move; that is, the perceiving of objects in their concreteness in the result of previous experiences of handling objects, enabling us to satisfy the needs which had resulted from the lack of balance between our internal structure and our environment.

Discussion

The author surveys the development of the idea of the relationship between motor activity and perception and thinking in the history of philosophical thought, considering, in particular, the contributions of Maine de Biran, who was the first philosopher to emphasise the importance of movement in our mental life, Bergson and Rignano. The last named argues, for example, that 'reasoning is nothing else than a series of experiments carried out in the mind alone' and that 'the logical process is identical with the activity on the perceptual reality, operated instead of actual performance by means of the imagination'.

Following this background survey, the author turns to an analysis of the role of kinaesthetic experience and movement according to modern schools of psychology, that is, behaviourism as examplified by Watson's theory of thinking, Gestalt psychology and Freud's psychonalysis. Thorndike, as an example of the Behaviourist School, came to the conclusion that animals do not learn by reasoning but by trial and error methods. They do not learn by watching or considering but by acting themselves. Consequently, Thorndike argued that even human reasoning has as its basis the same kind of motor skill and arguments for introspective methods of reasoning are inconsistent with the behaviourist's observations. The Gestalt theorists do not believe that action can be explained merely by stimulus-response bonds; on the contrary, every action is characterised by the state of tension which is relieved when the task has been completed. Every action consists in 'closing the gap' to bring the organism to a state of equilibrium. Perception appears to be the most essential factor in the process of animal learning. The animal reacts not towards any particular object, but towards the whole perceptual situation, which is organised in one dynamic unit with its striving towards a goal. The animal learns through its insight and, therefore, perception and organisation are important when motor activity is concerned. Freud also provides examples, showing the close connection between motor expressions of our abstract thought, and the motor experience corresponding to them, even though some of the experiences are turned into overt motor reactions.

The author suggests that each of the theories described above is limited in some sense or aspect, and consequently, five out of the six chapters in the thesis are devoted to a more detailed analysis of the concepts. He considers the active character of perception, the analysis of visual perception in relation to Berkeley's theory of vision, the active character of memory and the active character of memory according to Plotinus and other philosophers.

Similarly, he examines in detail the active character of imagination and of thinking, particularly the aspects of the biological function of thinking, its motor character, the role of symbols in thinking, and the meaning of symbols. Special attention is paid to the categories of thinking, 'substance' and 'causality' and to the problem of freewill, in the penultimate chapter.

Findings
The view that perceiving and thinking can be explained by motor experience must be tested by facts; and its applicability as the basis of their explanation constitutes the proof of its high probability. Because of the general character of this hypothesis the field which it can cover is very extensive, belonging to the many specialised domains of investigation as well as to the common property of the human race: to the observation of the behaviour of people, and of our inner processes in which we put our trust in our everyday activities.

Coding: 3d

A STUDY OF THE INCONSTANCY OF INTELLIGENCE by J. C. Daniels, M.Ed. thesis, University of Durham 1948.

Aim
a To question if there is, in real life, a unitary trait, ability, aptitude or mechanism which we can call intelligence, which is granted to individuals to a greater or lesser extent
b To examine the predictability of intelligence, the measurement of intelligence and the constancy of intelligence throughout an individual's life

Method

The author concentrates on the problems of the 11+ examination, but in passing touches on the question of intelligence in adults.

Discussion

One of the results of the 1944 Education Act was that secondary education ceased to be a 'type' of education, but became a 'stage' in an educational process, in the sense that every child reaching the age of 11 years passed into some form of secondary education. However, selection processes were introduced which imposed a system of vertical selection in secondary education and which considerably affected the adult lives of those who experienced these selection procedures.

The Intelligence Tests used were selected because they had been discovered to be a fairly accurate guide to what were desirable characteristics in our present form of society. Yet in the circumstances of the 1939-45 war, the Armed Services discovered many hundreds of thousands of men and women whose education had been confined to that of an elementary school to the age of 14 years and who proved to be as capable in the execution of difficult and complex tasks as their ex-grammar school colleagues.

Is an intelligence score constant and fairly measurable? On the question of constancy, the author argues that, although the average score of a large sample tends to decrease with age and after a certain age, individual performances vary considerably from the average, and in some cases the intelligence score of an individual may increase throughout his life-time. So far as measurability is concerned, the author considers that there is considerable evidence to show that intelligence score performance varies with environmental conditions, such as housing, family relationships, and so on. He suggests that this applies to adult performance, as well as to the performance of normal and handicapped children.

Consequently, he suggests that educators should perhaps be less interested in people's 'intelligence', which is a hold-all phrase for the infinite variety of human ability and aptitude, and be more concerned with 'capacity' which suggests a potential for growth, irrespective of the age of the individual.

Coding: 3a, 2b

THE EDUCATIONAL VALUE OF SELF-GOVERNMENT IN A YOUTH CLUB by V. S. Pate, M.A.(Ed) thesis, University of Birmingham 1948. [Main findings published in *Training worker citizens*, Macdonald and Evans, 1949.]

Aims

a To review, generally, the behavioural patterns of self-government in youth clubs
b To examine the techniques of self-government in particular youth clubs, (e.g.) the Warstock YMCA
c To consider if self-government helps the individual in the formation of his character

Method

The author reviews accounts of, and experiments in, youth clubs in the United Kingdom and overseas. Case studies of 50 members of the Warstock YMCA and the results of a questionnaire completed by 103 members of three clubs form the basis of the investigation conducted in the period 1945-1946. The correlation between sublimation and, firstly, length of membership, secondly, maturity, thirdly, home and lastly, intelligence, are examined by the chi-squared test method.

Discussion

The ages of members of youth clubs ranged from 14 to 20 years; each club is highly individualistic but all try to sustain their members' individual and social development. Four doctrines of behaviour are examined; viz the behaviourist (Watson), the psychoanalytical (Freud) the instinctivist (McDougall) and the functional autonomist (Allport). From this review it is argued that the key to character formation is the sublimation of innate emotional energy. Certain mental processes are considered to initiate the requisite deflection of energy which exemplifies sublimation such as, for example, that of experiencing actual situations, that of solving problems of concern to a group and that of bearing the responsibility for decisions. Sublimation is thus defined as, essentially, the deflection of an instinctual energy away from a natural goal determinded by an innate tendency, towards a new goal which is generally socially determined. Instinctual energy must find an outlet; the youth club provides such an outlet and, by example rather than by precept, attempts to indicate new goals which are ethically more worthy or socially more acceptable than the original instinctual goal. If these teleological assumptions are accepted, then self-government is an efficacious technique.

Findings
There is a direct association between sublimation and the home, but no direct association between sublimation and either the length of membership of the club or intelligence. The overall evidence suggests that clubs provide the setting and facilities for the individual sublimation of instinctive energy and for the integration of individual sentiments into a harmonious whole.

There was no direct evidence of the influence of work, and the conclusions about the influence of intelligence on the process of sublimation were limited because only boys of low intelligence were included in the study.

The principal practical conclusions were that clubs should be either small in number or be divided into small groups, that the leader should receive sufficient psychological training to deal with members' problems, that the leader should be acquainted with members' homes and that informality and self-government are essential ingredients for success.

Coding: 3d, 5b, 2b, 7c(viii), 8b

A STUDY OF THE PSYCHOLOGICAL REFRACTORY PERIOD IN RELATION TO AGEING by J. M. T. Brebner, Ph.D. thesis, University of Exeter 1965.

Aim
To study the 'psychological refractory period', that is, the period which follows the presentation of a signal during which responses to further signals (i.e. arriving within that period) are delayed by ageing beyond their normal latency.

Experiments
Three experiments are described; the first suggests that certain delays

in responding are longer for older adults than younger people. The second experiment suggested that delays in responding are not uniquely solely related to age; the third experiment tended to confirm the conclusions of the second. All three experiments suggest that the theory of Welford, that there is a single-channel decision mechanism limited in its capacity to deal with rapidly successive separate events, may be supported.

Discussion
The level of detail in this thesis is perhaps more appropriate for the specialist psychologist than the educationalist, but although Chapter 3 is highly technical, Chapters 1 and 2, particularly Chapter 2, the 'Study of Age', may be of some consequence to the adult education tutors concerned with older students.

Ageing is far from being a simple matter of the passing of chronological years. For example, Welford suggests that the effects of ageing upon skilled performance are:
a a slowing of performance with ageing
b increased intra-individual variation in performance as we move up the age-scale
c disproportionate changes in performance with age as the difficulty of the task increases
But Szafran, 1951, demonstrated that where the times taken to initiate and complete a response movement are measured separately, a greater increase in reaction, rather than movement-time, with age is evident. As the increase in reaction time with age outweighed any increase in movement-time, these findings, taken together with other experiments, suggest a central rather than peripheral locus for the slowing performance.

Of some interest is Welford's suggestion of three possible reasons why older people might be slower in the presence of irrelevant stimuli. These are:
a that older subjects may not be able to exercise the same degree of perceptual selectivity as younger people
b that older people may not have the same ability to overlap the taking of decisions with the making of movements
c that older people may need more sensory data for carrying out each task.

Coding: 3d

A STUDY OF THE EFFECTS OF T-GROUP TRAINING ON THE ACCURACY OF INTER-PERSONAL PERCEPTION IN STUDENTS AT A COLLEGE OF EDUCATION by H. J. Tinsley, M.Ed. thesis, University of Leicester 1967.

Hypotheses

a That individuals become more self-aware (self-perceptive) as a result of participation in a non-directive group of the study/T-group type

b That heightened self-awareness is linked with heightened awareness of others and that experience of a T-group increases with the accuracy of the individual's perception of others, both in group matters, e.g. status within a group, and personal matters, e.g. feelings and attitudes

c That this heightened self-awareness and increased accuracy of inter-personal perception are behaviour changes that are transferable to other inter-personal relationships, e.g. tutor/student

d That perceptive accuracy, inter-personal sensitivity is a skill that it is important for a teacher/tutor to possess and is of particular value in promoting effective inter-personal relations

Method

The learning technique studied is the T-group; that is, a small face-to-face group in which the participants have the task of creating a situation that meets the requirements of members for growth. Members have the opportunity to learn about themselves, inter-personal relations and the group structure.

The first half of the thesis outlines the research, states the problem and reviews the literature and development of T-group theory and 'conferences', particularly the contributions of L. P. Bradford of Bethel, Maine, USA, and of A. K. Rice of the Tavistock Institute, London.

The second half deals with the design, description, measurement and results of the experiment. 30 of an original sample of 40 students completed the experiment, initially meeting in groups of 5 and completing a slightly modified Suchman Social Sensitivity Questionnaire, re-forming into three groups, one of which was employed for control purposes. After further meetings of the two experimental groups, all three groups completed the Burke and

Bennis modification of Osgood's Semantic Differential at the beginning and end of the next period of experiment. This consisted of weekly meetings, totalling 11 hours over a period of 9 weeks. In a third period of experiment the original groups of 5 were reconstituted and re-tested on the Suchman Questionnaire. Tetrachoric correlations were established as part of the statistical techniques employed.

Discussion

There are common errors in perception which arise from the subject's own criteria of behaviour, from the tendencies to oversimplify, to stereotype, to rationalise one's own unwelcome thoughts to another, to be over-lenient or irrationally critical and to depend on general impressions. The objective of the T-group is to mobilise group forces to support the growth of members as individuals at the same time as they grow as collaborators and thereby to assist them both to avoid the common errors listed above and to develop positive characteristics. Rice particularly attacks the myths of the gifted amateur and the born leader, maintaining that leadership skills are painfully learned, although he doubts whether the pain associated with the experience of learning about oneself and one's relations with others is as yet accepted as an inevitable part of an educator's training. Such assertions require or deserve further scientific investigation.

Findings

The experiment did not prove that this form of group experience is more efficacious than any other in promoting heightened accuracy of inter-personal perception. Because the total number of participating subjects was so small, any generalisation is highly improper. However, bearing this stricture in mind, the results were sufficiently encouraging (in that they did not *disprove* the hypotheses) to suggest further experiment with a larger sample over a longer period.

Coding: 5d, 3d, 8c

THE TRANSFER OF TRAINING FROM T-GROUP COURSES IN HUMAN RELATIONS TO THE JOB SITUATION by D. Moscow, Ph.D. thesis, University of Leeds 1970.

Aim

To investigate the impact of T-group training on the subsequent interpersonal behaviour of participants in their job situations, including a cross-cultural comparison of outcomes following British, Dutch and American T-groups.

Method

'Students' were divided into three main groups:
1 an experimental group of participants from T-group laboratories;
2 a control group of non-trained subjects;
3 two comparison groups of participants from training courses involving human relations training, but not employing T-groups.

The subjects for the experimental group were obtained over a four-year period from five T-group laboratories conducted by the Department of Management Studies, University of Leeds, between 1964 and 1967 (27 male managers), and five T-group laboratories conducted by the Netherlands Institute for Preventive Medicine, T.N.O. Leiden, between 1966 and 1968. [52 subjects, 69% male; occupations included business, education, medicine and religion (13 nuns)].

Comparison Course A consisted of 15 participants from two nine-week middle-management courses with a human relations content; Comparison Course B of 12 participants from three two-week human relations courses for doctors and nurses. The American T-groups consisted of 101 subjects, of which 72.3% were male and in business, education, medical/social work, the Civil Service/public utilities and religion.

The author establishes a model, derived from the theoretical and empirical literature which he previously describes; he then presents this model in terms of a series of propositions, from which hypotheses to test the model may be readily derived. He considers the factors mediating in transfer of training to job situation. Background factors are readiness for change, voluntariness, self-perceived *security* in the job situation, self-perceived *autonomy* in the job situation, and self-perceived *openness* in the job situation. On-the-job change will depend on these background factors and, of course, on the training factor, which is, in this case, behaviour change in T-group.

The author describes every stage of the enquiry in detail; for example, the reader is told precisely the measure of inter-personal behaviour change during the T-group as applied to the British T-group population. Content analysis of tape-recorded T-group sessions was used to construct a measure of the degree of change in each participant's pattern of inter-personal behaviour from early to late in the laboratory. Participants' verbal behaviour during T-group sessions was then coded into eight behaviour categories:

opinions and information
initiating
analysing
supporting
facilitating
defensive
expressive
clarifying self and relieving own tension

The measure of overall inter-personal behaviour change was obtained by summating the percentage shift on each category, from early to late sessions. Information was also gathered by interview and questionnaire.

Findings

Positive transfer of training from T-groups to the job situation does occur. T-group trainees showed more change in inter-personal behaviour than a control group of non-trained subjects and the overwhelming majority of these changes were evaluated as being in the direction of increased inter-personal competence. British, Dutch and American T-groups were found to be equally effective in inducing change, though the specific learning emphasis differed.

There was some empirical support for the general proposition that 'social psychological' background factors mediate in the transfer of training to the job situation, whilst 'objective' (e.g. sex, length of job tenure) background factors do not.

Participants who show most readiness for change prior to the laboratory show most change during the T-group, and participants who have *median* self-perceived security, autonomy and openness in their work relationships show *most* inter-personal behaviour change in the job situation. Those with *high* or *low* self-perceived security, and so on, show *less* change.

Coding: 5d, 3d

ADULT LEARNING — A PSYCHOLOGICAL STUDY OF CONDITIONS OF LEARNING by G. H. Jamieson, D.Phil. thesis, University of Liverpool 1970.

Aim
To assess the effects of conditions of learning upon older persons; particularly cognitive learning.

Method
The research was carried out over a period of four years; it took the form of three separate studies which were linked by developments in the experimental procedures.

The first study was concerned with establishing the simple relationship between conditions of learning and response styles without regard to the meaningfulness of the task. 104 people (52 subjects over the age of 40, of median age of 55 years, and 52 subjects under 40, of median age 29 years,) who had previously been tested on the Raven's Progressive Matrices and the Mill Hill Vocabulary tests, were obtained from the voluntary panel of the Liverpool Medical Research Council Unit. One group of subjects had a task of grouping cards on the basis of outside form only, in which the condition of learning demanded a stereotyped response. The other group was given a task which demanded response flexibility; that is, the solution changed from outer form to colour (Shroder and Rotters' 1952 experimental design).

The second study involved the learning of binary notation. This task was chosen because it involves cognitive learning, and because it is relatively unfamiliar to most adults. In addition, it is a task that can be learnt in a relatively short time and therefore it is more free from 'interference' than other knowledge which requires more than one learning session. 80 females were chosen (20 from a state primary school, mean age 11 years; 20 from a college of occupational therapy, mean age 21 years; 20 from a college of education for mature students, mean age 40.6 years; and 20 from the Liverpool MRC Unit's panel, mean age 57.5 years). The subjects were randomly assigned to two different conditions of learning, programmed and guided discovery, within their own particular age groups. A standardised mathematics/arithmetic test was administered before the experiment and a post-test of knowledge of binary notation was given at the end of the learning session.

The third study was an extension of the second; it used similar experimental material, but it contained a 'transfer' task and a retention test. 80 female subjects were enrolled for the experiment, consisting of 20 members of the Liverpool MRC Unit, mean age 62.2 years; 20 housewives, mean age 32.7 years; 20 members from an extra-mural course, mean age 61.2 years; and 20 members of a course for district nurses, mean age 31.7 years. Information was obtained on the current educational status of the subjects and on their interests and hobbies.

Discussion
Besides describing the investigation and producing data in detail, the author reviews the literature. The early studies in adult learning, the work of Thorndike and others, the work of the Nuffield Unit, the contributions of Belbin, Belbin and Downs, the theoretical bases of adult learning, Hebb's model, the main theoretical problems and the conditions of learning are all discussed.

Findings
In the first study it was found that the conditions of learning had a significant effect upon the response styles of the subjects. When flexibility/rigidity was measured in terms of learning outcomes, there was no significant age effect. Thus, the *method* of learning, and *not* the age of the subject, was the main determinant of response style.

The results of the second study showed that when learning was measured in terms of performance on a binary notation criterion test, a significantly positive correlation was found between the initial arithmetic test and the criterion. It was also found that learning by the discovery method significantly helped subjects with lower arithmetic scores, irrespective of age.

The results of the third study showed that there was no age

difference in the ability to learn binary notation when the subjects were equated for arithmetical ability, whether they learned by programmed or discovery methods, nor was there any difference in transfer of learning. But a significant difference in favour of the younger subjects (under 40 years) was found on retention scores. However, there was no evidence to suggest that the discovery method conferred benefits on retention for the older subjects (over 50 years).

The research evidence suggests that response styles of all subjects of all ages can be the outcome of modes of learning; it shows that existing learning sets, in terms of subordinate capabilities are more important than age in determining the reception of knowledge; it also demonstrates that retention, and *not transfer,* of knowledge of binary notation is more affected, in a negative direction, by age.

Coding: 3d, 5a, KB1334

PERCEPTION, PERSONALITY AND MOVEMENT CHARAC-
TERISTICS OF WOMEN STUDENTS OF PHYSICAL EDUCATION
by M. G. Jones, M.Ed. thesis, University of Leicester 1970.

Aim
To examine the interrelationship of consistent modes of perceptual functioning, personality factors and consistent modes of movement behaviour.

Method
All students entering the second year of study at Bedford College of Physical Education, i.e. 140 women aged 19-21 years, intending to become physical education specialists, were given the following tests:
1 perceptual tests — rod and frame test   — embedded figures test (Jackson 1956, short form)
2 personality tests — Eysenck's personality inventory (1968) form — 16 personality factor questionnaire (Cattell 1962)
3 movement assessment — effort profile
4 sophistication of body concept — draw a person test (scored from the Hanna Marlens scale, Witkin et al, 1962)
5 laterality — eye; finger aiming; cone

— hand preference test (Whiting and Eastwood 1968)
— accuracy of throwing (Whiting and Eastwood 1968)
The whole sample (140) was divided into three sub-groups for the experiment:
Group A — students following a dance-stressed course (N=20)
Group B — students following a games-stressed course (N=91)
Group C — students following a combined P.E. course (N=29)
Initial tests were administered in September 1968, and re-tests taken in July 1969. The results are given in considerable numerical detail and were computer-analysed giving, for example, a Principal Components Analysis of Perception and Personality.

Discussion
The author has divided the thesis into three parts: an introduction and outline of related literature, a detailed account of the experimental work (the statistical terms are briefly explained in Appendix 4), and a discussion of findings with suggestions for further development.

Findings
The findings are detailed in the precise terms used in the disciplines of statistics, psychology and physical education. However, one of the conclusions is that movement education programmes may affect perceptual development and this implies that movement has a role in ameliorating the perceptual difficulties of some individuals.

Coding: 3d, 5m(xiv)

ISOLATION OF LEARNER TYPES — INDIVIDUALISED INSTRUCTION IN EDUCATIONAL AUTOMATION by D. H. Britt, Ph.D. thesis, University of Cambridge 1970.

Introduction
Computer Assisted Instruction is becoming increasingly popular. An ideal CAI programme would cater specifically for the needs of each particular individual, but it is impracticable to produce as many programmes as there are learners. Is it possible to create instructional

programmes scientifically designed, to fit the needs of large groups of individuals classified by Learner Type? A Learner Type consists of a group of individuals who share a similarity of reaction *during the,* as well as *to the,* process of learning.

Hypothesis
Individuals, both male and female, of varying ages and educational levels, having been clustered on the basis of similar performance on individual response patterns to a test covering a wide spectrum of capacity, ability, habit and environmental preference factors, will reappear in a like cluster based on the similarity of performance on individual response patterns to an instructional programme which presents the course material in a variety of ways, and which may have been administered several years after the test.

Method
483 GCE 'O' level candidates who took the Cambridge Local Examinations Syndicate's examinations in 1965 were questioned over a two-year period. Multivariate analysis procedures and sophisticated statistical techniques were applied by the investigator.

Findings
Individuals indeed formed into clusters, and remained within a particular cluster over a period of time, and thus Learner Types were identified. Consequently, there appeared to be some evidence to demonstrate that there was a need to create programmes to the exact needs and assets of these types, and that a programme written for one type was not suited for another. For example, Learner Type A seems to require programmes which do not frequently test retention ability. On the other hand, Learner Type B needs programmes which re-teach the course material, because B-type's predominant characteristic is low retention.

It is therefore suggested that the means of providing individual students with the learning material best suited to their needs, using completely computer-controlled teaching machines, may be through the identification of Learner Types.

Coding: 3d, 5a, 5k

Section 5

Curricula and courses

A PSYCHOLOGICAL AND SOCIOLOGICAL STUDY OF
STUDENTS IN HIGHER TECHNOLOGICAL EDUCATION by J. F.
Clark, D.Phil. thesis, University of London 1951.

Aim
To investigate various aspects of the problem of increasing the
number of technologists who can organise and administer or apply
research results to industrial development.

Method
A study of 130 technologists, mostly engineers, and 100 arts or
economic graduates, from a variety of universities and technical
colleges in Britain; by comparing their life histories, cognitive
abilities, attitudes, personality traits and characters, using interviews,
questionnaires, psychological tests and a limited form of participant
observation.

Discussion
The two groups revealed some interesting differences in family
structure and relations, harmony in the home and happiness during
childhood. More of the technologists were conservative in outlook,
conventional in behaviour, concerned with personal worthiness, not
very interested in people but interested in directing and organising

others, and strongly interested in active rather than intellectual pursuits. Large differences in favour of the arts group were obtained on verbal and general information tests. More technologists had definite vocational aims.

Findings
There was a need for a wider field of recruitment to technology, a more diversified form of education to school pupils to a later age, and particularly, *more scientific education for the bright. The teaching of English should be extended, as well as other cultural subjects,* to the scientific stream, both at school and university, and there was a need for the greater use of psychological resources in the design of technology courses and the counselling of students.

Coding: 4, 2b

PRESENT TRENDS IN PART-TIME DAY-RELEASE SCHEMES IN FURTHER EDUCATION by I. F. Rolls, M.A.(Ed) thesis, University of London 1960.

Aim
To review existing information about day continuation schools in general, and to compare their history with current practice as observed in the area of South-West and Central London.

Method
Principally by interview of members of organisations interested in schemes of day-release, that is, colleges, trades unions, industrial and commercial firms, and students in the London area.

Discussion
Part 1 of the thesis reviews earlier work, indicates the method of investigation, and defines the terms. Part-time day-release education describes the education of students who are released from what would otherwise be full-time employment, on the basis of one-half, two-halves or one-whole day a week, to attend some place of further education. Parts 2-5 deal respectively with a review of the history of

part-time day release education, from 1802 to 1959, the growth of day-release education (facts and figures), the background to further education, and a discussion of some problems of day-release education.

Findings
Perhaps one of the most interesting findings is that, in the area studied, the number of enrolments of 15 and 16 year, old students remained stable between 1952/53 and 1956/57, at about 6,000 enrolments in each age group. But in the same period the number of enrolments of day-release students of 21 years and over increased by 82%, from about 3,500 in 1952/53. Similarly, the number of enrolments of 18-20 year olds increased by about 61%, so that the numbers of released students (day, block or sandwich courses) in the 18+ age groups now constitute something like one-third to one-half of the total release figures.

Thus, if we consider the variety of maturity represented in the age-range covered by day-release schemes alone, we may anticipate that the author's main conclusion is that no uniform scheme of further education, whether it be day-release or any other arrangement, will adequately meet the needs of the country or achieve the aims of its supporters. He argues particularly for a less formal but more practical curriculum and emphasises the importance of 'coffee-table' education, that is, the freedom to discuss problems at leisure in an increasingly adult atmosphere.

Coding: 1c(ii), 4, 8a

SOME CONSIDERATIONS ON THE PROVISION OF GENERAL EDUCATION FOR YOUNG WORKERS by R. S. Miles, M.A. thesis, University of Birmingham 1961.

Aim
To examine the provision of 'general' or 'non-technical' education for young workers who are in occupations for which there is no apprenticeship or similar comprehensive training scheme.

Method
By questionnaires, testing ability in English and arithmetic and views on work and leisure, of 266 boys and 297 girls between the ages of 15 and 18 years, attending Bournville Day Continuation College. (All students, except 17, had previously attended secondary modern schools). Comparisons are made between this enquiry and other local and national enquiries, and the work of Bournville College itself is studied over approximately the period 1947-1954.

Discussion
Part 1 of the thesis deals with the young worker in his industrial and social setting, in various areas and at different periods of time. The author argues that the concept of the employer as exploiter is being replaced by that of commercialised entertainment and cheap literature. Coincidentally with this, industry is demanding higher standards of ability to cope with new techniques, machines and processes, and workers are tending to become robots in a caste system of managers, skilled and unskilled classes. In these circumstances young workers need special opportunities to develop as social beings.

Part 2 is concerned with Works' Schools in general, and Bournville in particular. Whilst at Bournville there was a great deal of informality, flexibility and choice, the curriculum was still too 'academic' and 'bookish'; not enough had been done in terms of accommodation and equipment to cater for practical interests – the main block to improving formal education is the, by definition, immature personal relationships of adolescents. Part 3 is concerned with the recommendations which cover all aspects of day-release or adolescent continuative education.

Findings
Fifteen years is too young an age for all compulsory education to cease. The absolute need is for matching the education of young workers with their interests and as, in virtually every case, the job holds supreme interest, then education must centre on that fact of vocation. The adolescent desires three things: freedom to experiment, security to fall back upon when his experiments go wrong and a purpose in life.

One of the problems of the young worker is that he is no longer of concern to the secondary sector of the education service yet not until the age of 18 does he come within the purview of adult education, as strictly defined.

Coding: 4

LIBERAL EDUCATION FOR INDUSTRIAL WORKERS IN THEORY AND PRACTICE by P. Simpson, M.Sc.(Social Science) thesis, University of Edinburgh 1970.

Aim
To examine the need for education among the manual working-classes in relation to the present provision of adult education.

Method
The author has based his research, firstly, on the evidence of documentary sources, such as the reports of the Trades Union Congress, the reports on liberal education schemes for trades unionists (e.g. Pickstock), training journals, and descriptions of the nature of industrial society. Secondly, 14 interviews were conducted with professionals concerned with education in industry, 24 interviews were held with students at Newbattle Abbey College, and 10 interviews were conducted with educators concerned with liberal education programmes.

Discussion
From a review of recent literature and statistics, the author argues that it is evident that not only are working-class people less represented quantitatively in their participation in adult education classes but that their participation is also geared towards the practical recreational sphere of adult education rather than towards the liberal arts.

The author refers to the notion of alienation — that is, that work, by its very nature, inhibits man from achieving his creative potential (Marx, Marcuse) — and argues that two basic types of workers exist. There are those who are alienated and dissatisfied, who may look to adult education for leisure satisfaction, and those who are alienated but satisfied. The latter form the real problem, and consequently, the adult education provision must be brought to the worker in the work situation if it is to influence the quality of his life. As Blauner showed in his study in the USA, 61% of the unskilled car workers thought their jobs dull or monotonous most or all of the time. However, the case for factory-based courses is not simple nor compelling, and the author provides the arguments for day-release courses outside the factory.

By interview and case study of residential students in Newbattle Abbey, the author discovered prima facie evidence that students wished to change not only their work situations but their total life style, and that alienation and the negative quality of work leads to a negative use of leisure.

The author then turns to the ways of meeting the needs for education on the part of the manual working classes, and describes the national provision of education for trades unionists, including a course arranged by the TUC, in conjunction with the BBC, called 'Representing the Union', day-release classes provided by university extra-mural departments, by the WEA and by local education authorities at technical colleges. He further compares in some detail the provision of liberal education for industrial workers in two regions, Sheffield and Edinburgh, and notes that the Sheffield region provides an example of the comprehensive development of education facilities, whereas the Edinburgh region has only just begun to develop its potential.

The author argues the case for an expansion of liberal education in two directions; firstly, by increasing high level courses for active trade unionists on day-release and, secondly, by persuading those unionists already educated to influence others to participate. Furthermore, he suggests that there is a case for increased provision of liberal education programmes based on the work place, as well as on day-release elsewhere.

Coding: 2b, 2a, 2d, 5h, 2e, 4, 3c, KB758b

AN ENQUIRY INTO THE ATTITUDES OF EMPLOYERS
TOWARDS LIBERAL STUDIES FOR PART-TIME STUDENTS IN
THE TECHNICAL COLLEGE by R. G. Morris, M.Phil. thesis,
University of Reading 1970. [Reported in *Liberal Education* No. 20
Summer 1971]

Aim

To assess the attitude of employers who released employees to day
or block-release courses that included an element of liberal studies,
for the session 1967/68 held in the North Oxfordshire Technical
College and School of Art, Banbury.

Method

188 firms, releasing a total of 589 students (the mean of students
released per firm being 3.1, the mode 1), were located from records;
176 postal questionnaires were sent out and 114 responded; 19
employers were personally interviewed.

Discussion

The preamble to the thesis describes the purpose of the research, the
characteristics of the College and the subject matter of what is called
liberal studies. The author notes that the attitude of many students
to liberal studies is one of tolerant scepticism, and that employers,
particularly in small firms, need to be convinced of the value of such
studies. Most employers regard day-release as a privilege. Having
reviewed previous research, the author then discusses the survey in
detail, together with other factual information which emerged, such
as, for example, the personal qualifications of employers, their
job-titles, and their responsibility for employees on day-release.

Two interesting facts emerged from the interviews; a few
employers' administrators (e.g. a civil servant) responsible for
day-release students rarely met them in the ordinary course of their
work, and a substantial minority of employers had no idea whatever
of the precise meaning of 'liberal studies'. One training officer
recalled a lecturer singing protest songs to a guitar accompaniment;
other employers emphasised English language as the central subject
of such studies. Some employers noted that if colleges treated liberal
studies as peripheral studies, then employers could hardly be
expected to believe otherwise.

Findings

On the whole, employers were more favourably than unfavourably disposed towards liberal studies, but most of the support was based on the assumption that there was some vocational centre in such studies, e.g. the study of English language. A minority showed disfavour and few respondents were prepared to support the mandatory introduction of the subject into all courses, even as a minimal proportion of the timetable.

The author argues the case for more research, particularly to enquire into industrial attitudes below executive level towards liberal studies, and to analyse the ethics of liberal studies' teaching.

Coding: 4

Educational methodology

Methods of learning: modes, techniques, styles and systems

A STUDY IN PROGRAMMED LEARNING by J. Hartley, D.Phil. thesis, University of Sheffield 1964. [part of thesis published as *Strategies for programmed learning*, Butterworths, 1972]

Aim
To compare studies between linear and branching programmes, particularly those developed by the author, and to measure the effectiveness of programmed instruction.

Method
The author reviews teaching machine systems, the previous research in linear and branching programmes, and in the social factors mundane to programmed instruction. In the second part he discusses the development of programmes — the linear programme and the skip branching programme — and describes a series of three comparison experiments. Finally, the programmes are evaluated and the research conclusions summarised. The people who took part in the experiments ranged from 68 secondary modern school girls to university students (3 experiments in Chapter 8).

Discussion
Essentially, in a linear programme, the student works through very small incremental steps in a linear sequence. The student's response,

which is almost always correct, is immediately reinforced by presenting the correct answer. In the case of multiple-choice branching programme, material is communicated in items larger than those in the linear programme, and is followed by questions designed to determine the effectiveness of the communication. If the student chooses the correct answer from a series of possible answers he continues to the next unit of information, but if he errs he may be allowed either to have a review of the initial item or directed to a further remedial sequence or sent back to an earlier stage in the programme. The skip branching programme is devised to meet criticisms of the two former types of programmed instruction. With the multiple-choice programme, each student is given a specific remedy, according to his error; with the skip branching system, the students making different errors on the same item all receive the same non-specific remedial sequence. The thesis, of course, describes the procedures in far greater detail and, thereby, with considerably more accuracy. Though the content will satisfy specialists in this field, the style of writing and the clarity of the thesis makes it easily understandable to the interested non-specialist.

Findings
Within the terms of particular experiments (the author considers generalisation inadvisable), three main findings emerge. Skip branching, when students were of the same initial knowledge, facilitated the test performance of higher-ability students more than an equivalent linear system; skip branching was superior to a linear system in terms of time taken when students differed widely in initial knowledge and ability and, finally, social factors affected results, for example, whether students worked individually or in pairs.

Coding: 5a

A COMPARISON OF GROUP AND INDIVIDUAL METHODS OF LEARNING FROM A SELF-INSTRUCTIONAL PROGRAMME ON ELEMENTARY PHYSICS by R. P. Amaria, M.Ed. thesis (2 vols), University of Birmingham 1966.

Aim

a To design a programmed course which would involve the solving of a scientific problem and in which there is opportunity for practical activity and experiment
b To compare the success of such a programmed course, given to individuals and to students in groups of two

Method

A 'linear' programme of 153 frames on the principle of moments with work on levers, involving practical work, was constructed. In a pilot study 36 10-year-old children from one class were allocated to homogeneous and heterogeneous pairs according to ability, or worked as individuals. A second study was conducted in a secondary modern (mixed) school, 72 12-year-old pupils from different classes of the first form being selected.

Discussion

Part 1 reviews programmed learning as a teaching technique, considers the problems of teaching science to different age groups, the suitability of programmed learning in various teaching situations, for example by CCTV, and the benefits of students working in pairs. The conduct of the experimental pilot study and the main study are described in considerable detail. As such, it provides a useful example of research in this field. Part 2 explains precisely how the programme on 'levers' was devised and presents the programme frame by frame. [The investigation is extended in 'A study of the factors influencing learning in Pairs', Ph.D. thesis, University of Birmingham 1970, using a sample of 745 secondary school pupils]

Findings

The results showed that in both the pilot and the main studies, group work as a whole achieved better scores than the work by individuals. Homogeneous pairs were significantly better than the heterogeneous pairs in the secondary school, but in primary school the heterogeneous pairs showed significantly better scores in the post-test on the content of the programme. The results showed more success for poor learners when working in groups than individually, and that high-ability pupils did not suffer, neither in their achievement scores nor by loss of time, by working with a low-ability partner.

The investigation results favoured group work in the use of programmed instruction involving practical work in science. The author suggests that further investigation into types of different groupings, *for different age levels,* in other disciplines are required to indicate the best criteria for grouping.

Coding: 5a

A STUDY OF THE EFFECTIVENESS OF A VARIETY OF TEACHING TECHNIQUES FOR REDUCING COLOUR PREJUDICE IN A MALE STUDENT SAMPLE (AGED 15-21) by H. J. Miller, M.Phil. thesis, University of London 1968.

Aim
To investigate the effects of a wide range of teaching methods employed to attack colour prejudice.

Method
About a thousand apprentices, principally in the London College of Printing, attending college for one day a week, and having one hour of each day timetabled for general studies, formed the sample. A pilot experiment testing 'personality' (feelings being stated by completing a modified form of the nine-point Bogardus Scale) and a pilot test of 'likes and interests' was first tried on 70 students of a similar type in another technical college. Attitude tests were administered at the beginning and at the end of the term to determine significant shifts in prejudice.

Discussion
The thesis is in five parts; the first contains a review of the literature, of reports of attempts to reduce colour prejudice, and of criticisms

of research into the reduction of prejudice. An analysis is made of the reasons for holding prejudices, of the problems of altering prejudiced attitudes and of the suggested techniques (vide P. Fordham and H. C. Wiltshire, 'Tests of Prejudice in an East African College', *Race,* vol 5, October 1963, pp 70-77 for a test of prejudice itself becoming a technique to combat the prejudice).

Chapter 2 is concerned with the problems of measuring attitudes; for example, the questions of disguised tests and the problems of validity and reliability. The experiment is described in Chapter 3 and the results are given in Chapter 4. Of interest are the particular teaching techniques used which fell into five categories: films, books, visiting speakers, discussion and other techniques. The other techniques included the use of an open attitude test, a gramophone record of Nelson Mandela's speech at the South African 'Riviona' trial, read by Peter Finch, formal debate, role-playing, and reviewing books about colour. Details are given of the backgrounds of the eleven teachers who took part in the experiment.

Findings

The results showed that colour prejudice was very high; that it increased during the period of the experiment; that most of the increase was caused by the attempts made to reduce it; and that the longer the attempts were maintained (up to a maximum of three hours) the greater was the increase in prejudice. Beyond three hours, there was an indication that prejudice may have been reduced.

It seemed better for the teacher to do nothing about the topic — especially so if he had a tender-minded and aesthetic temperament. If the topic was to be dealt with, a minimum of four hours' work would seem to be required. The only technique for which any success could be demonstrated involved the use of photographs of attractive coloured girls. Several techniques, including most forms of discussion and making incidental references to the colour problem, were shown to be particularly harmful.

Among the incidental conclusions was a piece of evidence favouring small classes; classes containing no more than twelve students did not in general increase in prejudice at all.

Coding: 5a, 3d

THE PLACE OF THE MUSEUM IN EDUCATION AND LEARNING by C. A. B. Steel, thesis for the Diploma of the Museums Association 1968 (28 pp). Available on application to the Education Officer, The Museums Association, 87 Charlotte Street, London W1P 2BX.

Aim
To examine the role of museums in education (with special reference to Sunderland).

Discussion
Surveys show that 50%-60% of visitors to the museum in Sunderland are under the age of 20 years, and that each child in the borough, in theory at least, visits the museum 2½ times per year. A survey of teachers in Sunderland revealed that 95% thought that their class would benefit from a visit to the museum, although 8% qualified their answer. However, there is some evidence that teachers receive insufficient instruction about museums in their training, and 45% of junior-school-teachers in Sunderland had no idea of what service could be offered to educationalists by museums; thus the success of the museum's schools' service was somewhat limited.

The place of the museum in adult education appears to be rather nebulous. Adults often buy publications and may learn from them. Adult associations, such as the WEA, use the museum for their activities, but few museums organise practical activities for adults, such as painting and sculpture classes in the galleries. Should not the museum be a social centre, an arts centre for adults? Perhaps education and learning ought to have a place in museums.

Coding: 5a, 5l, 7c(xxi)

THE EFFECTS OF DIRECTED AND UNDIRECTED ATTENTION ON THE RESPONSES OF COLLEGE OF EDUCATION STUDENTS TO PAINTINGS by W. A. W. Elloway, M.Ed. thesis, University of Manchester 1969.

Aim
To enquire into the nature of the aesthetic responses of College of

Education students and to discover the criteria, either implicit or explicit, which they apply when confronted by paintings. To discover the relative efficiency of undirected and directed attention in leading to the skills of aesthetic appreciation.

Method
109 male students who joined the Creative Design Department in Loughborough College of Education in 1967. In addition to aesthetic appreciation tests, tests of personality and cognitive factors (including verbal tests of intelligence) and questionnaires on previous art experiences were administered. Picture Preference Tests were given to an experimental group and to two control groups.

Discussion
The thesis includes a review of the literature concerned with experimental aesthetics, a description of the preparation of test materials to measure responses to paintings, an account of the development of an instrument to study the effects of directed perception and a discussion of 'what is meant by learning' in the context of the aesthetic appreciation of paintings.

The thesis also contains 30 transparencies used in testing — these include works by Gris, Braque, Rembrandt and Goya.

Findings
The effects of familiarity and past social pressures are revealed in differences between students' reactions to traditional and modern paintings, and the dominant part played by representation as a criterion of artistic excellence is demonstrated.

Mere exposure to pictures is unlikely to be very effective, although allowance must always be made for individual subjects whose attention is already directed by their informed interest. Indirect teaching techniques — those foregoing indoctrination — can be effective in producing many significant changes in the direction association with learning.

Coding: 5a, 5m(v), 3d

THE ROLE OF COMPUTERS IN EDUCATION by C. D. McBryde, M.Sc. thesis, University of Dublin 1969.

Aim

To review and assess the role of computer-assisted instruction.

Discussion

Chapter 1 deals with two groups of theories of learning: the Stimulus-Response Association Theory, arising out of the early experiments of scientists such as Thorndike and Pavlov, and the Gestalt Field and Cognition Theory, which began with Max Wertheimer (1880-1943).

Wertheimer considered that breaking consciousness into its parts destroyed what was most meaningful about it. As an example, one might consider the apparent movement in lighted advertising signs. To Wertheimer, this was striking evidence of the futility of breaking a whole into its parts; the components are separate electric lights going on and off, the resultant whole is an impression of movement. The word 'gestalt', which roughly translated means 'form', was applied to dynamic wholes.

Perhaps the most important contribution of Gestalt theory to our understanding of learning is the study of insight. One characteristic of good insight is reproductibility; that is when, for example, an ape is confronted with the same problem once more, it will quickly resort to the same solution. (Experiments of Wolfgang Kohler). Another characteristic of insight is the capability to transfer the method of attack to other similar problems. The two groups of theories are opposed to each other, although the differences between them are not as sharp as some of the more extreme protagonists would have us believe.

In Chapter 2 the author deals with programmed learning. He describes the linear type of programme, invented by Skinner, and shows how it follows precisely the Operant Conditioning theory of learning which is part of the stimulus-response group. Similarly, branching or multiple choice programmes are described, and the author shows how these types of programmes are essentially a tutorial process; the student's performance depends on what the tutor tells him; but what the tutor tells him depends in turn on what the pupil does. This continuous interaction provides a feedback which a branching programme uses to determine the next stage in the student's progress. Branching programmes do not follow any theory of learning in the way that linear programmes do, but by their use of whole units of information and by provision for insight in solving problems they are closely akin to the Gestalt theory. Remedial, review and skipping branching programmes are described and assessed.

Chapter 3 describes three systems of Computer-Assisted Instruction. Firstly, the system for organising content to review and teach educational subjects (SOCRATES), introduced in 1964. Secondly, the System Development Corporation type of programme which uses 35 mm. filmstrip (CLAS) introduced in 1961, and thirdly, Programmed Logic for Automatic Teaching Operations (PLATO) currently being developed at the Co-ordinated Science Laboratory of the University of Illinois.

The various types of programmes, their applications and their technological characteristics are discussed, with particular examples, in Chapter 4, under the headings: Branching Type Teaching Programmes, Tutorial Problem-Solving, the Making and Analysis of Tests, Desk Calculators and Simulators.

Findings
In his concluding chapter, the author writes '. . . the greatest hope for the future is in an improvement in the inter-action between students and computer. At the present time students are restricted to a fixed form of input . . . one would hope that . . . students will be able to phrase their answers as they please and the computer will interpret them'.

Coding: 5a, 3d

CONFLICT AND AGREEMENT ON THE EDUCATIONAL ROLE OF ART GALLERIES by D. Addison, thesis for the Diploma of the Museums Association 1971 (54 pp). Available on application to the Education Officer, The Museums Association, 87 Charlotte Street, London W1P 2BX.

Aim
To examine the role of the provincial Art Gallery in relation to formal and informal education, with particular emphasis on the Bradford and the West Riding of Yorkshire areas.

Method
A short, exploratory questionnaire was used as a basis for personal, informal interviews.

Discussion
Art galleries consist of collections and buildings; the task of their staff is to conserve and preserve the works in their collections, and then to make them available to the general public whenever possible. They catalogue their collections, purchase or borrow to supplement their collections, give information and advice, and identify and record works of art.

Representatives from primary schools, secondary schools, further education and local authorities and elected councillors all agreed that, in general, art galleries paid little attention to providing popular information, that is, information readily assimilated and understood by any member of the general public. But the staff of art galleries and museums felt that, whilst members of the general public understood the demands made upon the galleries, they did not comprehend the problems involved in providing such a popular service.

All those questioned gave priority to the role of the art gallery as a place of entertainment, as well as of education. Both an 'arts centre' and a 'resources centre' was implied in most answers to questions about the role of galleries. Generally, the need for personal contact between the gallery staff and the public was emphasised.

There was some disagreement about the location of galleries; some argued for a centre-of-town site, whilst others thought that car and coach parking facilities were more important than any particular location.

Findings

Art galleries should be regarded as the centre for activities related to the visual arts. Galleries should not impose an admission charge. They should provide refreshment rooms, rest areas and toilets.

Galleries should adopt a three-fold division of their premises; firstly, for permanent, on-view collections; secondly, for temporary exhibitions based on the permanent collection; and thirdly, for temporary and travelling exhibitions.

Due regard should be made to staging both 'popular' and 'educational' exhibitions, and far more importance should be attached to the extra-mural adult education role of galleries. For example, strong recommendations are made for the appointment of qualified educationalists to the staff of galleries, and the greater provision of publications, both specialist and popular.

Appendices give specific details or examples of the author's recommendations.

Coding: 5a, 5l, 5m(v), 7c(xxi)

Special methods for particular age groups or disadvantaged groups

---

THE PROVISION OF DAY-TRAINING CENTRES FOR THE SEVERELY SUB-NORMAL IN THE NORTH WEST 1959-1964 by R. Hertzog, M.Ed. thesis, University of Manchester 1967.

Aims

a To study the provision of day-training centre facilities by the Lancashire and Cheshire County Boroughs and the North West England and North Wales County Councils in the period 1959-1964
b To make a detailed study of the facilities and methods of education of four junior centres, three adult centres and a holiday centre for juniors

Method

The main aspects of the investigation are divided into two parts. Part 1 consists of a historical survey of the changing attitudes of the public to the mentally deficient, the consequent changes in legislation, the growth of state aid and the types of available centres, the pupils or students, the staff, the buildings, the curricula and the teaching methods. Part 2 deals with the conditions in day-centres in the North West from 1959-1964, and gives the impression of particular centres which the author visited.

Discussion

In 1958, 12,583 adults had been reported by authorities as suitable for training in the occupational and training centres, of whom only 5,999 were receiving such training. Priority had, after 1945, been given to children, 9,804 of whom, out of 12,387 regarded as suitable for training, were attending day-centres. A Ministry of Health circular 9/59 suggested that the provision of training for adults required that sufficient centres should be established to cater for a wide variation of individual needs, and that these should be entirely separate from junior centres.

Whilst many new methods, often translated from the methods used in primary schools, are being introduced in junior centres, many severely sub-normal boys and girls are subjected to a routine of senseless boredom. Therefore, they bring little in the way of accomplishment to the adult centres, measured in terms of personable behaviour. However, between 1960 and 1964 in 17 towns with a population of nearly 3 million people there were considerable improvements in both the quality of the centres and the provision of places for adults. But still about twice as many places were estimated to be needed as were provided.

Findings

Several areas had failed to provide separate adult training centres by the end of 1964; nevertheless, the number of adult places in separate centres per 1,000 head of population in the region studied compared favourably with the average provision in all centres in England and Wales. The undoubted progress in physical conditions should be matched by improvements in the organised educational programme and the author suggests, firstly, that more direction or control from the Department of Education and Science is desirable and secondly,

that training centres should reduce their isolation from the main-
stream of normal education.

Coding: 5b, 1c(ix), 7c(iv), 7a, 5l, 4

Reading and written work

THE ABILITY OF TRAINING COLLEGE STUDENTS TO UNDER-
STAND WHAT THEY READ by E. L. Black, M.Ed. thesis,
University of Manchester 1953.

Aim
To explore the problem of educated adult readers' understanding of
what they read.

Method
Examples of errors in comprehension were collected from the work
of students in one men's College of Education. These errors were
then classified under nine headings, so that an objective comprehension test for Training College students could be constructed.
Three experimental versions of the test were given to three groups of
270, 180 and 390 students, and from the results of the pilot tests
evolved a single test, consisting of seven passages and sixty questions,
all of which proved to discriminate sharply.

The various stages of the pilot-testing procedure were applied to a
sample of students drawn from 20 colleges, in which the sexes were
approximately equal. The final test was given to 240 students from
four colleges; test reliability being calculated by using the Kuder-
Richardson formula.

Discussion
The first chapter points to the importance of reading as a method of
weighing and considering problems, and the consequent need to
understand the written text. After reviewing previous research, for
example, that of Davis and Vernon, the author considers students'

errors in comprehension under nine headings, viz vocabulary, context, images, background information, allusions, the intention of the writer, irony, preconceptions and sentence structure.

Chapters 5-10 describe in detail the objective comprehension text, the construction of this test, some further technical and associated problems arising from test construction and the results. The final chapters are concerned with a discussion of the implications of the results, an examination of the possible causes of errors in comprehension, some suggestions for helping training students to read more effectively and the author's conclusions.

Findings

The errors in comprehension made by Training College students are important and frequent enough to merit the attention of tutors, but the types of errors are complex and varied. Many students do not recognise an author's intention, and many fail to detect irony.

The objective comprehension test of 45 minutes' time limit had only a slightly higher degree of reliability than the 20 minute test. Some of the evidence supports the view of Wall and Vernon that the most serious type of vocabulary difficulty for older readers occurs when the idea behind the word is complex, or abstract, or novel. Some evidence supports Vernon's view that there are important weaknesses in all mechanical methods of measuring the difficulty of a passage, (e.g.) the Thorndike Word List and the Flesch formula.

Finally, the author argues that not only English, but all subject specialist tutors ought to take account of students' difficulties in understanding text or reference books.

Coding: 5c, 6

BIOLOGICAL VOCABULARY IN SCHOOL AND ADULT LIFE — A STUDY OF THE VOCABULARY BURDEN OF SECONDARY SCHOOL BIOLOGY AND OF THE VALUE OF THE VOCABULARY IN ADULT LIFE WITH PARTICULAR REFERENCE TO THE NEEDS OF WOMEN by M. J. Tattersall, M.Ed. thesis, University of Birmingham 1964.

Aim

To identify the essential vocabulary of school biology and to find out

a how much of the vocabulary actually learnt is, in fact, essential for understanding and communicating the concepts of 'O' level biology

b how far this vocabulary prepares girls for understanding biological articles and broadcast programmes encountered in everyday life.

Method

The investigation is divided into two sections, of which Section 1 is concerned with the school biology vocabulary. This was suspected to be over-large because girls complained about it, and the work of American researchers carried out 20 years previously had shown it to be so. Ten textbooks were studied and a list of 2,028 terms compiled. When the criteria of frequency of usage in the textbooks and the teachers' judgments of each word were applied, only 45% of these were found to be needed for an understanding of the concepts involved and 16% were identified as really essential, that is, satisfying both criteria. Thus a great deal of wasted effort was judged to be expended.

Section 2 is concerned with the vocabulary encountered in everyday life. 60 women were asked to list their current reading material. From this, eight newspapers and magazines were selected because of their popularity. Added to them were *The Listener* for radio programmes and one television programme, 'Emergency Ward 10' studied 'live'. From these ten sources 1,705 terms were listed, of which 33.5% were found to be in common use and 10.6% were deemed to be essential. The two types of vocabulary were then compared and contrasted, using the essential lists as samples.

Findings

It was shown that, whilst many terms taught in school biology were unnecessary, a considerable number of terms which ought to have been taught were being ignored. This was felt to be due to schools' choice of topics to be studied, since the vocabulary used naturally pertained to the topic chosen. Too much importance was attached to the demands of examinations and too little to human interests. For example, perfunctory attention was paid in school biology to two physiological processes in the life of most women, the question of childbirth and the attendant problem of menstruation. Of a popular television programme the author comments 'a patronising exploitation of the layman's respectful admiration for professional expertise; a kind of cynical script-writer's one-upmanship, without any saving grace of explanation or demonstration'.

Coding: 5c, 5m(xvii), 5h, 2c

MULTI-MEDIA INSTRUCTIONAL SYSTEMS IN ADULT EDUCATION, WITH SPECIAL REFERENCE TO INFORMATION RETRIEVAL FROM TEXTBOOKS by G. T. C. Squires, Ph.D. thesis, University of Edinburgh 1970.

Aim
To analyse the concept of information in instructional systems for adults, outlining the implications of this analysis for the design and use of textbooks as information stores and to formulate hypotheses for further experimental research.

Discussion
Research has shown that both in mass communication and formal instruction, factors other than the medium are important. The instructional setting, the message or content, the type of audience, provide a framework for the use of any media.

Textbooks are a form of media; they provide a device which can be either source-controlled or receiver-controlled. In the first case, the learner follows the sequence of instruction devised by the source by reading the book from beginning to end in serial order; in the second instance, he uses retrieval devices such as the index, table of contents, and the headings, to devise his own sequence, thus controlling the information he receives.

An outline for the design of textbooks as information stores is given, which derives from an analysis of the retrieval process. For adult students particularly, the possible advantages of developing the use of retrieval systems in education are both short-term, in the form of increased learning and motivation over a single course, and long-term, in that learning to retrieve information can be considered as one aspect of learning how to learn.

Chapter 1 is a description of the general communication process; Chapter 2 turns to a systems approach in adult education which places media along with all other resources in a wider context of objectives, methods and evaluation. The analysis of the concept of information comes in Chapter 3, which is another possible starting point for the reader of the thesis. Chapter 4 deals with textbooks per se and analyses relevant research, whilst a similar approach to 'learner control' follows in Chapter 5.

The design of textbooks for retrieval is discussed in Chapter 6 and examples of various devices are discussed in Chapter 7. Chapters 8 and 9 are devoted to the investigation of structural tables and of non-linear texts respectively, and the final chapter offers suggestions for further research and contains the author's conclusions.

The thesis includes an extract from *Adult education for developing countries,* by R. Prosser, in which the problems of using radio, television, correspondence tuition and programmed learning to reach the mass of the people in Africa are considered.

Coding: 5c, 5a, 5k, 1c(x)

Broadcasting, closed-circuit and video-tape systems

EDUCATIONAL BROADCASTING AND ADULT EDUCATION by
D. F. Anderson, M.Sc.(Social Sciences) thesis, University of Edinburgh 1972.

Aim
To examine the idea of 'educative' as opposed to formal educational broadcasting, and to analyse actual examples of the 'educative' in the output of the British Broadcasting Corporation during 1970-1971.

Method
The author classified every programme, week by week, as printed in the *Radio Times*, into 'educative' and 'otherwise', and systematically listened, or viewed, over a period of one year.

Discussion
Chapters 1 and 2 consider the general rationale of the 'educative' as opposed to the explicitly educational, and places this idea in a setting of theories about mass education and educability during the past two centuries. He discusses in particular the theory of Baschwitz. Relevant sociological and psychological studies of the mass media, alienation studies, the idea of 'learning without involvement' and the contributions of Trenaman on communication and comprehension are the subjects of Chapter 3. In the fourth chapter, a 'curricula' type of analysis is made of the BBC's educative output during one year, from which study the author makes some recommendations.

Recommendations
Firstly, because enough has been achieved in educative programming in such series as 'Woman's Hour' or 'Doomwatch', or sufficient studies have been made to suggest that educative programming is a practical possibility, and, secondly, because, in spite of such successes, there is no overt policy-making or research and development in the field of educative programming, and, thirdly, because adult educationalists have, on their side, not been as active in this

field as one would expect, the author offers the following suggestions:

1. Adult education methods and principles could be included in the training programmes ot producers of educative series and, conversely, adult educators should learn something about the practicalities of radio or television production.

2. The author considers the BBC Advisory Committee structure is too narrow, and suggests a wider brief to include the educative as well as the educational.

3. Producers and adult educators should meet in workshop sessions rather than in the usual seminar situation, and should co-operate in forward planning.

4. Finally, he suggests some action research, the provision of experimental series to provide both producers and field organisers with the necessary feedback and evaluation, and, of course, pleads that the results of such research should be made available.

Two interesting features of this thesis are, firstly, the author's concern that the educative programme should not be exiled into a Fourth Channel educational 'ghetto' and, secondly, the record of the splendid contribution made by the BBC to education in its broadest sense. The author estimates the 'educative' accounted for 25% of television and Radio 2 air time, and amounted to about 35% of Radio 4 air time; in all, about 2,000 programmes during the year.

Coding: 5h, 7(xix), lc(x), 8b

THE USE OF CLOSED-CIRCUIT TELEVISION IN THE TEACHING OF GEOGRAPHY AND THE TRAINING OF GEOGRAPHY TEACHERS by D. G. Mills, M.Ed. thesis, University of Leicester 1966.

Aim

a To review the development of instructional television, particularly closed-circuit television in both the United States and the United Kingdom

b To review the investigation made into the teaching of geography by CCTV at Kidbrooke School and to compare the results of the teaching of other subjects in the school by the same method and the results obtained from Warblington Havant

c To investigate the use of CCTV in the training of geography teachers, with particular emphasis on the attitudes of students towards the medium and to compare what can be seen in the classroom with that which cannot be seen on a television screen

Method

The thesis examines the use of a CCTV system which linked Avery Hill College of Education to Kidbrooke Comprehensive School, a girls' school of about 2,000 pupils. The pubils' ability to recall was tested by written work and their attitudes by questionnaire; students' attitudes were appraised from the results of questionnaires and interviews.

Discussion

Chapters 1 and 2 discuss the subject matter arising out of the first two aims of the thesis. In Chapter 3 the students attitudes are examined in detail. Briefly, most students disliked the artificial atmosphere of television-monitored lessons, but liked the discussions arising out of telerecordings of lessons. Students agreed that, as CCTV lessons required thorough preparation, the use of CCTV improved their teaching skills.

Findings

Consequently, the principal conclusions of Chapter 4 are that, so far as students are concerned, the most useful attribute of CCTV for their training purposes lies in telerecording their lessons. Furthermore, they felt that if a bank of telerecordings could be created, these examples would provide an essential, practical focus for their discussions and lectures on education, and would provide a better method of cross pollination of teaching practices than exhortation.

So far as pupils are concerned, CCTV could be stimulating, provided that the teacher using the system was enthusiastic; without this fundamental teacher attitude there was no appreciable difference in the actual results of recall between CCTV and conventional lessions. lessons.

The author found that the equipment used by the College was less than adequate, and to some extent the technology used vitiated the conclusiveness of the results.

Coding: 5i, 5m(xix)

STUDIES IN LEARNING – WITH PARTICULAR REFERENCE TO LEARNING FROM TELEVISION by P. E. James, Ph.D. thesis, University of Liverpool 1972.

Aim

To report three studies in which various methods of presenting meaningful material for maximum learning efficiency are discussed: that is, comparing the effectiveness of video-tape and booklet presentation and testing various forms of video-tape presentation in combination with various forms of student participation.

Method

Experiment A – 49 students, aged between 17 and 22 years, were divided into two groups, one to be instructed in the use of a desk calculator by video-tape with a hand-out, the other to be taught by an instruction booklet presentation. Programmed-learning techniques were applied to both methods of instruction.

Experiment B_1 – 31 male and female student nurses in hospital x, and 43 female SRNs in hospital y, split into 5 groups, were shown a video-tape about X-ray procedures, to assess the amount of recall that occurred under four presentations of a video-tape. The video-tape was shown continuously for 22 minutes; the X-ray procedures were shown two at a time and the video-tape was stopped to allow the nurses to be questioned; the X-ray procedures were shown one at a time, stopped and nurses questioned; and the video-tape was shown twice.

Experiment B_2 – 50 second-year student nurses (including 3 males), in three hospitals, were shown a video-tape which was stopped at intervals to enable students to answer questions in a booklet. Post tests were administered, completed and collected, following which the motivation and post-educational achievement questionnaire was given.

Experiment C – Video-tape was used to provide a feedback of performance; 18 boys aged 11-12 years were taught a 7-bounce routine on a trampoline, 8 with video feedback (each boy being shown the playback of his own performance immediately) and 10 with non-video feedback. (The Fisher Exact Probability Test, Siegal 1956, was used).

The main burden of the thesis is the description of the three experiments in considerable detail, and the specification of the statistical techniques and scientific methods used.

Discussion

The author reviews research on the effectiveness of instructional television, particularly the most recent attempts to interpret findings on the basis of information and behaviour theory. The research literature argues for the value of student participation in learning from films, and suggests that the application of programmed-learning principles might provide a possible theoretical background by which to analyse experimental results. Her experiments are concerned with two main themes of investigation:

1 that which concerns different media for presenting the same learning material

2 that which concerns different presentation conditions of the same medium.

Findings

Experiment A — Both methods of learning were equally efficient, but the operation of a calculating machine is, perhaps, not the type of skill best taught by video-tape. The presentation methods used on the video-tape were criticised and both groups showed a lack of 'symbol similarity' between the calculating machine and past learning, which suggests that aspects of the task itself required extra analysis.

Experiment B — Programmed video-tape was a significantly better method of learning when compared with a double showing of the same material; this superiority was retained after one month.

Programmed-learning principles applied to video-tape worked successfully when:

1 response opportunities for the students were restricted to difficult parts of the video-tape

2 response opportunities were frequent and the responses required were short

3 response opportunities were given immediately after the information had been presented

4 a frame of reference indicated the number of points required in a detailed answer

5 verbal feedback of response was given.

The assessment of incorrect prior knowledge was an important aspect of the pre-test, as there was a tendency for these wrong responses to be repeated after the video-tape had been shown. This was less marked under repetition conditions. Too much existing knowledge was presumed in the video-tape programme; stressing of the principles of radiography did not seem to help retention, but the repetition of spoken items on the video-tape considerably helped recall.

Experiment C — The third study was concerned with the comparison of two methods of supplying feedback when learning a physical skill, whether visual (recorded on video-tape) or verbal. Although the expected advantages of video-feedback were not realised, the rate of improvement was faster when feedback was recorded on video-tape; learners with a wide range of verbal ability benefited from visual feedback. Visual feedback has an incentive value and encourages self-criticism.

Generally, the knowledge of terms used on a video-tape should be assessed by pilot sample before recording a programme. If specific objectives are outlined and the task is carefully analysed, then programmed video-tape is more efficient than repetition, but repetition is a valuable tool *in the programme construction*. Captioned items with accompanying speech are sometimes remembered best, but not necessarily so with every video-tape.

Coding: 5a, 3d, 5c, KB1335

Film

THE CRITICAL EVALUATION OF FILMS BY REFERATORY GRID — VALUE PATTERNS OF WORKING AND MIDDLE CLASS YOUTHS COMPARED TO THOSE OF PROFESSIONAL CRITICS by M.V. Carver, Ph.D. thesis, University of London 1967.

Aim
To discuss differences in taste in relation to the mass media as a problem in aesthetics and in psychological aesthetics.

Method
30 day-release apprentices of a mean age of 18 years 3 months, 30 middle-class direct-grant sixth formers of a mean age of 17 years 10 months, and 15 professional film critics, rated 10 films each (chosen from their ordinary filmgoing experience) on a 20-construct grid. This method relies heavily on George A. Kelly's *The psychology of personal constructs,* vols 1 & 2, published in 1955.

Discussion
The first chapter suggests that a distinction is made between personal preferences among aesthetic objects and aesthetic judgments of 'goodness' or 'badness' which are referred to extra-personal criteria. Since it is conceded that criteria vary from one judgment situation to the next, a question arises as to whether, when disagreements in overall judgments occur, different criteria are in use, or whether there are differences in experience, skill or sensibility in the individuals who disagree, such that the same criteria appear to be satisfied by different objects. However, a problem in the measurement of criteria arises from the fact that it is rarely possible, within the normal language of criticism (professional or lay) to separate completely the descriptive from the evaluative elements. But, by measuring the relationship of each concept in a value system to a succession of overall judgments, it becomes possible to trace, and to compare, value patterns. An examination follows of certain aesthetic theories concerning the differentia between art and non-art, particularly with reference to the cinema, and of certain critical attitudes to the mass media. The aim is to discover the value concepts most likely to discriminate between expert and mass audiences (if the hypothesis that different sections of the public use different value-systems is true).

Chapters 3-7 describe the investigative processes in detail; the design of the main investigation, the structure and content in individual grids and public systems, the content of the constructs, e.g. 'no moral' versus 'points to a good moral', the elements, i.e. 326 films, including 'Goldfinger' and some related experiments.

Perhaps the most interesting of the author's speculations is that both sets of young people have reached a certain level of maturity *in relation to their own subcultures.* The apprentices have, seemingly, 'settled' for a less sophisticated system at this point, but the sixth formers, on the contrary, have become aware of the possibility of mastering a higher-level system on their own.

From the author's study, the specialists in the system show the highest degree of consistency, modulation and (for its own users) meaningfulness. They employ a richer vocabulary which is highly developed and refined for the purposes of analysing and communicating the experience and value of a film. Consequently, although the values and tastes of 'expert' critics may be questioned, and although these may be difficult to transfer to the non-expert, some familiarity with the language of film criticism may be a pre-requisite to an awareness of a person's own capacity to respond fully to the experience of seeing a film.

Coding: 5g, 3d

Correspondence based courses

A STUDY OF DIFFICULTIES AND DISTASTES IN PRO-GRAMMED CORRESPONDENCE EDUCATION by C. K. Basu, D.Phil. thesis, University of London 1968.

Aim
To study the difficulties and distastes of adult students using programmed texts on modern mathematics.

Method
The participants in this field study were 381 men and women from the British Army and the Fire Service. 146 of them studied programmed texts on modern mathematics in a classroom situation; 135 studied modern mathematics in a conventional correspondence situation; 100 studied the same subject by programmed corres-pondence.

In addition to tests on the understanding of the subject matter, three questionnaires were constructed for identifying difficulties and distastes. Results were analysed by using the statistical techniques of factor analysis, the analysis of co-variance with multiple co-variates, stepwise regression analysis and chi-square tests.

Discussion

Education and training in a changing world imply that educational methods and techniques must become more efficient and more economic to cater for current mass needs. But how can we best combine a high quality of education with that quantity which will ensure the supply of manpower in a technological age, and at the same time preserve the individual's right to learn and develop? The author examines the role of instructional methods and media and the integration of modern media with self-instructional methods in the context of this question.

Correspondence education, firstly as a strategy of teaching, secondly as a part of an integrated newer media course, and thirdly as part of a systems approach, is examined in Chapter 2 (Solurov's theories). There is also a discussion of the historical development of correspondence education and of the student success rates. Chapter 3 reviews programmed instruction in a similar way. Chapters 4, 5 and 6 respectively describe the design of the field study, state and discuss the results and the conclusions.

Findings

84% of respondents preferred classroom mathematics lessons. Even when following a correspondence course, 87% would prefer to study with an instructor available to help them with their difficulties, rather than by working on their own. 67% of the respondents indicated that there was not enough information in the conventional correspondence course to set them right when they made errors. 74% indicated that, when they had answered a question, they wished to know whether they were right or wrong. 72% wanted tests before and after *each* lesson. These techniques were not used by the correspondence courses of the two colleges used by the Army.

Significantly, the lack of the human element was more frequently felt by the conventional correspondence course students than by those following the programmed correspondence course, possibly because programmed instruction has a better logical organisation, pays more regard to objectives, gives the opportunity to practise application and gives feedback on the results and provides re-inforcement facilities. The female sample seemed more favourably disposed than males towards programmed instruction in a classroom situation, but this could have been due to the greater appropriateness of the course to their immediate needs.

The effectiveness of programmed mathematics given in a correspondence situation does not differ significantly from that found in a classroom situation: conventional correspondence courses are less effective than either. All students' difficulties and distastes are increased when the content of the course is not clearly related to their needs. Finally, administrators of such courses in the Army are far from satisfied that these courses are really cost-effective when postage, printing and so on are taken into account.

Coding: 5j, 5a, 5m(xix)

A COMPARATIVE STUDY OF SOME ASPECTS OF EDUCATION BY CORRESPONDENCE by D. G. Toon, M.Ed. thesis, University of Manchester 1969.

Aim
A comparative study of the organisation of, methodology of, and courses offered by, correspondence institutions, principally those in the United Kingdom, North America and Australasia.

Discussion
The importance of education by correspondence cannot be gauged from the small volume of readily available published information. In Britain the annual enrolment in correspondence schools was estimated to be 300,000 in 1966; the New Zealand technical Correspondence Institute catered for 13,000 students. The Correspondence Schools for Higher Education in the USSR matriculated 1,205,600 students and produced 337,700 graduates in the ten years between 1945 and 1955. The Centre National de Télé-Enseignment at Vanves had 10,000 students in 1950 and 124,701 students in 1966/67. The University of Missouri's Correspondence Study Department reported a like expansion of enrolments. New national systems incorporating correspondence education divisions, e.g. Malawi, Zambia and Botswana, indicate the importance of correspondence tuition in the world today.

The author examines the reasons for the development and utilisation of correspondence education in eight categories:

1. geographical — the isolation of the individual
2. absence of tuition — traditional or otherwise in a required subject
3. medical reasons prohibiting student attendance
4. the effects of war producing an emergency system
5. socio-economic circumstances inspiring governments to provide correspondence tuition
6. the inadequacy of available traditional facilities — e.g. lack of accommodation
7. student preference
8. safety net or second chance education

Against this background the author attempts to explain the lack of prestige of education by correspondence and, in accounting for this, examines fraudulent practice and the pedagogical limitations of teaching at a distance. He traces the building up of government legislation to obliterate doubtful practices (in the United Kingdom there was established, in 1969, a voluntary accreditation scheme, i.e. through the Council for the Accreditation of Correspondence Colleges), and the devices used by the correspondence schools to overcome the isolation of the student. (The Open University, which began its operation in May 1969, is naturally not discussed in this thesis, other than in a mention of the deliberations of the Planning Committee.)

The claims made by correspondence educators for the correspondence method as a viable pedagogic tool are considered, as are the suggestions they have made for its future.

At least one-half of the thesis consists of appendices giving detailed examples of the literature and organisation of various types of correspondence schools. Example 29 is of a badly organised and printed correspondence course. An extensive bibliography is also provided.

Findings

The volume of provision of education by correspondence is likely to increase. There is an ever-present danger of exploitation by the unethical operator/entrepreneur. On the whole, the advances in correspondence tuition are through its incorporation in a 'systems' approach to education.

Costing estimates, comparing correspondence and traditional education, are highly complex; comparative costs of classroom and correspondence education per student per year in New South Wales,

Australia, in 1965 show that correspondence education cost 17% more. Similarly, Ewing reports that 'the cost of educating children by correspondence has been constantly the same as, or a little more than, the cost of classroom education, leaving the cost of school buildings out of the calculation'. However, given these reservations, the author considers that 'there can be no hard and fast rule laid down for the comparative costs'.

Coding: 5j, 5k

Composite and multi-media courses

HOW LECTURERS USED MULTI-MEDIA MATERIALS — A REPORT ON THE BBC/NEC LONGER COURSES 1969/70 (39 pp). Only available on request from the Further Education Officer, BBC, London W1A 1AA.

Aim
To investigate the success of tutorial classes using some or all of the components of the BBC/NEC Longer Courses produced in 1969/70, namely 'Square Two' (mathematics — television), 'Man in Society' (social psychology — television and radio) and 'Reading to Learn' (literature and history — radio).

Method
Each broadcast series was based on BBC textbooks which were extended by correspondence courses. Students could listen to, or watch, the broadcast programmes, read the BBC book, enrol at a tutorial class, take the correspondence course and, of course, do several or all of these things.

In May 1970, 400 questionnaires were sent to selected colleges, university extra-mural departments and adult education centres; 80% responded giving comprehensive background information about their use of the longer courses. In June 1970, 22 lecturers, or 15% of those running courses, were personally interviewed. Between January and June 1970, the BBC Further Education Officers visited tutorial classes and wrote detailed progress reports, and these were made available to the author.

Discussion

Two hundred tutorial classes were organised in January 1970 and by June 85% were still running. 2,500 students enrolled in January, most of whom were classified by lecturers as middle-class. Out of 133 colleges, 85% had BBC TV, 80% had VHF radio, 92% had audio-tape-recorders, 23% video-tape-recorders and 17% closed-circuit television.

Out of 44 colleges following 'Square Two', 32 classes met on Wednesday (TV evening), 43 met between 18.30 and 19.30 hours and 42 had classes lasting 2-2½ hours. In the case of 'Man in Society', followed by 58 colleges, 37 classes met on Thursday (TV evening) whilst only 7 met on Friday (radio evening); 5 met from 18.30 to 19.30 hours, and 53 had classes lasting 2-2½ hours. Perhaps it was because so many colleges had audio-tape recorders that they preferred to orient the classes around the TV programme. 'Reading to Learn' was followed by 49 colleges; 27 classes met on Wednesday, (radio evening), 47 met between 18.30 and 19.30 hours and 43 had classes lasting 2-2½ hours.

Findings

These are detailed in four sections; the organisation of courses, lecturers' views about the three courses, the patterns of use and suggestions for future developments. From questionnaire replies, it seemed that well over one-half of the 'Square Two' lecturers were satisfied with all the components, compared with over one-third of the 'Man in Society' group and just under one-third of the 'Reading to Learn' lecturers. The 'Square Two' lecturers interviewed had very few complaints about the course content, but three objected to the amount of work sheets and questionnaires sent to the students. On the whole, the 'Man in Society' lecturers liked the course content but criticised the co-ordination of components, the volume of material in the course and the lack of prior information. Half the 'Reading to Learn' lecturers were displeased with the course content and had 'virtually stopped' using the BBC book and the radio programmes; they complained of too much being in the course and of a lack of prior information.

In general two features stand out; the need for prior information before such a series and the dependence of a multi-media project, with a face-to-face element, on the tutor's favourable attitude.

Coding: 5k, 5h, 5j, 8c(xix), 8c(ix)

A SUMMARY OF THE REPORT ON LEARNING EFFECTIVE-NESS USING A TELEVISION LANGUAGE SERIES 1970 (9 pp). Only available on request from the Further Education Officer, BBC, London W1A 1AA.

Aim
To find out how much was learnt by people following the BBC TV series, Italian for beginners 'Si Dice Cosi'.

Method
Both written and oral language laboratory taped tests were conducted after the transmission of the final programme in the series.

Discussion
The series aimed to teach simple but correct spoken Italian orally to a wide general public assumed to have very little or no previous knowledge of Italian. A sample of 2,704 students, perhaps the keenest and most serious, was contacted by post immediately the series was completed. Those with no prior knowledge of Italian (Group A), 1,670, were sent a voluntary written test with the questionnaire, which they were asked to complete without reference to the supporting books. In addition, a group of 30 people were tested in a language laboratory.

47% of Group A returned completed questionnaires; their age distribution was slightly skewed towards those under 20 years, 61% were women, 50% were professional and highly skilled workers, 21% were students, 91% knew one or more other modern languages.

1,034 questionnaires were sent to those who said they knew 'some' Italian (Group B). This group obviously used the series to consolidate and improve their knowledge of Italian, so that reactions from this audience would be different from the reactions of Group A.

Findings

Given the dubious nature of setting a written test for an oral course, the doubtful theoretical nature of the selection of the sample and the lack of familiarity with the conditions of a language laboratory, the conclusions are highly tentative, suggestive rather than prescriptive.

The overall results of the written test of Group A were extremely encouraging; most would, it seemed, be able to understand spoken Italian and deal with straightforward tourist situations. But the results of the 30 language laboratory volunteers suggests that there is a far less satisfactory level of Italian than was inferred in the results of the written tests. Group B apparently gained more from the series than Group A; 74% of the former group said that the series was 'good', 4% that it was 'moderate'; none considered the series 'not good'.

Coding: 5k, 5m(xi), 5h, 2a

COURSE PRODUCTION AT THE OPEN UNIVERSITY by B. N. Lewis. Three of a series of papers published in the *British Journal of Educational Technology, No 1, vol 2; No 2, vol 2; No 3, vol 3 1971 (43 pp)*.

Aim

To highlight some of the problems that arise from the production of course materials when produced as part of a collaborative team effort.

Discussion

The Open University, inaugurated in January 1971, has a nationwide intake of about 25,000 students per year; by number of students it is the largest University in the United Kingdom and one of the largest in Europe. It is also the first full-scale multi-media system of higher education in the United Kingdom. Through the provision of correspondence materials, radio and television broadcasts, home experimental kits and the like, the University will enable a large number of adults to study for degrees (and other higher education courses) in their own homes and on a part-time basis. These courses are for adults who may have none of the usual university entry qualifications.

The first paper of this series describes the nature of the study materials, some of the problems of course writers, the problems of constructing home assignments, particularly if the marking is to be computer assisted, and the role of a planning and production system.

The second paper describes the main teaching arrangements; the correspondence units prepared for home study, the home experimental kits, the weekly broadcasts, the study centres and the summer schools. Networks of production flow diagrams which broadly summarise the processes are provided.

The third paper is concerned with a discussion of some of the recurring problems of planning and scheduling. The essence of the problem is the speed at which the staff have to produce materials in a world of deadlines and economic constraints. Regrettably, network planning methods, when at all specific, are almost totally inapplicable to the Open University's course production problems. The author amplifies this statement because the University has often been criticised for failing to make greater use of these methods. He argues that, because each course is created under different circumstances, with different aims and philosophies, and different target audiences in mind, the more precise the network system planned, the less acceptable it becomes to particular individual course teams. Thus, the Open University has developed practical methods of signalling the four main variables, the activities, the products, the people who perform the activities and the time over which the activities are carried out.

Coding: 5k, 5j, 7c(ii), KB846

Learning environments — physical

A RECREATION PLAN FOR THE NORTH EAST COAST by K. Laidler, M.Sc. thesis, University of Wales 1970.

Aim

To detail a series of co-ordinated proposals for the optimum development of recreational facilities along the North East coast of England (from Berwick to Teesmouth).

Method

By use of a tabulated sieve technique taking into account such factors as 'water sports suitability' and 'historical interest'.

Discussion

The thesis is an inter-disciplinary study, linking the problems of environmental planning to a particular recreative aspect of adult education, that is, the development of water sports. The author begins with a statement of the problems encountered in undertaking such analyses, and the need for a regionally integrated plan at this level to overcome them. On this basis he formulates goals and objectives.

As an example of the problems, he notes that recreational associations exist at differing geographic levels and at differing levels of participation. Allowance must, therefore, be made for the whole spectrum of recreational activities, from individualistic to intensely communal. Also, it is difficult to estimate the latent demand for facilities; cost, awareness, accessibility are obviously important, but in fact many participants are not members of official clubs, so that their needs and demands are 'unregistered'. Demand can change with fashion; the demand for bowling alleys assessed by club membership changed from 10,000 in 1963 to 25,000 in 1964, to 15,000 in 1965.

However, given these problems, the inter-related factors of demand and supply are examined, and a synthesis of these complementary facets leads logically to the formulation of high level regional proposals.

As special attention is given throughout the study to coastal water sports provision, a matrix technique is developed to give a greater degree of objectivity to the sitings and standards of marinas and other water-orientated facilities. The results of this technique are incorporated into the section on detailed policy proposals, along with the other information. Some areas of the coastline are examined individually, and a section of photographs providing a visual record of the coastline is also included in the thesis.

It is worth noting that, although leisure time is increasing, 42% of the working population have no more than 2 weeks' annual paid holidays. Moreover, one-third of adults still work on Saturdays, so that 'free' weekends are far from universal. (BTA Survey 1967)

Coding: 5l, 2b, 5m(xiv)

Particular subjects

THEATRELESS DRAMA by D. S. Baker, M. Phil. thesis, University of Southampton 1971.

Aim
To examine the respective characteristics of 'drama' and 'theatre' in their historical and theoretical contexts, so that the work in some schools, drama centres and colleges may be clarified.

Discussion
The author suggests that 'drama', like 'play', is a means of exploring one's emotional, intellectual and physical capabilities; that it is essentially an experimental *process*. Theatre is the *product* of a process in which experiences considered to be significant by a playwright are presented by actors to an audience. Drama is an activity which requires the total physical involvement of the participants, and it need have no aesthetic value. Theatre, on the other hand, can be judged in terms of art and depends on empathetic audience participation for its effectiveness.

Theatreless drama begins at the point where 'drama' becomes purposive to the extent that the participants evaluate their work and seek to improve it. The author suggests that this initial experience occurs, or should occur, at about the age of seven. The concept of theatre is introduced when a group of actors improvise within a predetermined scenario, even though they retain the exploratory element of drama. Such theatre depends on the technique of the 'commedia dell'arte'; it is sometimes described currently as 'the theatre of participation'. The first part of this study deals with the theory underlying the concepts of drama, theatre, and the phases of 'theatreless drama' from childhood to maturity.

The second part describes current work in these developments and discusses the role of the teacher/tutor. The author reasons that everyone must have some means of discovering the measure of his personal involvement in the community and that the 'theatre' provides just this opportunity.

Coding: 5m(ii), 5a, 3d

A STATISTICAL STUDY OF THE PREFERENCES OF A GROUP OF CHILDREN AND ADULTS AS SHOWN BY CERTAIN TESTS OF AESTHETIC APPRECIATION by E. A. Peel, Ph.D. thesis, University of London 1945. [Published in part as 'On Identifying Aesthetic Types', in *British Journal of Psychology,* Vol 35, Part 3, May 1945; and as 'A New Method for Analysing Aesthetic Preferences', in *Psychometrika,* Vol 2, No 2, 1946]

Aim
To enquire into what aspects of pictures and designs appeal to children, adults (laymen and experts); to find out whether children agree better among themselves than adults and whether laymen agree better than experts. An attempt is made to discover what evidence there is of development from the choice of the child to that of the untrained adult.

Method
Artistic qualities, called criteria, were used in conjunction with eight tests, each of which was designed to emphasise certain aspects of appreciation. For example, the criteria, 'rhythm and symmetry' in a design test the 'formal' quality in appreciation. By using the

technique of correlating persons and criteria, and by applying factor analysis to the correlations, it was possible to relate the factors which characterise a group of individuals to the artistic criteria selected for use with each test. This was carried out by asking a group of 12 adults and a group of 12 adolescents, aged 13-16 years, to arrange a number of pictures into an order of 'liking'. It was assumed that the pictures liked most were the most aesthetically pleasing.

Discussion
To clarify the nature of the problem of aesthetic experience, the author examines some of the theories of beauty (Listowel, Kant, Schopenhauer, Ruskin, Fechner, Lipps, Wilenski and others). He maintains that there is a common element in most discussions of aesthetics; that is, that there is some insistence on some kind of formal unity, together with certain objective conditions such as composition, harmony, rhythm, balance, proportion and symmetry. These formal qualities are insufficient to explain beauty. Art also appeals to the senses and purely sensuous qualities are factors in aesthetic enjoyment. As the thesis is concerned with the art of painting, the influence of colour on aesthetic appreciation is also discussed.

Some authorities question whether so fragile and evanescent a flower of the mind as beauty can ever be investigated by empirical or statistical methods. Chapters 2-5 inclusive are concerned with answering this question, firstly, by reviewing previous experiments in the psychology of beauty and, secondly, by describing the author's own tests and statistical analysis.

Findings
In general, the children (or adolescents) prefer well-drawn, naturalistic pictures, symmetrical designs and balanced patterns, and brilliant colours. The untrained adult seems to show a tendency to prefer naturalistic painting, although to a less extent than children. The adult's response to colour is in marked contrast to that of children; the adult prefers more restrained colour schemes.

The expert demands more than mere reproduction, symmetry and brilliance of colour. He responds to emotional and expressive elements, insofar as they are related to the criteria 'spontaneity' and 'modernism'. He has a greater preference for formal abstraction, subtler balance and rhythm.

As people develop from childhood to maturity there is an evident increase in individual and personal tendencies to influence their aesthetic choice. The need for a continued education is firmly supported in this research by the results shown by a group of adults in their artistic preferences. The author described how their preferences show almost no development from the preferences of adolescents with respect to representational art. There was some evidence of development in their response to abstract art and colour.

He argues that the art education of adults should be coupled with discussion groups and visits to museums and art galleries. Creative art work should be linked to aesthetic analysis, for adults are continually confronted with situations demanding an ability to distinguish the genuine from the counterfeit.

Coding: 5m(v), 2b, 5a

AN INVESTIGATION INTO THE VALUE OF FIELDWORK IN THE TEACHING OF GEOGRAPHY IN SECONDARY AND FURTHER EDUCATION by D. Edynbry, M.A. thesis, University of Sheffield 1966.

Aim
The principal aim is to discuss the value of fieldwork in secondary education, but one chapter examines the amount of fieldwork carried out in a sample of ten establishments of further education.

Method
Analysis of questionnaires.

Discussion
The thesis is in three parts, the first section of which is concerned with theoretical considerations, and includes some of the ideas on the meaning, use and importance of fieldwork by writers on education and geography. There is a review of possible fieldwork topics, of the opportunities provided for fieldwork, field-study centres, ship adoption, broadcasts and local studies, and of the attitudes of examining boards.

The second part is a description and analysis of the questionnaires, and recounts some personal experiments by the author in further education. Part 3 consists of conclusions and appendices.

Of 18 colleges of further education offering courses in geography to full-time students, 8 offered no courses which included fieldwork. Therefore 10 colleges, distributed from the South Midlands, southwards, were chosen as a sample; these offered a variety of courses to full-time day and part-time day and evening students, leading to several examinations.

Three colleges offering meteorology used instruments beyond the sophistication of ground and grass thermometers. During 1964-65, one college had arranged 30 visits to a factory; 3 had each arranged one visit to a factory, 6 had arranged no visits. 2 colleges arranged visits to farms, 2 to power stations, 4 to steel works, and 6 had arranged miscellaneous visits (e.g. Kew Gardens).

Why were there no more visits? 8 colleges of the 10 reported time-table difficulties, 6 out of 10 were worried by expense, 6 out of 10 by travelling time, 4 found it difficult to leave the college and one teacher recorded lack of experience as his stumbling block.

However, most college lecturers were of the opinion that, without fieldwork, geography was an academic grind. In fact, those lecturers who organised fieldwork often did so in their own time, and sometimes at their own expense. 7 out of 10 colleges organised fieldwork during holidays, evenings or weekends.

The author argues that applied geography, perhaps urban fieldwork, is a necessary part of both liberal study courses and CNAA degrees concerned with environmental studies. He suggests that greater support for these activities could come from principals and local authority officials.

Coding: 5m(xix), 5a, 5e

AN ENQUIRY INTO THE FACTORS INVOLVED IN THE LEARNING OF HISTORY BY ADOLESCENT PUPILS BETWEEN THE AGES OF SIXTEEN AND NINETEEN by H. Abouzied, Ph.D. thesis, University of London 1955.

Aim
To investigate the various factors involved in the learning of history and to construct various tests for assessing the development of these factors.

Method
Parts 1, 2 and 3 survey in considerable detail the principal philosophical issues inherent in such an enquiry, and Part 4 deals with the problems of measuring interests and of testing aptitudes such as recall and critical thinking. 31 new tests were devised and subjected to factorial analysis, using a sample of 245 fifth and sixth form boys and girls in four different schools

Discussion
Part 1 of the thesis consists of a philosophical discussion of the nature of history, as described by various schools of thought, and an examination of the relation between philosophy and psychology and its bearing on the learning of history. In Part 2 the author considers the attempts of various agencies of society to bridge the gap between the learner and the subject of history. The aims of teaching history, the value of the subject, its place in a social studies curriculum, the question of content and the methods of teaching history are all discussed. Part 3 is concerned with the psychological aspects of the problem of learning history. It includes a discussion of the contributions of various schools of psychology, the nature of students' interest in history and of the methods of measuring such interest.

Coding: 5m(vii)

AN ENQUIRY INTO CHANGES OF OPINION, ON THE PART OF ADULT READERS, WITH REGARD TO CERTAIN POEMS — AND THE REASONS UNDERLYING THOSE CHANGES by J. N. Britton, M.A. thesis, University of London 1952.

Aim
To study preference ratings for poems, by setting up reliable orders for each of Eysenck's bipolar criteria from the ratings of 13 experts on 31 contemporary poems; and by studying the preference ratings of 220 adult students, including 18 Services personnel, and sixth form pupils on the 15 poem test.

Method
Factorial analysis of the results of the 31 poem test, and two 15 poem tests.

Discussion
A poem is good to the reader with whom it succeeds; the critic is good who recommended the poem and, perhaps, foretold to some extent the terms of the reader's own reactions to it. Of course, the maturing of individual judgment may lead an individual to agree with critics and other, more mature, individuals. It is suggested that such a consensus of mature opinions may imply that a poem may be judged on some sort of objective basis. In this thesis the author limits himself to a statistical analysis of the responses to poetry: he accepts that critical interpretation begins where statistical analysis ceases. The true poems (there are spoof poems as distractors) include the work of Sitwell, Thomas, Pound, Graves, Yeats, Macleish, Read, MacNeice and Fuller.

Findings
There are, for the specialist tutor, many detailed findings and suggestive results; for example, science forms' boys and girls show, in addition to a significant preference for the restrained poems, a significant preference for the false poems.

In general, however, he found that, although poetic judgments were highly individual, they could be complementary. An observer's angle of view of a statue may be unique but his view is yet complementary to other views of the same statue from other angles: so some greater objectivity in poetry appreciation may be gained by pooling poetic judgments to form 'composite orders' rather than by the measurement of the overlap of individual views.

Poetic judgments are not made in cold blood; the mood of poetic creation has been called 'a storm of association' of which 'poetry is reverberation'. It would appear that this is also true of appreciation.

The sign of the reader, adult or young adult, least experienced in poetry is that he rejects what he cannot comprehend; the prime obstacle to poetic judgment seems to be the intervention between the reader and the expression of the poet, of the reader's preconceived ideas, attitudes and sentiments — for example, readers' comments suggested that it was frequently the tone of the poem or the attitude of the writer to which they took exception.

Coding: 5m(iv), 2b

THE EXPERIENCE OF STUDENTS IN ADULT CLASSES IN ENGLISH LITERATURE IN RELATION TO THE AIMS AND METHODS OF TUTORS — A STUDY BASED ON WORK IN CLASSES PROVIDED BY UNIVERSITY EXTRA-MURAL DEPARTMENTS by H. E. Hodgkinson, M.Ed. thesis, University of Manchester 1968.

Aim

To show how literature is taught in extra-mural classes, and to find out whether tutors' aims, approach and teaching methods accord in any way with the students' expectations and experience of classes.

Method

97 completed questionnaires were received from 170 tutors, full-time and part-time, who were conducting literature courses, under extension or joint-committee rules, during the session 1965/66. Tutors replying supplied, as a sample, 272 student names and addresses from the register of their 1966/67 classes; 241 of these students returned completed postal questionnaires. 100 students' responses were analysed, the remainder served as reference material. The numerical results of the analysis of the questionnaires (which

include students' age, social class, period of full-time education, etc) are presented graphically or in percentage form.

Discussion

Part 1 of the thesis is concerned with an introduction to subject matter, and to a discussion of the broad problems of the research project. The historical background is dealt with in Part 2, in four chapters entitled 'Opportunities for the Study of Literature in Adult Education in the 19th century', 'The Development of English as an Academic Subject', 'Changing Attitudes in the 20th century towards the Study of Literature in Adult Education', and 'Past and Present in the Defence of Literature'.

The author reminds us that, although in 1821 Shelley was moved to write 'A defence of poetry' and in 1851 the library of the Mechanics' Institute at Sheffield officially excluded the works of Shakespeare, by the end of the 19th century literature was a popular subject for study in extension classes. Neither has literature gained acceptance easily within the universities; the author describes the struggle for academic recognition and notes that within the universities there is a tendency to move away from the claim for literature as a unique source of human values to an appreciation of its value in multi-disciplinary courses. But the literature tutors in the extra-mural classes and, indeed, their students, seem content with the establishment of a place for their subject. How will they react to the changes likely to occur within the intra-mural field?

The author also doubts if the position of literature as a proper academic subject and as an appropriate study in adult education is completely secure. Is the whole concept of the purpose of literature threatened by the new media, such as television, which are able to project material previously the prerogative of the printed word? Having established the background, the author describes in Part 3 the details of the enquiry, and, in Part 4, the findings.

Findings

50% of tutors are influenced by currently popular literary topics when constructing their syllabus. The novel is the most popular topic, followed by drama. 57% of tutors construct syllabuses according to principles associated with the teaching of literature, 23% according to considerations concerning students. 'A syllabus must hold together so that the parts illuminate and reinforce one another'. The general tendency is towards a detailed textual study but half of the tutors are reasonably favourable towards a general survey-type course, particularly as an introduction to the study of literature. For the majority of tutors, historical questions are discussed as they arise from the study of a text; but over 70% of tutors extend their field beyond English literature to encompass American literature and foreign literature in translation.

The largest group of students, 31%, was in the 35-45 age group; a further 22% in the 45-55 age group. 61% are housewives, 19% teachers, and the remainder represented many occupations. 34% completed their education at 21 years of age, and a further 26% at 18 years. Thus, the sample consists principally of well-educated, middle-class housewives in early middle or middle-age.

84% of students joined the course 'to enjoy literature'; 70% 'to hear an expert on a chosen topic'. In general, the aims of tutors and of students matched. 64% of students rated their class experience as 'exceptionally good' or 'above average'. 72% of students contributed to discussions 'frequently' or 'quite often'. 66% of students took notes in class and 40% of this group took notes on points raised by other students.

Individual tutorial help was not given in 62% of classes, but most students did not wish to receive such aid. 54% of tutors did not encourage creative writing (according to students) but 39% of students admitted engaging in creative writing, though only 14% of this group showed their work to their tutor.

But tutors and students, somewhat surprisingly perhaps, reported a use of visual or aural aids; for example, of 97 tutors, 45 reported using visual aids, 56 gramophone and tape recorders, 7 gramophone alone and 6 tape recorder only.

Though the essay is, perhaps, the most difficult exercise for students, the essay was the chief kind of work required of students.

In general, classes were enjoyable occasions; the tutor played a part in setting standards and the students had high expectations, usually confirmed by experience. Indeed, a number of students recorded unexpected gains, such as 'changed opinions', 'development of new interests' and 'mental stimulus'.

It is of interest that, although tutors tended to favour informal methods, some 44% of students expressed a preference for the lecture method of teaching. Both tutors and students, however, showed a favourable attitude towards the use of teaching aids; 68%

of students found them 'useful' or 'fairly useful'.

Coding: 5m(ix), 7c(i), 8c, 7c(iii), 2a, 2b, 1b(ii), 1b(iii), 1b(iv), 1b(ix), KB1617

THE EXTENT AND METHODS OF MANAGEMENT EDUCATION IN BRITAIN TODAY by R. Connell, M.Ed. thesis, University of Manchester 1967.

Aim
To examine the provision for management education and the teaching methods used in the United Kingdom.

Method
The study is based on the collection of material from various books and publications, visits to some of the institutions mentioned in the text and, in particular, a questionnaire to institutions preparing students for the Diploma in Management Studies.

Discussion
Part 1 of the study describes the development of the 'British movement' for management education, and refers to the influence of the general system of education on management attitudes. The author notes that until about 1950 two systems of education catered for different classes and provided education, different in quality and content, for rulers and the ruled. As a consequence, the recruiting base for managerial positions was much narrower than it might have been. The 1963 National Economic Development Council's Report called for an improvement in the quality of management to sustain a faster rate of economic growth and inspired the Government to take steps to implement and develop formal management education and training schemes.

Management is not a homogeneous professional group; they differ as to the nature of the functions they perform within a firm and their responsibilities vary according to the size of the firm and the nature of the industry. Accordingly, this diversity calls for a provision of a multitude of courses with various aims and objectives.

Educational methodology

In Part 2 of the study the roles of the main institutions engaged in this work are examined. In 1965 the British Institute of Management listed 256 colleges as offering courses; these colleges were estimated to be providing nearly 2,000 courses per year, with just under 50,000 full-time and part-time enrolled students. The universities have, since about 1960, taken an active interest in management education on a substantial scale. They offer a variety of courses (that organised by the Cambridge Board of Extra-Mural Studies is described) but perhaps their main concern is with quality, and the research procedures that sustain that quality.

The London Graduate School of Business Studies and the Manchester Business School (to use the shorter title), opened in 1965, are concerned with postgraduate and/or post-experience studies, with the specific aim of integrating academic discipline in the study of management. Their main contribution has been to establish a closer rapport between the educational system and the needs of industry. Although there are 32 independent colleges offering management courses, the author confines himself to describing 4. On the whole, courses are offered to meet the needs of middle and senior managers and the courses are usually residential and short, 12 weeks being the maximum. Courses are also organised by Management Consultants, by companies, by industries and by the British Institute of Management.

The teaching methods and the teaching staffs are described in Part 3 of the thesis. There is considerable disagreement and uncertainty as to how managers may best be developed, and thus a variety of methods are used. These include the formal and informal lecture, the syndicate exercise, the case study, role-playing situations, the business game, the T-group dynamic participatory learning method, and job rotation and coaching within the firm.

A chapter is devoted to a consideration of the academic qualifications and business experience of management teachers engaged in the Diploma in Management Studies. From replies received from 22 colleges, out of 231 full-time teachers, 68.8% were graduates and 43.2 were graduates with professional qualifications.

Sadly, the author notes that there has been little progress in persuading management teachers to undertake courses in the art of teaching adult learners.

Coding: 5m(x), 7c(i), 7c(v)

288

MODERN LANGUAGE STUDY IN FURTHER EDUCATION,
WITH SPECIAL REFERENCE TO THE TEACHING OF ADULTS
AND TO THE AREA COVERED BY THE MANCHESTER AND
DISTRICT ADVISORY COUNCIL FOR FURTHER EDUCATION
by C. L. M. Harding, M.Ed. thesis, University of Manchester 1969.

Aim

To ascertain the extent and the nature of modern language provision
and teaching in further education (excluding university internal, but
including extra-mural provision) with special reference to adults.

Method

The thesis is composed of a detailed historical survey, an extensive
examination of publications which deal with or touch upon the
problem and a thorough survey by four questionnaires, i.e. a
questionnaire to local education authorities, to institutions, to 113
teachers serving in 33 institutions, and to students from whom 500
were returned (including 38 from Holly Royde College).

Discussion

The first four chapters deal with the historical and contemporary
background of language study including, for example, broadcasts,
and review the pertinent literature. Of the ten most important
languages (in terms of numbers of speakers) apart from English, only
four (Russian, Spanish, German and French) find a place in the vast
majority of institutions teaching languages for industry and
commerce. Although there was a rapid development of new methods
of teaching since 1962, many writers have reiterated the unsatisfactory state of language teaching as regards training, course
materials, validation and wastage but few have attempted to assess
the motivations which bring adult students to classes and the reasons
for the high drop-out rate. Yet the number of students enrolled in
language classes in evening institutes and evening classes in major
establishments of further education in 1967-1968 reached nearly
110,000, 45% of whom were studying French and 28% German.

   Chapter 5 deals with the aims and objectives of language teaching
to adults, describes the administrative pattern, the recruitment,
training, servicing and assessment of teachers, the teaching methods

in languages for adults, the role of the linguistic sciences and considers the motivation and aims of students.

The last section of the thesis is concerned with the design of the enquiry, the results and an evaluation of those results and with a series of appendices summarising the wealth of detailed information gleaned from the questionnaires, e.g. the proportions of teachers using precise categories of audio-visual aids and the numbers of teachers who regularly read foreign newspapers.

Findings

National and regional machinery need strengthening to bring about a more effective rationalisation of language courses and the recommendations of the Redcliffe-Maud Report need to be put into effect to end the fragmentary nature of local administrative areas and the unevenness of the provision.

The types and objectives of language courses need to be much more clearly defined to avoid confusion of aim in the minds of students. Adult classes should be held near to the location of the specialised equipment used in language teaching and the classes should be reasonably small. No class should be closed whilst a nucleus of keen students, however small, attends. Fee structures should be rationalised to allow students to move from one type of course to another and higher fees should not be charged for non-vocational classes. The author pleads for closer liaison between responsible bodies in the area and other further education establishments and between the educational sector and industry and commerce.

Part-time teachers should be systematically trained in the techniques of adult teaching and its psychology and in the new methods in audio-visual and audio-lingual teaching of languages. A more professional system of recruitment and remuneration is suggested and a plea made for better facilities to evaluate and discuss new materials and techniques, including greater participation in the teaching provided by the mass media.

The author argues that adult students need continual counselling, that streaming is essential, that the students' personal problems need to be identified and remedied but that examinations should only be set in classes where they are part of the stated objective.

The author considers that student wastage should not be regarded as a reflection on the teacher, but that the reasons for student drop-out should be collated to indicate possible future improvements.

Coding: 5m(xi), 1b(xiii), 1b(ix), 5f, 5b, 5a, 2a, 2b, 2d, 4, 6, 7b, 3d, 8a, 8b, 8c, KB1647a

---

MUSIC IN ADULT EDUCATION – WITH SPECIAL REFERENCE TO UNIVERSITY TUTORIAL AND SESSIONAL CLASSES IN THE LONDON AREA by R. Dugmore, nee Lowe, M.A.(Ed) thesis, University of London 1956. [Published in part as 'Structure and Stricture: R. O. Morris and Adult Education' in *The Musical Times*, Novello & Co, 1960 under the pen-name R. Lowe.]

Aim
To trace the growth in demand for musical appreciation classes, to examine teaching methods and to consider the appropriateness of musical appreciation as an extra-mural subject of university standard.

Method
By questionnaires to a representative body of tutors in the London area, and to 80 students in 6 tutorial classes in music, of whom 27.7% were housewives and, at the most, 8% were manual workers.

Discussion
The growth of music classes from 1919 to 1954, the syllabus of the first London class under R. O. Morris, and Sir Henry Hadow's Memorandum to the 1919 Committee of Reconstruction, are the subjects of Part 1 of the thesis.

Part 2 is concerned with an analysis of the replies to the questionnaires. The tutors' questionnaire covers such topics as the syllabus, grading of classes by previous musical ability, text-book harmony, sight-singing methods, written work, discussion work, and what values are inculcated. The students' questionnaire asks for background information, previous training, liking for written work, voluntary study time per week, listening habits, studies of other arts and views on class organisation.

Findings
Part 3 sums up the findings, which are that musical appreciation *is* an appropriate study at university level, but that there might be a new approach to musical terminology and more attention might be given to group work, discussion guidance, and class preparation.

Coding: 5m(xii), 1b(xi), 5a

INTERESTS IN NATURAL HISTORY AMONG ADULTS by R. W. Crossland, M.Ed. thesis, University of Manchester 1955.

Aim
To investigate the interests in natural history of three groups of adults:
a What are the most popular topics in natural history among, firstly, persons who attend residential weekend courses and, secondly, members of the Youth Hostels Association?
b What are the patterns of interest in natural history of men and women of different age groups?
c Is the provision for courses in natural history for members of the YHA adequate?

Method
Questionnaires were completed by 248 adult students and 1,721 members of the YHA. The author administered the questionnaire to the student sample; the hostel wardens to the 1,373 YHA members; a smaller group, of 348 YHA members, answered the questionnaire privately, and returned the answers by post; thus, there were three separate samples.

Discussion
About half of the YHA members' sample were under 21 years of age and were included in the research in order to provide information concerning changes of interests from 11 years onwards. The YHA groups are biased samples, representative of the better-educated section of the YHA membership. The quantitative evidence in this report is in the form of percentages of total numbers in groups and sub-groups, giving A ratings (interest levels A, B or C) on either a five

or a three-point scale for each topic. The thesis includes statistics showing the composition of the samples according to age, sex, education and occupation, and information on the reading habits of students, and the causes of the origins of interests — about one-third of votes ascribed initiation of interest as due to a 'personality' and about 10% to 'school'.

Findings
In all three samples, four topics — birds, trees, wild flowers and geology — were popular at all. ages between 21 and 70 years. Students had a moderate interest in plant and animal ecology and YHA members had a moderate interest in mammals. Interest in the remaining 11 (or 12) topics suggested, e.g. fungi, was slight.

Differences in interest due to sex were so small that they could be disregarded, but in the YHA groups there were clear changes of interest between 15 and 26 years of age in both sexes. The interest pattern for men appeared to be stable from the age of 25.

Women and girls had wider interests than men and boys, and adolescent interests were more numerous than those of adults.

On the whole the better-educated section of the YHA (sampled) has interests in natural history similar to those of adult students, and as adult tutors had already correctly identified the predominant interests of their students, then their provision as regards content matter for this section of the YHA was adequate.

Coding: 2b, 4, 5m(xxi), 5m(xiv), 7c(i)

PHILOSOPHY AS AN ADULT STUDY — AN ENQUIRY INTO CURRENT THOUGHT, ATTITUDES AND PRACTICE IN ENGLISH ADULT EDUCATION by E. R. Holmes, M.Ed. thesis, University of Nottingham 1964.

Aim
To examine the study of philosophy in adult education classes in England, Scotland and Wales.

Method
Essentially by postal questionnaire to 128 tutors in 1962/1963, of

whom just over 50% replied, through visits to tutors, and by questionnaire to 336 students, of whom 247 replied. Both question-naires are given in full in the appendices.

Discussion
Part 1 of the thesis begins with a discussion of the general questions concerning philosophy in adult education, the character of the work, its relation to the teaching of philosophy in universities, student attitudes, the role of the universities in adult education, the qualities of the tutor, the aims of the teaching, the minimum length of courses and some possible effects on life in general of a study of philosophy.

Part 2 deals with matters connected with classes in greater detail; for example, the procedure, teaching methods, work done and ground covered, together with details of the provision and the types of the classes. Next comes a discussion of the students, from four aspects, philosophical, cultural, educational, and personal and social, and a further description of the tutors.

The thesis refers to a number of other surveys; the Manchester 1948/49 survey, reported by W. E. Styler, the East Midland 1952/53 survey made by R. Peers, the East Midland 1954/55 survey of 2,102 students made by the University of Nottingham Extra-Mural Depart-ment, the East Midland survey 1962 (unpublished) by F. Bayliss, the Nottingham 1960/61 (unpublished) survey made by the Nottingham Adult Education Centre, and the Derby survey 1953 made by T. Cauter and J. S. Downham.

Findings
Philosophy accounts for about 2% of what is commonly regarded as adult education in liberal studies; two-thirds of this work is done in tutorial, sessional or terminal classes, mainly provided by University Extra-Mural Departments. The students are fairly typical of adult education students of liberal studies in general; on average they have had a longer, full-time education than the rest of the population and they have a greater affiliation to religious institutions than the population as a whole. Manual and labouring workers are under-represented compared with the population as a whole, and there is a large turnover of new students, about half each year being newcomers.

However, there is one difference between philosophy students and adult education students in general; in philosophy classes, men, on average, slightly outnumber women, whereas in adult education generally, women outnumber men. Philosophy classes attract people of all ages but, as is the case of the general picture, there is a dearth of young, married people. In 1961/62 there were about 4,000 students in philosophy classes.

Whilst most of the tutors are full-time university teachers, there are also some clergymen, school teachers, and so on.

Coding: 5m(xiii), 2a, 4, KB1669

THE EDUCATIVE ELEMENT IN PHYSICAL EDUCATION by P. J. Arnold, M.Ed. thesis, University of Leicester 1965.

Aim
To study various aspects of physical education and to consider the role of physical education in contemporary society.

Discussion
Part 1 of the thesis deals with the theoretical and social framework of physical education. The educational process is life-long and all-embracing and not confined to school-age or school-time. If the phrase 'education of the whole man' means anything, it connotes the harmonious development of the physical, mental and spiritual aspects of man. In this respect, individual development may be summed to describe social benefit.

In Part 2 the author considers the biological basis of physical education, the connection between health adjustment and academic achievement, the relation between physical growth and physical education and the need for exercise to ensure balanced muscle and bone growth. The author emphasises the role of physical education throughout an individual's life, discusses the problems of different Somato-types and argues the case for respect for the individual personality. The mental, the emotional and the social element in physical education, particularly the role of play in the growth of understanding in the young child, the significance of dance to adolescents and older students and the question of competitive activities are discussed in this section.

Part 3 briefly considers the role of physical education as part of continuative and recreational education.

Coding: 5m(xiv), 3d

THE EDUCATION OF ADULTS FOR METRICATION by A. L. Kelsall, M.Ed. thesis, University of Manchester 1970.

Aim

To find out what, in 1970, selected adults thought about metrication, and how the education of adults for metrication was being carried out by selected agencies.

Method

725 adults engaged in adult educational activities, including 25 Weights and Measures Inspectors and 300 men and women students at the Adult Centre in Manchester, completed a Likert-type test. After three pilot studies, the sample was assessed as accurately representing the total population. Consequently, six hypotheses were tested from the results of these respondents.

In addition, 125 agencies concerned with the education of adults for education were sent a short questionnaire. The groups approached included 17 Ministries and Nationalised Industries, 27 Industrial Training Boards, 20 Colleges in the Manchester area, 38 Professional and Trade Associations, and 23 Local Government Offices and Manchester business firms; 90 replied.

Discussion

The thesis is in three parts: the first dealing with the historical background and implications of metrication in the United Kingdom; the second describing the experiments to establish attitudes to metrication of selected adults in the Manchester area; and the third considering the steps being taken to inform, educate and train adults in Manchester for metrication.

Findings

The groups most favourable towards metrication proved to be the men, the better educated, the younger adults, adults who had been taught about metrication since 1965, the adults who travelled abroad and those who were prepared to move for promotion.

How far were agencies taking such attitudes into account and what were they doing to educate adults about metrication? Where such agencies were doing anything at all in this field, they were found to be primarily concerned in giving information. They tended to show little understanding of how best to educate adults for metrication and they themselves showed incomplete understanding of what is meant by metrication.

The author considers that there was an indifference to human relations, and that this was likely to delay the progress of metrication.

Coding: 5m(xix), 7c(xviii), 2a, 2b, 8c

Section 7

Guidance and counselling

A PSYCHOLOGICAL ANALYSIS OF DIFFICULTIES AMONG
DAY AND EVENING STUDENTS by W. M. Dawson, M.A. thesis,
University of London 1951.

Aim
To find out more about the root causes of adult student difficulties;
to observe the extent to which educational and vocational guidance
could be introduced. To explore the effectiveness of training for
management and to suggest a practical method of teaching
management students some of the arts of investigation.

Method
This study may be described as clinical, being either by personal
interview or by group interview. Intensive work was carried out
during the years 1948-1950 on a small observational sample group of
101 male day-students and 148 male evening-students — a sample
derived from a previous pilot investigation on 650 men and women
students.

Discussion
Less than 7% of day-students attended secondary modern schools,
whereas 41% of evening-school students had attended these schools
(at pre-war standards). 82% of day-students had a grammar school

298

education compared to 39% of evening-students, but over 20% of evening-students had full-time technical education, compared to 11% of day-students.

The part-time student frequently studies under adverse conditions; he often studies in a family living room, he must contend with the modern menace of noise, and he must do his fair share of household chores.

The major part of the thesis gives the results of the analysis of the interview questionnaires and, by individual or group case study, details of the personalities and circumstances of the students; for example, the incidence of broken homes, types of school failure, reactions to training processes, anxieties about promotion and so on.

Findings

The most characteristic deterrent to study of day-students was a preoccupation with the traumatic aspects of family life; the incentives were keen interest in work which gave satisfaction and the definition of future goals. Day-students would, perhaps, have been less anxious if placed in employment before embarking on full-time training. The most characteristic deterrent to study among evening-students was found in physical and social conditions, although, like day-students, the incentives were satisfaction from work and study.

Both day and evening students realised their deficiencies in social skills. Both types of students would have benefited from re-considered forms of selection, grading, training and placement, and from closer liaison between employers, training specialists and organisations specialising in leisure-time occupations.

Coding: 6, 5m(x), 2b, 2a, 4

A STUDY OF MALE INDUSTRIAL WORKERS AFTER RETIRE-MENT by W. E. Beveridge, M.A. thesis, University of London 1964.

Aim

To examine attitudes to retirement in relation to six variables: job attitude, post-retirement activities, planning for retirement, occupational differences, financial and domestic circumstances and job stability.

Method
101 retirees from five firms in North West London, retired for not less than six months and not more than six years, completed a questionnaire and were interviewed in their own homes.

Discussion
In 1960 in England and Wales, 11.6% of the population, or about 6 million people, were aged 65 years and over, compared to 6.7% of the population in 1911 and to an estimated 14.7% of the population in 1979. For this reason, studies of the problems of retirement are becoming increasingly relevant and important.

The author reviews previous research in Chapter 1, noting principally that the mass of unskilled and semi-skilled are, by definition, least equipped to find themselves new, satisfying occupations in retirement (Tronchin-James, Heron). The Nuffield Foundation reported in 1963 that 'comparatively few of the older manual workers seem to prepare their minds for the years of "leisure" that must follow their retirement'.

Having described the definitions adopted and the sample in Chapter 2, the next six chapters are concerned with the results of the investigation. Interviews were held with 24 managers and supervisors, 28 skilled manual workers, 43 semi-skilled and unskilled manual workers, and 6 technicians and clerks; of this total sample, 27 had been retired for 1 year but less than 2 years, 54 had been retired for 2 years but less than 5 years.

Out of 101, 49 said that retirement was much the same as working life, and 40 found retirement fairly satisfying; 21 found retirement less satisfying than work and 20 found retirement per se somewhat unsatisfying. On the whole, supervisory workers were more satisfied with their retirement situation than were workers in the semi-skilled and unskilled group.

What do retirees miss most by no longer being at work? 75 mentioned companionship and only 27 mentioned money. What do retirees enjoy most in retirement? 40 mentioned independence, 28 the chance of an easier time, 22 the freedom to do new things.

The most frequent social activity in retirement was shopping for the household, and 77 out of 101 claimed to shop regularly. 67 retirees said they had visited friends in the previous fortnight; during the same period 24 had watched sport outdoors, 17 had visited a social event (bingo, old people's club), 15 had played an outdoor game, such as golf, 14 had attended church and 13 had been to a cinema or concert. 93 of the 101 possessed television sets and TV was their regular source of information and entertainment.

86 worked around the house, 71 in the garden, 33 had an indoor hobby such as oil painting, and 45 had read a novel or other book during the previous fortnight. More than half offered 'take up an activity or get a job' as retirement advice. The supervisory grades were, as may be expected, the most active group proportionately in social activities.

One interesting factor brought to light in this thesis is that retired people demand little; when they speak of standards of living, they refer to basic essentials, food, heat, etc. Holidays, visits to pubs, etc were luxuries they did not expect to continue in retirement. A man's ability to handle retirement depended on his wife's capacity to shop wisely, and the degree of her understanding. Many retired men did not understand the degree of change in life style that their retirement brought about in their wives' daily routines. Surprisingly, the link that binds the retired to their adult children is not as strong as may be expected, even though about one-third lived in the same house as their children.

The loss of money income is more a loss of status, the inability to buy a round of drinks; similarly, loneliness is a function of the feeling of a lack of belonging to a group. A man's attitude to his job and social group at work are likely to give little or no indication of his attitude to retirement.

Findings

Loneliness, rather than isolation, is the principal difficulty facing retired men. Consequently, there is the need for social activities which give status and acceptance. There is a need for opportunities to earn a little money to make life more comfortable. Of the sample of 101, only 2 were using further education opportunities; the others did not know these facilities existed!

Planning for retirement is essential; the author asks for courses, not only for the man but also for his wife, not only of lectures but also of discussion, and finally, courses which stem not only from the adult education service but which originate from the co-operation of employers unions and education services.

Coding: 6, 2a, 1c(v)

A PSYCHOLOGICAL STUDY OF HOME, JOB, FRIENDSHIP AND
PERSONAL PROBLEMS IN LATE ADOLESCENCE by V. P. Varma,
Ph.D. thesis, University of London 1968.

Aim

To study the theoretical work on adolescence, to examine the
problems of adolescence and to offer suggestions to help adolescents.

Method

The attitudes and problems of adolescents were assessed on an
attitude inventory and on direct and indirect versions of a questionnaire given in a free interview. The abbreviated version of the
Wechsler Intelligence Scale and attainment tests in reading,
arithmetic and spelling and a drawing test were given individually to
100 average and 50 backward boys aged 16-21 years.

Discussion

In the first part of the thesis, the author surveys the literature on
adolescence, describes what happens in adolescence and emphasises
the continuum of human growth. Thereafter the research plan is
described, a statement is made of the principal hypotheses and
details of the tests are given, together with a description of the
fieldwork procedures. The final five chapters deal with the analysis,
the detailed results of the tests and the provision of community
services to help adolescents.

Findings

The author suggests that the adolescent boy of today is not a
thoroughly sick person, but that he (whether average or backward in
ability) has, on the whole, approximately three serious problems, and
a dozen other problems in the following areas, and more or less in
the following order: personal problems, employment and money
problems, home problems, problems of friendship and a miscellany
of other problems (vide L. Cole, *Psychology of adolescence* 1954).

There are some highly interesting findings; for example, average
teenagers were more hostile towards adults than the backward ones;
66% of the former and 48% of the latter blamed adults for many of
their problems but 52% of the average and 56% of the backward
teenagers would rather go to their parents for advice about their

problems than to their friends. Nevertheless, 84% of both the average and backward young people recommend that there should be a place where teenagers can get advice — someone 'one can trust and respect and who will keep confidence'.

The grown-up backward boy is often left to himself, yet, unlike the feeble-minded, the dull are not so dull as never to feel their own innate shortcomings. All adolescents in the sample wanted friends; indeed, the author considers that the whole matter of social education for the late adolescent today cries out for more careful consideration than it has received in the past. The picture that emerges is one of responsible and generous young people, sometimes confused, sometimes distracted, often willing to seek advice, and nearly always displaying the astounding resilience of human common sense.

Coding: 6, 2b

PUBLIC KNOWLEDGE OF SOCIAL WORK AGENCIES IN GLASGOW by I. Lindsay, M.Sc. thesis, University of Strathclyde 1969.

Aim
To investigate public knowledge of social work agencies in Glasgow and to investigate the related problem of consumer attitudes towards social workers.

Method
Two distinct 'problem' areas were chosen for sampling, one a typical older slum area, the other a new housing scheme. A random sample was chosen — 215 people over the age of 21, the ratio of women to men being deliberately weighted in favour of women, i.e. 146 to 69. Interviews based on a schedule were conducted by women (men are associated with authority); *no prior notice* was given of the interview and there were only 3 refusals. Results are presented in percentage form.

Discussion
It is useful to distinguish three different categories of social work:
casework, group work and community development. The social work
services are going through a period of change and development; there
has been a growing awareness that individual casework is not of itself
the solution to all the social problems with which the individual has
to deal. The individual has to be seen in his full setting, the potential
for self-help in any community has to be encouraged and directed,
the extent to which problems are not those of deviant individuals but
of deviant communities has to be examined — all of these are the
responsibility of community development workers.

The author describes the socio-economic background of Glasgow
and the principal agencies operating in Glasgow. Of particular
interest to adult educationalists are: the Society for Social Service,
which holds weekly clinics in the Community Centres and dealt with
1,400 problems in 1967/68; the University Settlement which, in
1968, dealt with 329 families; and the Marriage Guidance Council,
whose staff of 45 voluntary counsellors dealt with 900 families in
1968.

The major part of the thesis is concerned with the analysis of
responses to the interview and the collation of results.

Findings
The roles of the Welfare Department and of the Children's Department were not immediately familiar. Knowledge of School Welfare
Officers was almost non-existent. However, the sample knew of the
services of the Probation Department. Almoners were well known;
working in an institutional setting would not appear, on its own, to
have an adverse effect on public knowledge of an agency.

The voluntary agencies compared favourably with the statutory
services. The RSPCC, Alcoholics Anonymous, and the Marriage
Guidance Council (especially among men) were well-known. There
were few references to church or to the general practitioner. The
offices of the Ministry of Social Security were regarded as a 'helping
agency', not just a collecting point. However, little was known of the
location of most agencies, but on the whole social workers were
regarded as kindly and helpful.

The response to the voluntary social work services leads the author
to suggest that statutory services must give greater consideration to
the community potential for voluntary social work. Perhaps public

authorities have, for too long, been prepared to spend money on services without any attempt to find out whether the service reaches those in the greatest need, whether it is appreciated and whether it is effective.

Coding: 6

PATTERNS OF WORK AND LEISURE OF DAY-RELEASE CRAFT STUDENTS AT A TECHNICAL COLLEGE by A. Rowlands, M.Ed. thesis, University of Wales 1970.

Aim
To trace patterns of development of work and leisure, in the late secondary school and post-secondary school era of the 'average' and 'below-average' secondary school child who carries on with part-time education at a technical college.

Method
Information was gathered, by two questionnaires together with two short essays, from 120 students, aged 15-21 years, about education, socio-economic background, attitudes to work and college and leisure activities. Staff opinion was ascertained by a questionnaire and interview/discussion. The statistics are expressed in percentages and illustrated histogrammatically.

Discussion
The thesis begins by describing the research plan, the college, staff, students and the day-release system. Thereafter the author examines in detail the student at school and the transition from school, the student at work and at college, and the students' leisure activities.

Findings
In 1967/68, of 46 full-time teaching staff at the college, 9 were graduates and 12 had a teaching certificate recognised by the Burnham Committee. 65.8% of the students were on day-release; 20.2% attended for evenings only.

76.5% of students in the sample came from a manual background, and fathers were mainly in skilled or semi-skilled employment. 91.6% had attended secondary modern schools and 81% of the sample left school at the age of 15 years. The predominant influence in informing the individual about further education was the employer

(55%), followed by parents (28.7%), careers masters (20.8%), Youth Employment Officer (17.5%). But who gave the most help in finding the first job? Family (50.8%), YEO (32.5%), own effort (27.5%) — only 7% were influenced by the school. 76.6% of students 'like my job a lot' — having accepted the role they are to play in life they rarely venture out of it, even in fantasy.

50% of students would prefer not to attend college, but staff/ student relationships were generally satisfactory. 67.9% prefer practical work to theory; 58% regard the General Studies course as valuable but about 58% suggest less time should be devoted to it. Their socio-economic background does not favour continuous study — 55.8% have no separate room for study at home.

22.5% were members of local youth clubs and a further 17.5% of sports clubs; 46.6% were not members of any club. Most students, 71.7%, did not consider that the college equipped them socially — only 2.5% participated in Students' Union activities.

55.6% had not read any book recently and only 20% of the sample were members of a public library. The most popular daily paper read was the *Daily Mirror,* 80%. About 30% watched television on 2 evenings and 20% on 3 evenings; 32.6% watched for 3 hours each evening, 22.2% for 4 hours, 15.9 for 5 and more hours. Comedy (81.6%), films (71.6%), detective stories (65.8%) and westerns (59.1%) were the most popular programmes.

38.3% actively participated in soccer and another 24.1% in rugby football. 62.5% frequented the public house more than twice a week (often during the lunch break on the day they attended college); 30.8% drank on four occasions or more each week. 'Are the activities available so meagre that the only place the teenager can find relaxation and enjoyment is the local pub? 21.6% attended church often; 47.5% never.

Generally there is evidence for excessive hours of work, 31.7% working 50 hours or more per week, of a lack of facilities for careers guidance or counselling about further education opportunities, of a lack of motivation to work at college. The vast majority are unambitious, happy in their work choices, and truly the product of a manual socio-economic background and the Secondary Modern School.

Coding: 6, 2a, 4

EASING THE RESTRICTIONS OF AGEING Report of a Seminar arranged by Age Concern and the University of Cambridge Board of Extra-Mural Studies at Madingley Hall, September 1972. Published by Age Concern, 55 Gower Street, London, WC1E 6HJ (62 pp).

Aim
To examine four areas of possible restriction or limitation for the elderly; i.e. of economic resources and income, of psychological and mental changes, of social roles and relationships and of physical health.

Method
In each area, given above, the proposition was that, with age, certain restrictions emerge for some or all old people. What are these restrictions, what is their impact, can they be prevented or delayed in onset and can they, once they have arrived, be ameliorated? Five eminent lecturers attempt to answer these questions. Professor Kathleen Jones examines the social and cultural context; Professor A. B. Atkinson looks at problems of economics and finance; Professor Michael Hall considers physical health; Dr Sheila M. Chown surveys psychological and emotional aspects of the problem; and David Hobman reviews the changing roles and relationships implied in ageing.

Discussion
The papers provide, inter alia, pithy accounts of research and some principal facts; for example, in 1968, 21.1 out of every 1,000 people were over the age of 80 years, compared to 6.0 per 1,000 in 1911.

Findings
Perhaps the main conclusion is contained in the Epilogue, written by A. J. Willcocks: '. . . repeated discovery of the limited data available about the process of ageing, the restrictions it causes and the needs it creates . . . we need to know more . . . the time seems more than appropriate to suggest some form of major enquiry (perhaps a Royal Commission) into the whole issue of the elderly'.

Coding: 2d, 3d, 7c(i), 7c(xxi)

Section 8

Organisation and administration

National administration and policies

NATIONAL ADULT EDUCATION SURVEY (THE REPUBLIC OF IRELAND): Interim Report presented to the Department of Education, April 1970, (139 pp).

Aim
To survey the needs of the community in the matter of Adult Education, and to indicate the type of permanent organisation to be set up in order to serve those needs.

Method
Since the Minister indicated that he would wish for a speedy report, the Advisory Committee decided to conduct a survey which would discover immediate and fundamental needs on which action might be taken forthwith. Consequently, the survey methods are concerned with systems of a practical value. In any case, the Advisory Committee argued, without a proven structure and a general national and local working system for adult education, detailed research would be unrewarding.

Discussion
Adult Education is defined as 'all the educational activity engaged in by people who have broken with full-time continuous education.'
'The purpose of adult education (formal or informal) is change, in knowledge, skill and attitude, leading to personal, social, moral,

political, religious and community development.'

'We recognise that although education and training may be divided by definition, they cannot be easily divided in practice.'

'This concept (education permanente) is not identical with adult education or continuing education; it is a new integrating concept comprising the whole spectrum of educational activity from nursery school to educational institutions attended in the "third age".'

When the family education system, the sequential system (primary, secondary and higher) and adult education 'collectively provide the opportunities for anyone to learn whatever he needs to learn, whenever he needs to learn it, the community has reached a stage of excellence in using its total resources for the deliberate education of all its members. This what is meant by the Educative Community.'

Thus, having stated the objectives and basic concepts of adult educationalists, the Committee proceeds to review the general needs of people for adult education. Technological advances give opportunities, such as more leisure-time, for education. But such advances also pose problems; we must re-educate ourselves throughout life to meet the demands of rapid change.

There are many other needs, which the report examines, but it suggests that the proof that these are real needs may be seen in the diversity of voluntary bodies providing a varied range of aspects of adult education, such as theology classes, shop steward education, floral arrangement classes and tree growing.

To these general educative activities, the Committee adds the need to inform people facing particular problems — poverty groups, functional illiterates, the handicapped — and the need to help particular groups at particular times of anxiety or pressure, for example, parents facing the generation gap, or those about to retire. A specific example of an organisation concerned with informal adult education is given in Chapter 5.

The formal adult education services, often described as the Vocational Education System, is described in Chapter 6. 86,171 people (17,290 in part-time day courses and 68,881 on part-time evening courses) enrolled for courses organised by Vocational Committees in 1967/68. Various recommendations are made; to quote but two; 'the whole approach in adult education must be flexible' and 'Adults should have an adequate counselling and guidance service . . .'.

Members of the Committee were particularly exercised by the need to support leader-training for all the various types of voluntary organisations having educative functions as part of their purpose. They were equally insistent on the need for the training of teachers, tutors, etc. in the new means and methods of learning at the disposal of students. Similarly, the Committee asked for the use of buildings at times when they are not being used for the principal purpose; for example, schools during the evenings, weekends, holidays and hotels in off-peak periods. Indeed, learning may be undertaken in the students' homes.

Turning to the media of communication, the Committee extends the definition of the 'library' to connote a 'house of culture', recommends the exploration of a link with the British Open University, and emphasises the educative role of Radio Eireann.

In order to facilitate co-ordination of adult education interests at national level the Committee recommends the establishment of a permanent Council of Adult Education and at local level it recommends the appointment of a County Officer, the Adult Education Development Officer, to be 'Mr Adult Education' for his county or area. (An elaboration of his functions and training requirements is given in Appendix F).

AONTAS, the National Association of Adult Education, is seen as carrying out an essential and important function, . . . principally that of monitoring, auditing and informing.

The Committee recommends research in adult education, and argues that its recommendations will lead to the better use of resources currently being applied to adult education, rather than divert new resources to it.

Appendix B consists of a directory of agencies and voluntary bodies engaged directly or indirectly in adult education in the Republic.

Coding: 7a, 7b, 8, 3b, 6

EDUCATION – AN ECONOMIC PROBLEM OF RESOURCE
ALLOCATION by M. O'Donoghue, Ph.D. thesis, University of
Dublin 1968.

Aim
To examine the implications of the application of various economic
models to the national problem of allocating resources to education.

Discussion
As the educational sector of public expenditure is increasingly
absorbing a larger share of total national resources, economists have
begun to use their particular scientific methodology to consider the
optimum use of resources. At the same time, contemporary
educationalists often appeal to economic principles to support their
case for the increase in the allocation of resources to education as a
whole, or for extra expenditure in particular sectors of their service.
In many cases they argue that the benefits from increased expenditure on education are sufficient to justify a re-allocation of resources
to this sector.

The author examines four different theoretical approaches to the
allocation of resources to education and describes the problems of
applying principles of economics to 'real' situations. The 'rate of
return' approach relies on the market mechanism and treats
education as an investment activity, the expenditure on which may
be calculated in the same way as the expenditure on any other type
of investment asset is justified. The contributions of Becker, Blaug,
Wiesbrod and Vaisey to this approach are considered in detail;
unfortunately their analysis often refers to historical experience,
whereas the decisions to acquire education are concerned with a
future which, in many instances, does not confirm the trends of the
past.

An alternative approach, the 'manpower' approach, which was
applied in various forms in Sweden, France and Holland, deals with
the educational system in its role of providing the skills and
knowledge needed to sustain some specified level of production.
Consequently, various types of education are viewed as being derived
demands from the pattern of employment. Even amongst economists
actively concerned in such studies, the role and usefulness of
manpower forecasts are still matters of belief rather than knowledge

and, therefore, to allocate educational expenditure on the basis of such forecasts is a highly suspect operation.

The 'social demand' approach considers the demand for education as a whole, whether motivated by economic or non-economic considerations. However, the demand for participation in education is a subtle reflection of the social structure; for instance, the education of girls is bound up with other aspects of their expected sex role, and even the structure of the educational system itself may be relevant to the problem of participation. Early streaming by ability in primary schools may, for example, be associated with inequalities of participation in secondary and continuing education. This approach may be nearer to reality, but it poses many methodological problems.

A fourth approach is the 'cost-effective' approach; the objective to be attained is defined and then the least-cost combination of inputs of resources per pupil is calculated. But objectives have to be agreed with some precision.

Having established the methodological difficulties involved in such approaches, the author deals with the problems of education and migration, education and inflation and the financing of education.

Findings
Economists frankly admit that there is little statistical data; that the products of the educational system are defined in a vague and amorphous manner, that the application of the principles of economics to educational problems is relatively new. The author pleads for more research, particularly of an inter-disciplinary nature and implies that the application of economists' complex models, with their assumptions, to the problems of education is a highly sophisticated process deserving, at times, a healthy scepticism.

Coding: 7a

THE MEASUREMENT OF THE ECONOMIC BENEFITS OF RECREATION − A THEORETICAL AND EMPIRICAL STUDY by R. J. Smith, D. Phil. thesis, University of Birmingham 1969.

Aim
To test, both in theory and practice, methods for measuring

recreation benefits, rather than merely to produce a figure of benefits for a particular recreation area.

Method

Clarification and examination of the approaches to the problem, followed by an empirical example (i.e. fishing at Grafham Water) to identify problems which arise, an assessment of their importance, and an indication of the extent to which such problems may be overcome. A questionnaire was distributed to a sample of 1,000 of the anglers at Grafham Water in 1968, and another questionnaire was distributed to a selection of 34 anglers travelling over 160 miles to fish at Grafham Water in 1968.

Discussion

The pressure of an ever-increasing demand for outdoor recreation has made it impossible for us to ignore the recreation potential of our rivers and reservoirs. If the possibilities of providing for recreation are to be taken into account at the planning stage in all water resource projects, then it is necessary to have a monetary value of recreation benefits; this figure may be attached to other benefits such as increased domestic water supply, flood alleviation and irrigation. We also need to know the costs of a particular recreation to compare it with other recreational possibilities, and to estimate yields of greatest net benefit.

Chapter 1 examines various methodological approaches; the author considers that proposed by Marion Clawson as the one most soundly based in economic theory. Chapter 2-4 inclusive are concerned with the derivation of an empirical demand curve for trout fishing, using the data obtained from Grafham Water and utilising the Clawson approach.

Empirical estimates of travel costs are analysed in Chapter 6, and attempts to improve the specification of the demand curve are discussed in Chapter 7. The final two chapters draw together the analysis of the economic benefits of trout fishing, and state the conclusions.

Findings

The findings are essentially relevant to economic planning; of particular interest is the remark that 'It is difficult to see how any reliable results (for predicting future demand) can be obtained without undertaking large-scale social surveys. This is a matter which should receive some attention'.

Also of interest are the statistics of the socio-economic background of people with an enthusiasm for fishing, e.g. nature of employment, hours of work, gross annnual income, etc.

Coding: 7b, 2b

PRESSURE GROUPS, FURTHER EDUCATION AND THE 1944 ACT — THE INFLUENCE OF PRESSURE GROUPS ON FURTHER EDUCATION SECTIONS OF THE EDUCATION ACT OF 1944 by B. J. Evans, M.Ed. thesis, University of Manchester 1971.

Aim
This is a case study in the history and politics of further education. Its aim is to examine what lay behind the clauses of the 1944 Education Act devoted to the subject of further education. Why was further education included in the reform? What causes determined the shape of the proposed system of further education, and how far did the efforts of interested parties contribute to the result?

Discussion
The influence of pressure groups in education has been largely neglected. The main hypothesis tested is that pressure group activity existed, and that it contributed to the formulation of the relevant further education provisions of the Act. Pressure group activity is not considered in isolation; it is related to other elements which helped to create a given situation.

Therefore, a second hypothesis emerges which is also considered; that is, that the impact of total war provoked the ferment of ideas, and accelerated the growth of pressure group activity. In the introduction to his thesis, the author examines the definition and role of pressure groups in a dynamic political system and reviews the literature concerned with the relationship between war and social change.

He suggests that the physical condition of evacuated children, especially from the London area, awoke people's consciences, that the Council for Educational Advance established in 1942 was an effective body, and that R. A. Butler, the President of the Board of Education, responded to a general desire for a measure of far-reaching reform with sympathy and vision. Chapter 1, 'The Impulse for Reform' deals with the general; Chapter 2 turns to the specific 'The Necessity of Technical Education' and shows how industry, commerce and education agreed that a new approach to industry and technical education was required if Britain was to prosper.

In Chapter 3, 'The Emergence of the Technical Education Lobby', the author reviews the reactions to various proposals and the suggestions made by various associations, for example, the British Association for Commercial and Industrial Education. He judges how far each body acted as an independent pressure group and evaluates how far, taken together, the individual groups formed a lobby. Turning to adult education, the author describes how new impetus was given to a re-appreciation of the value of adult education, particularly through the experience of adult education in the armed services, such as the Army Bureau of Current Affairs. In Chapter 4 he argues that the build up of the adult education pressure group was slow but, nevertheless, a group emerged which found the government fairly responsive to its demands. 'The Emergence of the Adult Education Lobby' is described fully in Chapter 5.

Individuals played their parts; Ernest Green, Harold Shearman and W. E. Williams were as much social reformers as they were educationalists, and all three played a leading part in the activities of the Council for Educational Advance. Similarly 'The local education authorities did not merely exercise pressure behind the scenes; they set in motion schemes to demonstrate exactly what they were capable of providing. Essex County Council set up residential colleges'. But 'Adult education was served by an inchoate, untidy lobby. That lobby obtained . . . recognition and kind words but failed to secure a sufficiently generous financial allocation. It was, perhaps, a hollow triumph'. The extent of Parliamentary concern with the promotion of further education is established in Chapter 6, 'The Parliamentary Debates'.

Findings
The evidence is weighed and assessed in conclusion; two sentences have, perhaps, a timeless quality: 'The adult education campaign was the least well organised and the least effective. For all the enthusiasm

of its supporters, much energy was dissipated, particularly as far as the voluntary bodies were concerned, over the issue of voluntary versus statutory control of adult education'.

Coding: 1a, 1b(xiii), 7a, 7b

Regional and local administration and policies

LEADERSHIP IN INDIAN AND ITALIAN IMMIGRANT COMMUNITIES by L. Blaxter, M.Phil. thesis, University of Sussex 1967.

Aim

To examine the relationship between immigrant communities and the society which encapsulates them; in particular, to study the relationship between Southern Italian immigrants and American society and the Indian and Pakistani communities and British society.

Discussion

The thesis is not an examination of race relations nor of the 'colour problem'. It is the study of relations between communities, with different cultures, where one community is encapsulated and dominated by another. These relationships between the communities are examined in terms of roles, especially the role that immigrant leaders play in organising the inter-action of the communities.

However, this is not to deny the extra dimension that colour gives to the problems of immigrants; but by taking the case of the Southern Italians, certain comparisons may be made, and certain problems identified, which are basic to all immigrants, regardless of colour.

The thesis is in five sections; the first deals with modes of migration, the pattern of settlement, in both Indian and Italian communities. The second logically considers the encapsulating society, the host community. The third and fourth sections consider in detail the values and resources of leaders, the ties between leaders and followers, some examples of leaders and of the criteria of leadership and the external contacts made by leaders. The fifth section concentrates on the Indian Communities in British society.

Regrettably, the pattern of behaviour that exists between communities of different cultural origin is, in part at least, conditioned by stereotypes. The relationship is that both host and immigrant expect members of the other group to behave in a certain way; if these expectations are not met then there is conflict, unless people can think in terms other than of stereotypes. Leaders of immigrant communities may find that, because the host community does not offer them the roles which their intellectual qualifications deserve, they have no alternative but to maintain the cultural distinction of their immigrant community as a sub-group in the host society. As the P.E.P. Report on Racial Discrimination, 1967, noted 'it is those immigrants with the highest qualifications and general ability (language ability, familiarity with British life and customs, etc) who experience most discrimination'.

Coding: 7b

COMMUNITY DECISION-MAKING IN A GEORGIAN CITY by B. S. R. Green, Ph.D. thesis, Bath University of Technology 1968.

Aim
To make an analysis of decision-makers and decision-making in a medium-sized English city, with the aim of providing empirical data of theoretical relevance and attempting conceptual clarification in the area of community power studies.

Method
By questionnaire, but respondents were encouraged to be discursive and conversational, so that the questions provided a starting point for discussions, rather than a structured framework for the classification of short answers as in sample surveys. Reputation items and newspaper reports were also used.

317

Discussion
The major problem initially was how to identify actors significantly involved in decision-making. A review of previous literature suggested a useful distinction between structural power and interactional power, relative to community decisions. Structural power refers to the ability to set conditions, make decisions and take actions regarding community-wide facilities and institutions. Such power resides in political-administrative positions, and the wielders of such power are easily identifiable. Officials, however, in contrast to elected members, play a more active role in initiating policy and securing desired outcomes than their formal role of advisers, consultants and implementers would indicate.

However, there is no evidence in Bath of a conspiratorial coalition of chieftain officials. The pattern of power corresponds rather to independent sovereignties with spheres of influence, where each issue area is controlled by a different set of top leaders whose goals and strategies are adapted to the particular segments of the community that happen to be interested in that specific topic. Each sphere is dominated by a small group of officials and elected members, but, increasingly, elected members and 'interested parties' are invited to enter the decision process as modifiers, critics, commentators and preliminary legislators, as the decision process comes to fruition. Thus, there are limitations on those exercising structural power. Nevertheless, more research is needed on the extent and importance of official co-operation as a basis for the exercise of power.

Inter-actional power refers basically to the ability of one actor to influence another. In analysing community decision-making, we may consider the situation where an actor, subject to such influence, is in a position to exercise structural power. Actors, in this study, fell into three distinct categories; firstly, those in the external environment, such as central government personnel; secondly, actors within the community but outside the authoritative role structure, such as the Chamber of Commerce; and thirdly, the incumbents of authoritative positions, for example, the Committee Chairman, and the Town Clerk. These actors elected or appointed to authoritative political or administrative positions are called 'prescribed decision-makers'.

This study is concerned with situations where one of the actors is a prescribed decision-maker. Described, therefore, are recruitment to decision-making roles, the roles and resources within the prescribed power structure, the university issue as a case study in decision-making and the changes in community decision-making between 1930 and 1965.

Pluralism, which is regarded as desirable, demands a balance between structural power and interactional power, not a domination of one by the other. In the concluding section the author examines the conditions under which pluralism prospers. He is cheered by the movement towards greater diversity of council members in Bath, by occupational type and political affiliation, since 1930. For example, the number of 'managerial executive' rose from 3 to 10 between 1930 and 1962 and 'local family business' fell from 24 to 12. But there are revealing statements; for example: 'I was brought in just after the meeting with the Minister when I became Chairman of . . . The Chairman of Planning took over from the officials – he is a spellbinder – he took us by the nose and dragged us in. He said we don't want any dissension or the Minister won't give it to us. We all accepted this'; (the university issue was in question). 'The Trust is a big headache – some of their demands are not economically possible – they are a bit tiresome'.

Coding: 7b, 7c(xii)

A REVIEW OF THE DEVELOPMENT OF THE EDUCATION SERVICE IN THE BOROUGH OF CHESTERFIELD 1944-1967 by K. H. Wood-Allum, M.Ed. thesis, University of Durham 1969

Aim
To examine the growth of the Education Service in the Excepted District of the Borough of Chesterfield from 1944-1967.

Discussion
The thesis describes the negotiations leading to the granting of Excepted District status, the formulation of the Scheme of Delegation, the establishment of managing and governing bodies and the production of the Development Plan for the Borough.

Building programmes of both Major and Minor works are examined and related to the proposals of the development plan. There is an analysis of the philosophy of secondary education which was applied by the Borough officers to create a system of Secondary Schools in the decade after 1944 and an examination of the struggle from 1965 to reorganise this sector on the principle of non-selective secondary education. The primary sector is also included in this survey, particular attention being given to the introduction of ita (initial teaching alphabet) and French. Consequently, the growth of Special Services, the Further Education and Youth Service and the Library Service, within the functions delegated by the Scheme of Divisional Administration, is outlined within the context of a review of the total local education service.

The Scheme of Delegation gave the Borough the power to provide adult education in evening institutes. Enrolments increased from about 1,400 in 1958 to 6,300 in 1967. During 1951-1958 enrolments varied between about 1,200 and 1,800. The author argues that enrolments always fall after fees are increased and cites Chesterfield's experience as a particular case of a general rule.

The percentage of the adult population attending evening institutes rose from 2.27% in 1960 to 3.8% in 1964. In the author's view this rise was largely due to the appointment of the first full-time organiser for further education and the youth service in 1963. Indeed, in 1967, 6.55% of the adult population of the Borough attended classes in what had now been renamed adult education centres. The range of subjects listed as being offered shows that the mainstay of their programmes was the leisure-time activity. In May 1967 a second officer was appointed, a principal, adult education centres, and 'the service can be expected to grow even more'.

The WEA and Sheffield University Extra-Mural classes are held in a permanent 'home' — Hurst House, near the centre of the town.

Findings

Of eleven chapters, the adult education sector occupies one-half of one chapter; as the author shows, the controversies concerning, and developments in, the other sectors have occupied a greater part of the stage. Nevertheless, he concludes that, since the appointment of officers with particular responsibilities for the adult sector, it is true to note 'the successful growth of the service in all its aspects'.

Coding: 7b, 7c(iv), 8a, 2a, 7c(iii), 7c(xv), 7c(i)

ADULT EDUCATION IN THE ROMAN CATHOLIC CHURCH, THE CHURCH OF ENGLAND AND THE SOCIETY OF FRIENDS
by P. D. Brennan, M.Ed. thesis, University of Manchester 1970.

Aim

To investigate religious education as it is at present and as envisaged in the Roman Catholic Church at national, diocesan and parish levels, and, by way of contrast, to examine the provision of the Church of England in a similar way, and the Society of Friends at General Meeting, Monthly Meeting and Local Meeting levels.

To examine areas of agreement or inconsistency between the various levels of each religious organisation – a vertical study; and to contrast the position of each corresponding level of each religion – an horizontal study.

Method

By informal interview with a questionnaire to guide or focus the interview, and by reference to the relevant religious organisations' literature, papers, etc.

Discussion

Arguing that the Church of tomorrow is decided by adults of today, and that the speed of scientific and technological discovery poses special problems for the contemporary Christian, the author sets out to answer four questions as applied at national, diocesan and local level. The four questions are:

a What structures exist that are directed to the education of adults?
b Who are the participants?
c What types of education are offered?
d Are the religious agencies providers or stimulators?

The educational provision of the Roman Catholic Church is examined nationally; if there is one ruling principle, it is that 'Christian education embraces the whole sum total of a man's activity, sensible and spiritual, intellectual and moral, individual, domestic and social . . .' As an example of diocesan organisation, the Diocese of Brentwood is described, and the Parish of the Immaculate Conception, Chelmsford, is taken as a typical local organisation.

Similarly, the national educational organisation of the Church of England, the Diocese of Manchester, and the Parish of St. Matthew's,

Stretford, are considered. Of some interest is the fact that the Diocesan Officer was appointed, in 1967, Honorary Staff Tutor in Religious Studies in the Extra-Mural Department of the University of Manchester.

Both the Roman Catholic Church and the Church of England may be correctly described as hierarchical. The Religious Society of Friends has no episcopacy, ordained clergy and, indeed, in spite of encompassing about 21,000 members, no official spokesman. The organisation nevertheless ascribes areas of responsibility, and decisions are taken at various levels. The author describes the yearly National Meetings, the Lancashire and Cheshire General Meeting, the Hardshaw East Monthly Meeting and the Mount Street Meeting in Manchester, and the educational work which revolves around such corporate activities.

Findings

The Roman Catholic hierarchy in England has now officially appointed a Laity Commission to explore, in the light of the teachings of the Second Vatican Council, the role of the laity. Adult education has not been identified as a specific discipline and at present, for practising Catholics, the sermon is the only occasion for adult education.

In the case of the Church of England, the Board of Education has an Adult Committee with three full-time staff providing a Consultation and an Application service. At diocesan level, there is also an Adult Education Committee. In the parish, the clergy's pastoral work, the sermon and, for example, the drama group and a club were all used for religious adult education.

The Home Service Committee and the residential college of Woodbrooke all provide help to individual members of the Society of Friends in the area of religious adult education. Participation by members is greater than in the other two organisations, but the smallness of numbers, and the social and educational background of members may account for the participative dimensions of the Society.

In all three religious bodies there is a growing emphasis on the establishment and use of small groups both for education and worship.

Coding: 7c(xxi), 7c(i), 7c(v), KB1091

POLICY FOR FURTHER EDUCATION IN ENGLAND AND
WALES SINCE 1944, WITH PARTICULAR REFERENCE TO
MANCHESTER by G. Harrison, M.Sc. thesis, University of Salford
1970.

Aim

To study decision-making and the outcome of the decision-making
system and processes within the field of further education, as defined
in Section 41 and Section 8(b) of the 1944 Education Act, in
England and Wales.

Discussion

Further education is defined as 'Education primarily intended for
persons who have left school, through provision secured either by the
Minister of Education, or by the Secretary of State for Education
and Science acting in the capacity of the former Minister of
Education; or by Local Education Authorities in accordance with
appropriate schemes of plans approved by either of these Ministers'.

The thesis consists of five parts; the early history of Further
Education (origins to 1944), the national system, 1944 to about
1968, an interpretation and assessment of the national system, a case
study and critical evaluation of further education in Manchester
1944 until about 1968, and the conclusions.

By 1967 there were 738 further education establishments in
England and Wales, serving about 1,800,000 students (including
evening institute students following courses leading to recognised
qualifications). The author describes and assesses the types of courses
provided and the student membership in Parts 2 and 3 of the thesis,
and includes sections showing the links between further education
and the secondary school sector, further education and the youth
employment service, and further education and the adult education
providers. He notes that, by the late 1960s, three-quarters of
enrolments in evening institutes were for single, non-vocational
subjects, with women over the age of 21 predominating.

Part 4 deals with a specific local authority area, and details the
following five aspects: the provision existing in 1944 and proposals
for the future; the development of physical facilities; government
and finance; the consolidation and growth of provision; and the
relations with the Authorities, Bodies and Individuals. The causal

influences on policies are identified and the effectiveness of these policies are evaluated.

Findings
The decision-making processes are complex, sophisticated and usually dependent on the goodwill and commonsense of individuals. For example, although Manchester Corporation has always been characterised by a strong party political system, there has, fortunately, been a substantial measure of agreement on educational policy within the Education Committee itself.

However, the evidence suggests that the role played by the governing bodies of FE institutions has not been as active as could be expected; for example, 'library facilities are inadequate in all colleges . . . the same applies to office services'.

'The adult education field has been much affected by the limitations imposed by scarce resources. What has been attempted is of a very high order, apart from community centre work which had made indifferent headway . . . There is ample evidence of social needs being met on a geographical basis . . . but the facts clearly show that the pattern has remained virtually unchanged'.

The thesis also includes a detailed critique of courses, of staffing problems and policies, of co-ordination successes and failures, and of the training of external teachers. This criticism is placed in the context of scarce national resources and the local difficulty of a large city whose recent history is rooted in the Industrial Revolution.

Coding: 7b, 1b(xiii), 7a, 1c(xi), 2a, 7c(i), 8c, 4

Section 9

Staffing

Recruitment

RECRUITMENT OF SISTER-TUTORS IN THE NURSING PRO-
FESSION — A STUDY OF A ROLE CHOICE AND ITS DETER-
MINANTS by E. A. Dutton, Ph.D. thesis, University of London
1971.

Aim
To study the situation and attitudes of hospital nurses, particularly
ward-sisters, to discover why the tutor's work was not sufficiently
attractive to ensure a steady supply of candidates for training within
the context of a social psychological study of role choice.

Method
Questionnaires were based on a pilot survey consisting of 30 long
interviews, usually tape-recorded. Six separate questionnaires were
used in the main field work, and distributed to a sample consisting of
87 sisters in teaching hospitals, 388 sisters in general hospitals, 209
sisters in psychiatric hospitals and 40 prospective tutors, embracing,
in all, 54 different hospitals.

The first questionnaire was concerned with personal characteristics
etc. — the background data; the second consisted of a semantic
differential to discover the differences in the sisters' perception,
firstly of their own role, and then of the role of the tutor and the
role of the assistant matron respectively. Questionnaires 3, 4 and 5

were devised as a means of discovering the attitudes sisters held towards tutors and their work, each from a slightly different point of view, i.e. the work of a tutor, reasons for being anti-tutoring and reasons for tutoring. The final, sixth questionnaire, assessed the hospital climate to see if there was any relationship between 'hospital climate' so measured and a willingness to become a tutor.

Responses were analysed in various ways, e.g. the Hendrickson White Promax system of factor analysis and Kendall's Cluster Analysis Technique.

Discussion

The first part of the thesis reviews the previous research in the subject area, describes the historical background to the problem of the poor recruitment of sister tutors and presents a socio-psychological analysis of the research problem.

The previous research literature showed that the way the nurse's role should be interpreted was a major and continuing source of controversy. Some were striving to gain full professional recognition for nurses by pressing for an increase in the technical/academic content of training courses and demanding exclusive right to control admission. Others saw nursing as a practical vocation requiring little theoretical knowledge. Nurses were bureaucratic employees rather than autonomous professionals. It is against this background that we may examine the problem of tutor recruitment, in that tutors are necessarily seen as the agents of those concerned with raising professional standards. The second part of the thesis, three-quarters of the volume, is concerned with the field-work and results.

Findings

It emerged that attitudes to tutors and tutoring were influenced by the conception held of the nurse's role. In Great Britain, where a majority of well-qualified nurses held to the traditional vocational conception of nursing, work as a tutor tends to be much less popular than in America, where professional striving is widely supported. Most sisters in British hospitals paid tribute to a vocational conception of the nurse's role, and were sceptical of the tutor's work, and many felt that present training courses were wrongly conceived and that this in itself was a deterrent to potential recruits.

These general conclusions are supported by a wealth of detailed evidence; for example, approximately one-third of sisters in general and psychiatric hospitals are from manual, working-class backgrounds, and consequently are, other things being equal, less likely to be interested in tutoring than sisters in teaching hospitals who generally come from higher social strata. Ward sisters were particularly insistent on the bad effects of poor communications between training schools and wards, and it may be that an administration course for matrons and their assistants is a pre-requisite for improvements in tutoring and in attitudes to the role of tutor.

The thesis raises an important general question: that is, the need to develop more precise middle-range theories; for example, more understanding is needed of the effect that particular organisational pressures have on individuals with different types of self-concept and different basic role affiliations. There seems to be a need for a closer link between the two disciplines of sociology and psychology (vide G. G. Stern) as so much individual action is more truly seen as a reaction to group pressures of various kinds.

Coding: 8a

Training

THE USE MADE BY PART-TIME TEACHERS OF ADULTS OF FACILITIES FOR TRAINING by A. K. Stock, M.Ed. thesis, University of Manchester 1969.

Aim
To survey the use made by part-time teachers of adults of facilities for training in the North-West of England, with special reference to part-time teachers employed by local education authorities.

Method
Pilot questionnaires were administered to trainees on courses, principally to find out what type of students were available for in-service training, what sort of courses existed, and what were the attitudes of students to courses. A final randomised working sample of 592 part-time teachers of adults was selected, and data from the questionnaires transferred to punch-cards and subjected to computer analysis. The findings are tabulated throughout the text.

Discussion

The training of all or any teachers in further and adult education is a comparatively recent notion; though references to this idea date back to the Ministry of Reconstruction, Adult Education Committee, Final Report of 1919, adult education work has been regarded as a marginal activity, so that general acceptance of the need for training and certification really only dates from the 1960s.

The background to this research project is described, including the increase in the provision of courses, the Leverhulme project, and the report on the 'Recruitment and Training of Staff for Adult Education' issued by the NIAE in 1966. Though the growing interest in professional training was encouraging, nevertheless the author estimated that in 1968 only about 42% of part-time teachers were Department of Education & Science recognised teachers.

In the period 1963-1968 in the North West of England there existed quite a large variety of training courses provided by an equally large range of institutions; for example, 412 courses were offered by Lancashire County Council alone.

Course attendance is greatest when the part-time teacher is under the direct supervisory control of full-time personnel and courses are provided by his own LEA, and most popular for those specialising in drama as their teaching subject and for those with less than 2 years' adult teaching experience. Twice as many 'non-professional' as 'professional' teachers attended DES recognised courses.

Within the 41.7% 'qualified' part-time teaching force, 77% were employed full-time in the secondary education sector, 10% were in the 'further' sector, but, by course attendance, 26.1% were from the secondary sector, 57.1% from the 'further' sector. 30% of the subsample in school-teaching grades held the full-time office of Head of Department. Of nearly 60% of part-time teachers from occupations outside teaching, 42.7% were housewives, 18.4% were in manufacturing industry, 31% had no certificate relevant to the subject they taught. On the whole, the lower the terminal education age, the greater the propensity to attend courses.

Chapter 6 deals with five aspects of the courses attended; the organising bodies by subject matter, the organising bodies by date of course, the course-duration by subject matter, the course timing by subject matter and course residence by subject matter. Subject to considerable variations, the modal course likely to be attended by a part-time teacher in North-West England was one of two-weekend days, was non-residential, had about 10 hours of formal course work and was promoted by a local education authority.

In Chapter 7 the author analyses opinions on courses, the types of provision by opinion on future development, the attitudes to types of promotion and method and the 'open-ended' opinions. Most teachers were concerned with their personal effectiveness in the classroom rather than with the 'common core' of adult educational method.

Most teachers would have liked teaching demonstrations by experts, a series of courses leading to a definite qualification, and an element of teaching practice in the course. Curiously, trainees favoured the lecture method; predictably they would have liked courses to be free of charge.

Findings
The stress is on the dynamic nature of the adult education system, the need for experiment in training and the desirability of continued descriptive research of this type at regular intervals.

Coding: 8b, 8c, KB 1534

A COMPARATIVE STUDY OF THE TRAINING REQUIREMENTS AND CERTIFICATION OF TEACHERS AND INSTRUCTORS OF MOUNTAIN ACTIVITIES IN SELECTED COUNTRIES IN WESTERN EUROPE by K. I. Meldrum, M.Phil thesis, University of Nottingham 1970.

Aim
To examine the provisions made for the training and certification of instructors and teachers of mountain activities in Britain, Belgium, France and Switzerland.

Discussion
Chapters 1, 2 and 3 deal respectively with the historical development of outdoor activities, the historical development of mountain activities and of mountain activities in Britain. The other countries are considered individually in Chapters 4 to 6, and these chapters

illustrate how centralised and decentralised administrations affect the interpretation of the mountain activities in both alpine and non-alpine regions. This allows for an adequate system of cross-referencing in the comparative analysis.

The chapter devoted specifically to Britain begins by placing mountain activities in the context of the British educational provision. The author then examines the promotion of outdoor recreation in Britain and considers, in order, the development of mountaineering and mountain training, of canoe training, of caving and caving training, and of skiing and skiing qualifications. He describes the work of the British Mountain Centres, of which there were 2 in 1945 and 40 in 1966, and the Mountain Activity Training of students in higher education.

Findings

The number of active participants in each of the activities is increasing rapidly; skiing is the most popular in each country examined, and caving the least popular. Climbing and canoeing were generally of equal popularity, except in the case of Switzerland. The degree of popularity is a function of the accessibility of the facilities and the degree of encouragement which is provided through various educational media. The provisions made in the decentralised systems in both Britain and Switzerland tend to respond to public demand, responding flexibly but not anticipating needs. In contrast, the centralised provision tends to be more rigid but offers a comprehensive system of certification which anticipates needs.

The provision in Britain differs from other countries in that there is a greater emphasis on the educational content of training and certification. But detailed examination of this training shows that in general the courses available are neither sufficiently extensive nor sufficiently detailed to enable those responsible for establishing outdoor activities to forego further in-service training.

Coding: 8b, 4, 5m(xiv), 1b(xiii)

Attitudes, motives and behavioural patterns

A STUDY OF THE SOCIAL SENSITIVITY OF STUDENT TEACHERS, WITH SPECIAL REFERENCE TO MATURE STUDENTS by R. P. Meldon, Ph.D. thesis, University of London 1968.

Aim

To examine the contribution of social sensitivity to teacher competence during student teachers' courses.

Method

Social sensitivity was defined generally as a process of empathy — as the ability to predict the likely, subjective, verbal responses of the following predictees:
a) men and women in general within the students' tutorial groups
b) two lesser-known individuals, a male and a female member of staff
c) an individual boy and girl, chosen by each student on a school practice

Two media of prediction were employed, the British version of the Allport-Vernon Study of Values for the adult predictees, and, for the two children, a devised questionnaire concerning self-concepts. Of the 132 subjects of the investigation, 91 (68.9%) were over 25 years of age. The age range was 18-50 years, and the mean age 31.3 years; 69.7% of the sample were women.

Social sensitivity was measured by the calculation of 'D' scores; intelligence and personality by reference to the Manual for the Group Test of High Grade Intelligence A.H.5, A. W. Heim, 1956, and the Myers Briggs Type Indicator respectively. The complete data was analysed generally, and subjected to a quantitative analysis by computer which included factor analysis and regression programmes.

Findings

Social sensitivity is significantly related to success in practice teaching — particularly to the understanding of two chosen children. However, sensitivity to others is not significantly related to either

331

intelligence, sex or maturity, but appears to be associated with the intuitive type of personality. The author suggests further research, on the grounds that, if these findings are confirmed, then such a personality test would be a useful part of a counselling service for intending teachers and tutors.

Coding: 8c, 6, 8a

A POST-WAR ENGLISH TECHNICAL COLLEGE – THE DEVELOPMENT, STAFF STRUCTURE AND CLIMATE OF AN EDUCATIONAL ORGANISATION by B. F. A. Tipton, M.Phil thesis, University of Reading 1969.

Aim
A study of an area technical college offering both elementary and advanced courses on part-time, and full-time bases, and including evenings-only courses with recreational objectives.

Method
Relatively unstructured interviews with senior members of staff; 15 pilot structured-interviews, and 57 interviews conducted over the period 1966-1967. Official documents and various college files were also scrutinised.

Discussion
The thesis is divided into three parts, the first of which introduces the area of study; for example, the general environment of technical colleges, and describes official policy and technical college goals such as the levels and breadth of work. The second part, in the course of four chapters, deals respectively with 'Jones' College, its setting and development, some of the characteristics of the staff, the staff climate of activity and the staff and the college goals. The final part summarises the results of the project and provides, for example, details of references and of the interviewing schedule.

During the period 1951-1966 'Jones' College changes from being an institution working preponderantly at a junior level to one which classified almost one-third of its work as 'university' level and less than one-quarter as 'school' level. It had changed also from being an institution where the great majority of students attended on an evenings-only basis to one where the number of part-time day students outstripped those on evenings-only courses, and where over 900 students were attending full-time or sandwich courses. In terms of volume of work, these 900 students accounted for 40% of the total student hours in 1966/67.

The reasons for the growth and change, the tensions caused and the consequences of such rapid developments are discussed in detail. Of particular interest are staff attitudes to adult recreative education: 'In 10 years' time this college will have an important function in training for leisure' and 'I think that facilities like judo and flower arranging should be available, but not at 'Jones' College'.

Findings

The diffuseness of official goals made it possible for 'Jones' College to acquire a multiplicity of educational functions; this brought into the college, as teachers, people of widely differing educational and occupational backgrounds. The growth of a staff group-identity was hampered by the considerable yearly additions of new staff members. Few teachers had undergone any training for teaching in further education – a fact which, perhaps, suggests calculative rather than moral reasons for joining the profession.

Most teachers welcomed the intrusion of non-teaching tasks into their work; the author considers that promotion often depended on the ability to administer, and administrative ability could most easily be proved by the starting of new courses.

The atmosphere felt competitive because success came not only in the form of promotion into 'dead men's shoes' but also as a self-made new position in the hierarchy of departments and lectureships; failure, therefore, did not simply mean non-promotion, but a re-structured hierarchy in which old positions could be vulnerable.

In this environment of rapid expansion, the methods of social control that are associated with a professional group tended to be ineffective. Indeed, 'Jones' College appears to provide an example of an organisational situation lacking in a complete system of bureaucratic controls and containing conditions unpropitious for the operation of supplementary, or complementary, professional controls. Is 'Jones' College typical of post-war technical colleges?

Coding: 8c, 8b, 8a, 1b(xiii), 1c(ii), 1c(xi), 4

THE ROLE OF THE YOUTH WORKER IN CONTEMPORARY
SOCIETY by M. H. Bristow, M.Ed. thesis, University of Leicester
1970.

Aim
To explore what role the youth worker has in contemporary society
by building a picture of the expectations that shape the role and
which prescribe the worker's actions.

Method
The investigation deals with four aspects of the problem; the social
field or attitudes and values that affect the 'climate of opinion'
within which the work is conducted, the structure and organisation
of the service, the personnel and the ideas that motivate the service.
During 1967-68 observations were made of 40 full-time youth
worker situations and 170 past students of the National College for
the Training of Youth Leaders were contacted. In addition, 190 field
workers responded to a postal questionnaire and various local
authority officers assisted.

Discussion
Part 1 considers the status and role of the youth worker; the
relationships between the youth worker, contemporary society and
young people; the purpose of the work, the growth and development
of the service in England and Wales and the problems inherent in this
type of work. Part 2 describes the contemporary structure of the
service, its organisation, the ideas and ideals of the service and the
place of the worker in the local chain of command. The actual tasks
of a youth worker, the facilities he can command, the membership of
clubs and a study of the workers themselves are the subjects of Part
3.

Findings
Youth work is organised on the basis of partnership between
statutory and voluntary agencies. It exists to meet needs of young
people that are not met by other institutions. Clients (members) are
mostly in the age group 11-20 years with the modal age about 15
years.

Role expectations by employing agencies, workers and clients are complex and thus vary widely. This leads to variety in interpretation, diffuseness and conflict in the work. The number of full-time, professionally trained youth workers is small; most workers are part-time, the majority voluntary, but some are paid. The role of the worker is essentially in the area of social learning and one of the principal duties is counselling.

Generally, there are too few workers in too many inadequate premises. Sadly, many young people over the age of 18 years (legally adult) felt that some workers were loth to allow them any substantial responsibility in running the club or to recognise that their needs, as a group, differed from those of the younger members.

Coding: 8c, 2a, 1b(xxii), 5b, 6, 7c(xxi), 8a

AN EXPLORATION INTO THE ROLE OF THE PHYSICAL EDUCATION LECTURER IN FURTHER EDUCATION by A. L. Curtis, M. Ed. thesis, University of Birmingham 1970.

Aim
A study of the physical education lecturer's role expectations and those of his role set, the college principal, fellow members of staff and the students, in establishments of further education, particularly those in the Merseyside area.

Method
The method used to collect the data is based upon the Q-techniques of Stephenson and Kerlinger. Briefly, this means that individuals are asked to sort decks of cards in relation to some cognitive objects, the result of which is a distribution of cards unique to each individual. A sample of 61, 20 students, 20 members of staff, 13 physical education lecturers and 8 principals, in 10 Merseyside colleges was taken. The statistical analysis of responses is a detailed variance analysis, but computations are described fully and factor analysis was attempted.

Discussion
Physical education lecturers are almost always trained teachers, but

their training had been directed towards primary and secondary education. As students in colleges of further education are often adults (especially in club activities), there is some force in the argument that training for teaching adults, which is somewhat different to training for teaching in the schools, should receive some attention.

It is argued that, of the three functions of a physical education teacher, viz instruction, socialisation and classification, the socialisation role is increasingly the most crucial, and this is particularly so in colleges which cater essentially for young adults.

The central section of the thesis is concerned with a description of the collection and analysis of the data. The author relies on a dichotomy between an open-minded attitude and a restrictive attitude, and offers statements to the sample population for ordering. Open minded would be, for example, 'to fit his programme to the students and not the students to his programme', and restrictive would be 'to maintain a certain distance between himself and his students'. Each statement was prefixed 'I expect the PE lecturer to . . .'. On the basis of an eleven point scale, the respondents' expectation was assessed between the two poles of restrictive and open-minded.

Findings

The opinions of the PE lecturers and members of staff have much in common, those of the lecturers and the principals have a certain amount in common whilst those of the PE lecturers and students differ significantly. All four groups as a whole favour an 'open-minded' approach to the PE lecturers' role. Curiously, the principals appear very sure amongst themselves about what a PE lecturer must do, but not at all sure about what he must not do, whilst students are uncertain on both counts.

Coding: 8c, 5m(xiv), 8b, 2b

THE REGISTERED NURSES' VIEW OF GENERAL STUDENT
NURSE EDUCATION by N. K. Lamond, M.Litt thesis, University of
Aberdeen 1970. [To be published in 1974 as *Becoming a nurse — the
registered nurses' view of general student nurse education*, Royal
College of Nursing, London.]

Aim
To investigate the role expectations held by nurses of the teaching
responsibilities pertaining to the role of ward sister as she influences
the education of the student nurse.

Method
By 124 interviews with administrative personnel, teaching personnel,
ward sisters, surrogate sisters, part-time staff nurses and full-time
staff nurses. The ward sisters were, at the time of interview, working
in medical wards, surgical wards, 'specialities' wards, psychiatric
wards or paediatric wards. The questionnaire included an analysis to
responses to the following concepts: nursing as a career; conditions
of service; satisfaction of human interaction; nursing as a vocation;
nursing as a profession; nursing as a humanitarian service; bedside
nursing; the duties of a ward sister; the patient as an individual; and
the patient as a participant.

Discussion
The activities of the ward sister in a training hospital fall into three
broad categories: bedside nursing, administration and teaching.
Though the latter aspect of a sister's daily round is the subject of this
study, the author emphasises that teaching duties are but one aspect
of her total responsibilities and, consequently, in Chapter 1 the
teaching role is placed in the total sociological context. Chapter 2
describes the interviewing method. The following chapters deal
respectively with 'what is nursing?', 'nursing at the level of task
performance', 'the management of death', 'the relational aspects of
nursing', 'nursing as a profession', 'teaching the teachers', 'the nurses'
perceptions of their needs for planned education' and 'the place of
nurses in the community'.

Findings
The organisation of daily nursing is much more complex today than

in the past; consequently, learning by practice alone is not enough. It is very difficult for a nurse-tutor to objectify her perception of student nurse education; in addition, it was found that nurses are not unanimous in their interpretation of nursing as a concept.

It was noted most markedly that nurses no longer believed that the ward sister should be very involved in transmitting her skills at the level of job competence.

The management of death was notable as requiring both instrumental and expressive components of patient care, and consequently requiring an experienced nurse as a teacher.

The ward sister'was seen to be the most appropriate role model upon which the recruit should base her expectations of social behaviour and, in the main, the ward sister was seen by nurses as the vehicle for the transmission of the values of nursing to the novitiate.

Present-day nursing was shown to be a process of socialisation rarely, if ever, completed; continued education was seen to b: important. Most nurses 'felt' that there was a barrier between themselves and the non-initiated public.

There is little consensus of opinion on key issues in the socialisation of student nurses; hospital ward sisters seemed to be particularly at variance with college personnel categories.

Coding: 8c, 5a, 3c

CONCEPTS OF THE ROLE OF THE CRAFT TEACHER IN FURTHER EDUCATION by D. Hurst, M.Ed. thesis, University of Manchester 1972.

Aim

To examine the part played by the teachers of craft subjects in the further education colleges (including an adult education centre) in Liverpool.

Method

Evidence was collected by administering, in 1972, four questionnaires. Firstly, 150 out of a possible 232 craft teachers in Liverpool, identified in a pilot survey, completed questionnaires. Secondly, personal interviews were conducted with 31 teachers (short profiles are given to each teacher, six of whom were selected for more extensive treatment and an activity/behaviour group analysis is also included). Thirdly, interviews were conducted with 10 heads of craft departments; and, fourthly, 153 students completed questionnaires which were distributed by 15 of their teachers.

Discussion
The thesis is in three parts: Part 1 is concerned with the aims of the research, the design of the questionnaires, and the implementation of a pilot study. Part 2, the field study, describes the methodology and findings of the main research efforts, and Part 3 describes the conclusions.

Findings
The average age of craft teachers was 44 years, 93% were male, 84% were Lecturers Grades I or II. About three-quarters had, before appointment, six or more years of industrial experience; 65% were 'early school leavers'; 39% had been formerly students at the college in which they were teaching. 70% considered that craft teaching had a low status in further education teaching. 85% considered that teaching methods in further education were improving.

Of particular interest in the interviews conducted with heads of departments was the emphasis placed on team-teaching. This is not solely a matter of pedagogy; dangerous machinery is used and college workshops are not covered by the Factories Act. Consequently, a craft teacher is constantly concerned with safety, and one safety measure is to double-up the staff in the workshop.

113 out of 150 students considered that the best teachers were those who used visual aids; 132 of the 150 liked teachers to accompany them on visits to industrial plants. Generally students supported and respected their teachers, to the degree that the majority expected from them a counselling service. These demands, made on teachers by their students, highlight two questions. Do craft teachers have sufficient professional training as educators and is there a case for appointing worker-teachers?

Coding: 8b, 8c, 5m(vi), 6

Appendix I

Content of theses coding system

Introduction

Subject topics are given, either in the order of importance indicated in the original thesis or in order of relevance to the interests of the adult movement.

Example — if the thesis is solely concerned with adult education then the subject coding shows the 'weighting' of the original author BUT if the thesis is primarily about schools but nevertheless contains a wealth of information about parental attitudes, reading habits and membership of voluntary organisations, then the coding system will record only the latter constituents.

Thus:

5m(iv), 2c, 3b, 2a, KB19 means

5m(iv)	= prime subject matter in the original thesis	=	educational methodology, teaching and learning processes, concerned with English language
2c	= usually less than prime subject matter in the original thesis	=	participation in adult education — the problem of literacy
3b	= usually less subject matter in the original thesis	=	theory of education — philosophy of adult education
2a	= usually less subject matter in the original thesis	=	participation in adult education — student personnel

KB19 = the thesis is also listed
under that number in
Professor T. Kelly's
*Select bibliography of
adult education in Great
Britain* (3rd edition)
published by NIAE

Sometimes a thesis covers many subjects, not all of which can be mentioned in the summary. Thus, to take the example above, 2a would indicate that the thesis does deal reasonably extensively with 'participation in adult education', but I have judged it more helpful to dwell in my summary on the other topic areas, 5m(iv), 2c and 3b.

CODE	SUBJECT

1. HISTORICAL DEVELOPMENTS IN ADULT EDUCATION

a.	General historical and descriptive surveys
b.	Particular movements and organisations
(i)	Adult education in association with Day schools
(ii)	Adult schools and evening classes
(iii)	Literary and philosophical societies and other learned societies
(iv)	Mechanics' Institutes and similar bodies
(v)	Political and religious reform societies
(vi)	Cooperative education
(vii)	Working Men's Colleges and similar institutions
(viii)	Working Men's Clubs
(ix)	University extra-mural teaching
(x)	Workers' Educational Association
(xi)	University tutorial classes
(xii)	Trade unions and allied organisations
(xiii)	Adult and further education under the auspices of local education authorities
(xiv)	Non-residential adult education centres
(xv)	Residential adult education
(xvi)	The Open University
(xvii)	Education in H.M. Forces
(xviii)	Adult education in the Merchant Navy
(xix)	Adult education in hospitals
(xx)	Adult education in prisons
(xxi)	Women's organisations
(xxii)	Young people's organisations
(xxiii)	Organisations for the promotion of music and the arts
(xxiv)	Other organisations concerned with adult education

(xxv)	Libraries
(xxvi)	Museums and art galleries
(xxvii)	Community centres
(xxviii)	Community associations
(xxix)	Community colleges and village colleges

	Special aspects
(i)	Rural adult education
(ii)	Adult and further education and technical training
(iii)	Adult education for women
(iv)	Adult education for the unemployed
(v)	Adult education for retirement
(vi)	Religious adult education
(vii)	Youth work and adult education
(viii)	Immigration
(ix)	Adult education for the handicapped
(x)	Adult education and the mass media
(xi)	Full-time studies

2. PARTICIPATION IN ADULT EDUCATION

    a   Composition of students in adult education — student personnel
    b   Motives, attitudes and behavioural patterns
    c   Problems of literacy
    d   Problems of attendance

3. THEORY OF EDUCATION

    a   General education and social theory as applied to adults
    b   Philosophy of adult education
    c   Sociological goals and functions of adult education
    d   Psychology of learning in adult education

4. CURRICULA AND COURSES

5. EDUCATIONAL METHODOLOGY — TEACHING AND LEARNING PROCESSES

    a   Methods of learning, modes, techniques, styles and systems
    b   Special methods for particular age groups — disadvantaged groups and so on
    c   Reading and written work
    d   Discussion systems, seminars and other special groups
    e   Educational visits
    f   Audio-visual aids

g	Film
h	Educational broadcasting
i	Closed-circuit television
j	Correspondence-based courses
k	Composite courses
l	Learning environments — physical
m	Particular subjects
(i)	Classics
(ii)	Drama
(iii)	Economics
(iv)	English language
(v)	Fine arts (except music)
(vi)	Handicrafts
(vii)	History
(viii)	International relations
(ix)	Literature
(x)	Management
(xi)	Modern languages
(xii)	Music
(xiii)	Philosophy
(xiv)	Physical and health education
(xv)	Psychology
(xvi)	Religion
(xvii)	Science
(xviii)	Social work education
(xix)	Other subjects
(xx)	Literacy education
(xxi)	Interdisciplinary subjects

6. GUIDANCE AND COUNSELLING

7. ORGANISATION AND ADMINISTRATION

a	National administration
b	Regional and local administration
c	Particular movements and organisations
(i)	University extra-mural departments and departments of education
(ii)	The Open University
(iii)	The Workers' Educational Association
(iv)	Adult education centres
	Education centres specifically for adults
	Education centres for adults and secondary education
	Education centres for community purposes
(v)	Residential education
	principally long-term
	principally short-term

(vi)	National Adult School Union
(vii)	National Co-operative Education Association, Co-operative Union
(viii)	National Council of Young Men's Christian Associations
(ix)	National Extension College
(x)	National Federation of Community Associations
(xi)	National Federation of Women's Institutes
(xii)	National Union of Townswomen's Guilds
(xiii)	Seafarers' Education Service and College of the Sea
(xiv)	Trades Union Congress
(xv)	The Library Service
(xvi)	The Young Women's Christian Association of Great Britain
(xvii)	Professional associations (see the current NIAE *Yearbook of Adult Education*)
(xviii)	Industrial Training Boards
(xix)	British Broadcasting Corporation
(xx)	Independent Broadcasting Authority
(xxi)	Other organisations (see the current NIAE *Yearbook of Adult Education*)

8.   STAFFING THE SERVICE — PERSONNEL

    a   Recruitment
    b   Training
    c   Attitudes, motives and behavioural patterns

Appendix II

The following list includes a number of significant research publications which have not been presented in thesis form.

We have given the 'coding' after each title so that readers may identify the principal content areas from Appendix I. Photocopies of the summaries in this list are available from the NIAE (30p each) and a printed summary of the Russell Report, prepared by NIAE itself, can be obtained from the Institute at 2p per copy.

Author	Title	Coding
Badley, F.S. (ed)	Second Symposium on Broadcasting — Determinants of Broadcasting Policy, published by University of Manchester Department of Extra-Mural Studies, 1970	5h, 5i, 2b, 7c(xix), 7c (xx)
Bailey, K.V., McQuail, D. and Halloran, J.D.	Preparation and Exchange of Information and Research, published by BBC, 1966	5h, 8c, 7c(xix)
Belbin, R.M.	The Discovery Method — An International Experiment in Retraining, published by OECD, 2 rue André Pascal, Paris 16, 1969	5b, 3d, 2b
Belbin, R.M.	The Discovery Method in Training, published by HMSO, 1969	3d, 5b, 2b
Glatter, Ron	Management Development for the Education Profession, published by George C. Harrap, 1972	8b, 7a, 7b, 5a
Glatter, R., and Wedell, : E.G. (with the collaboration of W.J.A. Harris and S. Subramanian)	Study by Correspondence — An Enquiry into Correspondence Study for Examinations for Degrees and other Advanced Qualifications, published by Longman Group, 1971	5j, 5k, 5l, 2d, 2b, 2a, 5b

Appendix II

Author	Title	Coding
Groombridge, B.	Television and the People, published by Penguin Books, 1972	3c, 2a, 5h, 7c(xix), 7(xx), 8c
Halloran, J.D. (ed)	The Effects of Television, published by Panther Books, 1970	3d, 2b, 5h
Halmos, P. (ed)	The Sociology of Mass Media Communications, published by the University of Keele, 1969	8c, 2h, 7c(xix), 7c(xx), 3c
Hancock, A., and Robinson, J.	Television and Social Work, published by NIAE, 1966	5k, 5m (xviii), 5h, 5b, 2a
Harris, W.J.A.	Home Study, published by Manchester University, 1972	5j, 5k, 5l, 2d, 2b, 2a, 5b, 2e
Lee, T.	A Null Relationship between Ecology and Adult Education, published in the British Journal of Educational Psychology, Vol 36, February 1966	2d, 2b
Macfarlane-Smith, I.	An Experimental Study of the Effect of Television Broadcasts on the G-Courses in Engineering Science, published in The Vocational Aspect, Vol 17, No 37, and Vol 20, No 46, 1965-68	5h, 5a, 5m(xix)
Robinson, J. and Barnes, N. (eds)	New Media and Methods in Industrial Training, published by BBC, 1967	5a, 5h, 5j, 5k, 7c(xix), 7c(xviii), 7c(xx)
Ruddock, R.	Sociological Perspectives on Adult Education, published by Manchester University, 1972	3c, 3b, 3a, 3d
Shaw, R.	Training Arts Administrators — Report of the Committee of Enquiry into Arts Administration Training, published by the Arts Council of Great Britain, 1972	8b, 8a, 5d, 7c(xxi), 4
Taylor, F.J.	Adjusting the Amount and Level of Information to one's Audience — A Practical Approach to the Problems of Teaching by Radio, Television and Lectures, available on request from the Further Education Officer, : BC	5h, 3d, 5a
Wedell, E.G. (ed)	Structures of Broadcasting — A Symposium, published by Manchester University Press, 1970	7c(xix), 7c(xx), 8c
Wiltshire, H., and Bayliss, F.	Teaching through Television, published by NIAE, 1966	5k, 1b(xvi), 1b(ix), 5h, 5j, 5m(iii)

346

Index of authors of original theses

General index